P9-CET-008

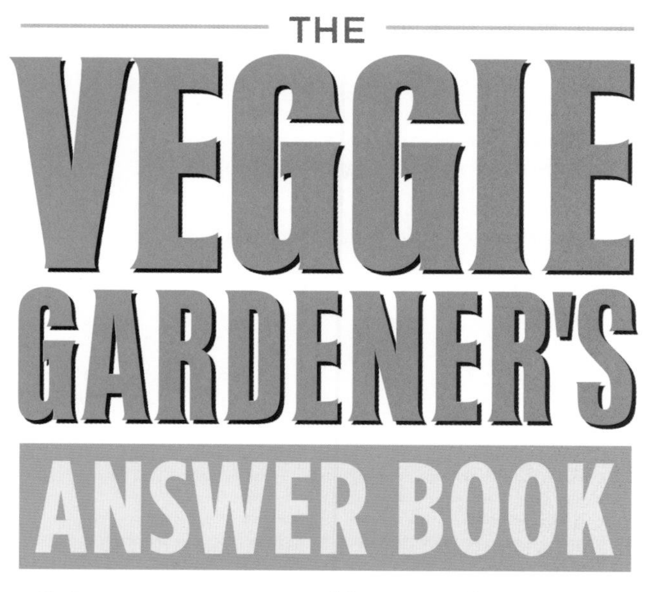

Solutions to Every Problem You'll Ever Face

Answers to Every Question You'll Ever Ask

Barbara W. Ellis

Storey Publishing

The mission of Storey Publishing is to serve our customers by publishing practical information that encourages personal independence in harmony with the environment.

Edited by Gwen Steege and Fern Bradley
Art direction and cover and text design by Jessica Armstrong
Text production by Ponderosa Pine Design, Vicky Vaughn Shea

Cover illustrations and chapter opener backgrounds by © William Howell Golson
Interior illustrations by Alison Kolesar, except those on pages 13, 19, 20, 21, 25, 29, 90, 93, 97, 114, 131, 148, 149, 151-154, 158, 178, 242, 254, 302, 310, 321, 345, 358, 369, and 397

Indexed by Nancy D. Wood

Printed in China by R.R. Donnelley
10 9 8 7 6 5 4 3 2

LIBRARY OF CONGRESS CATALOGING-IN-PUBLICATION DATA

Ellis, Barbara W.
The veggie gardener's answer book : solutions to every problem you'll ever face; answers to every question you'll ever ask / Barbara W. Ellis.
p. cm.
Includes index.
ISBN 978-1-60342-024-2 (pbk. : alk. paper)
1. Vegetable gardening–Miscellanea. 2. Vegetables–Miscellanea. I. Title.
SB321.E48 2008
635–dc22

2007049728

CONTENTS

CONTENTS (*continued*)

Questions, Anyone?

From a distance, those tantalizing glimpses of backyard vegetable gardens make growing tomatoes, squash, and other crops seem like a simple and straightforward hobby. It's easy to imagine that the plants take care of themselves from the day they're planted until the day the gardener shows up with harvest basket in hand. After all, the crops are arranged in neat rows further organized by an orderly collection of stakes and trellises, with everything blanketed by a thick cover of mulch. Take more than a brief glance at that garden, though, and you'll discover a hub of activity, with overlapping tasks that ebb and flow as crops are planted, tended, harvested, and replaced.

The devil is in the details for all this gardening activity, and that's where lots of questions arise. This book is designed to help everyone, from beginner on up, understand all the activity that's at the root of a successful organic food garden. Whether you want to plant a veggie garden for the first time or find new ideas and tips to help you grow vegetables more successfully, this book offers helpful, uncomplicated answers to all sorts of questions about what you need to do when and why. There are questions and answers on planning and planting your garden, improving soil, and caring for crops, as well as safe ways to control pests and diseases. In addition, beginning on page 168, you'll find detailed answers to all the cultural quandaries that arise for the most popular vegetable crops, from starting seeds and scheduling transplanting dates right through to knowing when and how to harvest. Throughout, you'll find plenty of regional advice, too, since what works for a garden in Maine, Minnesota, or Montana won't always work for one in Alabama, Texas, or California.

Don't try to read this book from cover to cover. Instead, think of it as a knowledgeable gardening friend you can turn to whenever you need help with a particular crop or gardening technique. One of the great things about gardening is that there are always new things to learn, new techniques to try, new crops to grow, and new questions to be answered. As you gain experience, you'll learn what works for you in your garden. You'll also discover, if you don't know it already, that there isn't just one way to approach any gardening chore or grow any crop. So experiment, and have fun! Along the way, you'll discover how to appreciate and easily manage the hub of activity that results in a beautiful and bountiful organic vegetable garden.

PART ONE

Digging In:

Creating and Maintaining a Great Vegetable Garden

Starting a vegetable garden is exciting, but it can be a little intimidating, too. Every gardener dreams of a bumper harvest, but it's hard to know how to manage the details of planting and caring for so many different crops. Here are some basic principles to keep in mind:

- **KEEP IT SIMPLE AND START SMALL.** Don't try to grow everything! Plant just a few easy-to-grow crops.
- **START COMPOSTING.** Once you've used it, you'll realize you can never have too much!
- **MULCH.** To control weeds and retain soil moisture, cover garden beds with a thick layer of organic mulch.
- **VISIT YOUR GARDEN OFTEN.** Pull weeds as soon as you see them, add mulch where it's thin, water plants that are dry, redirect wayward stems, look for signs of pests and diseases, and check for produce that's ready for harvest.
- **TAKE NOTES.** Start a journal to record spring weather, what and when you planted and transplanted, when certain pests emerged, and how much you harvested.

CHAPTER 1

Planning and Planting a Vegetable Garden

Selecting Crops to Grow

Q As a new gardener I'm completely overwhelmed by all the choices on the seed racks and in the catalogs. How do I narrow down my choices?

A Every gardener – beginning and advanced alike – has trouble deciding what to grow, since each selection seems a little better than the last. And although each gardener approaches this problem a little bit differently, here are some guidelines that may be helpful.

- **GROW WHAT YOU CAN'T BUY.** Concentrate on crops that you can't find at your local supermarket and ones that offer unusual color or taste.
- **PLANT CROPS YOU LOVE.** If you adore tomatoes or peppers, grow several cultivars of those. Try to avoid growing the same selections offered in the grocery store.
- **TRY CROPS YOUR NEIGHBORS SWEAR BY.** It helps to know what crops are easy to grow in your area – and *when* they're easiest to grow. Ask your neighbors, along with experts at garden centers, garden clubs, or the local Cooperative Extension Service.
- **BE ADVENTUROUS.** Experimentation is one of the most enjoyable aspects of having a garden. Try growing some unusual edibles just for fun – purple-fleshed potatoes, white pumpkins, or kohlrabi, for example.

Q **I see vegetables marked "hybrid" and "heirloom" in catalogs. What's the difference? And what are OP vegetables?**

A A hybrid vegetable is the result of cross-pollination between two genetically different parent plants. Plant breeders develop hybrids to increase disease resistance, to improve yield, or to select for special fruit characteristics such as color, flavor, or shipping quality.

Heirloom vegetables are cultivated forms of crops that have been perpetuated by gardeners who save seed (or propagate by some other means such as taking cuttings) from year to year. Some heirloom vegetable varieties have been around for more than a century! Gardeners have kept these varieties growing for generations because the crops performed well in a particular area or because they have outstanding flavor, unusual color, or other appealing characteristics.

OP stands for open-pollinated, meaning that wind, bees, or other insects, rather than plant breeders, transferred the pollen to fertilize the flowers. While all heirloom vegetables are open-pollinated, not all OP vegetables are heirlooms, since all seed companies offer modern-day varieties of vegetables that have been pollinated by wind or other means.

Q I've checked with experts, both at my Cooperative Extension office and at a local garden center, and I'm also planning to ask some local, dirt-under-their-fingernails gardeners for advice about what to grow. What else I should ask them?

A Gathering information on local gardening — sources, schedules, problems, and events — is a great way to benefit quickly from the experience of others. Gardeners are nearly always happy to share what they know. Here are some subjects that are worth asking local gardeners about:

- **SCHEDULES.** When do they plant spring crops like peas or cabbage and warm-season ones like peppers and tomatoes? Have they tried growing fall crops?
- **FAVORITE CROPS.** Do they grow your favorite crop? What are their favorite cultivars? Any problems?
- **SOURCES.** What are the best garden centers around? Where else do gardeners buy seed or transplants? Is there a good free or cheap source for finished compost, compost ingredients, or mulch around?
- **PROBLEMS.** What pests are the most bothersome? What other major problems cause headaches?

CATALOG LINGO

The crop descriptions in seed company catalogs and Web sites include lots of abbreviations — such as V, A, DM, and VF. Most, but not all, refer to disease resistance or tolerance. Look for a guide to symbols at the beginning of the catalog or at the beginning of each crop entry. Here are some common abbreviations you'll encounter:

AAS	All-America Selections Winner
A	Anthracnose
CMV	Cucumber mosaic virus
DM	Downy mildew
F	Fusarium wilt
F1	Hybrid variety
LB	Late blight
N	Nematodes
OP	Open-pollinated
PM	Powdery mildew
TMV	Tobacco mosaic virus
V	Verticillium wilt

Q **I want my first vegetable garden to be a big success. What are the easiest crops to grow?**

A While the list of easiest crops varies from region to region, there are a few super-simple standouts. Radishes and green beans top most gardeners' "no fail" lists. Other easy crops include cucumbers, summer squash, zucchini, garlic, leaf lettuce, snap peas, Swiss chard, and kale. Tomatoes are a bit harder but not by much. The newer compact hybrid tomatoes developed for patio culture are especially easy.

Sizing Up Garden Size

What's a good size for a first garden?

A Carefully managed, even a 4'×4'/1.2×1.2 m plot (16 sq. ft./2.4 sq. m) will produce quite a bit of food and will leave you time to learn about and enjoy caring for a vegetable garden. If you have lots of space and want to try a larger garden, make it no more than 10'×20'/3×6 m (200 sq. ft./18 sq. m). Keep in mind that the ideal size for your garden depends on the types of crops you want to plant, too. Crops like bush beans, lettuce, spinach, peppers, and carrots are perfect for a small garden, since the plants are small enough to allow you to fit in a variety of crops in the available space. However, if pumpkins and winter squash are high up on your planting list, you'll need to prepare a bigger garden, since just one of these plants can cover an entire 4'×4'/1.2×1.2 m plot.

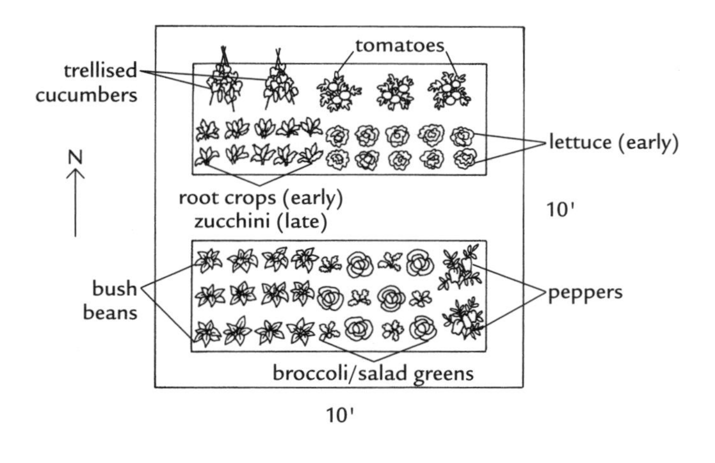

Q **I had a small garden last year, but it still got out of control. How do I keep my garden manageable?**

A Even in the smallest garden, an important technique for keeping the work manageable is to plant in dribs and drabs: Plant a little lettuce seed now and a little more 2 weeks later. While there are crops you'll want to plant all at one time – like peppers or tomatoes – planting small batches of many crops is a good garden habit to cultivate. Whatever size garden you tend, you'll find that staggering the planting spreads out the harvest and much of the attention that plants need in between, too. Instead of having a 20'/6 m-long row of lettuce or beets to thin on a given day, you'll have only a foot or two of seedlings to thin. In part 2, you'll find staggered planting recommendations for many crops. Use them as you cultivate the habit of planting a little at a time. Cover soil that's not yet planted with plastic to help it warm up, or cover it with grass clippings to keep it moist and suppress weeds. Or let the weeds germinate as a short-term cover crop and then slice them off before you plant your seeds.

Q **I plan to keep my first garden small, but I'm really excited about having a big food garden in the future. Is there something I can do this year to make it easier to have a big garden next year?**

A If you want to enlarge your garden next season, mark out the additional space you plan to plant, then start improving the soil and getting weeds under control this season. Set up compost bins on the site so you'll have plenty of compost at hand once you're ready.

SEE ALSO: *For no-dig strategies you can use to start preparing soil for next year, pages 83–84.*

Q **I have a small backyard plot, but I want to grow as much of my own food as I can. How should I go about that?**

A You can produce an amazing amount of food in even a small garden if you use some of the principles from the various forms of intensive gardening, also called biodynamic or French intensive gardening. Intensive gardening involves using raised beds, wide rows or close spacing between crops, succession planting, companion planting, and crop rotation. You'll also need to follow a soil-improvement schedule like the one outlined on page 78 to ensure rich, well-drained conditions.

Intensive gardening can be complicated, and it does demand some initial extra work to build the beds, enrich the soil, and plan out your planting scheme. It's best to switch your garden over gradually, and there are any number of ways you can do that. For example, start with a soil-improvement system, then try experimenting with succession plantings and wide rows during the first growing season. Add raised beds the first fall, and then work out a basic crop-rotation system the following winter. You'll find more information on row spacing, succession planting, and crop rotation later in this chapter.

SEE ALSO: *For companion planting ideas, page 139; for instructions for building raised beds, pages 81–85.*

Picking a Perfect Site

Q How do I decide where to put my vegetable garden? I have a good-size yard and live outside Indianapolis, Indiana.

A To find a great site, start by looking for a site that receives full sun, ideally at least 8 hours a day. Also take the following into account:

- **WELL-DRAINED SOIL.** The site should drain well after a rain, since wet soil is difficult to work, most vegetables don't like wet feet, and wet soil also is very late to warm up in spring. Plan on installing raised beds if your site doesn't drain well.
- **EASY WATER ACCESS.** Carrying water is no fun. You'll want a site that you can reach with a hose.
- **LEVEL IS BEST.** Look for a site that's fairly level. Plan on terracing if you don't have a level site.
- **KEEP IT CLOSE.** While you probably want a garden that's not smack-dab in the center of everything, you also may not want one that's out on the back forty. A spot you routinely pass daily makes it easy to pull a weed or two, check to see if plants need watering, or pick a few ripe tomatoes.
- **OUT OF HARM'S WAY.** Locate your garden out of the center of the yard and away from play areas and walk-

ways, so it doesn't have to compete with softball games, barbecues, and foot traffic to other parts of the yard.

- **CONSIDER UNDERGROUND PROBLEMS.** Consider the location of underground wires or cables as well as plumbing and septic systems. Also, stay away from sites where tree roots will compete with your vegetables.
- **CONSIDER FENCING POTENTIAL.** If deer and other pests are active in your neighborhood, choose a site that you can fence.
- **PLANT PROTECTION.** Select a site protected from prevailing winds, or plan to create some kind of windbreak.

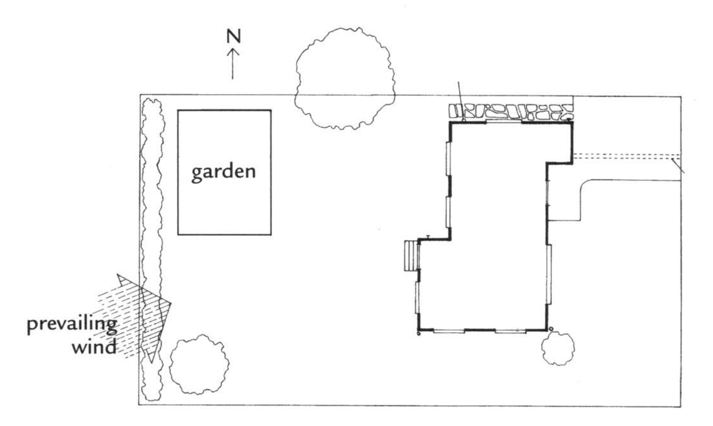

Hedge at left blocks the wind

I live near Dallas, Texas. What kind of site will be best for my conditions?

A In the South, vegetables like tomatoes will produce acceptable crops with less than full sun. Locating your garden where at least some of it receives partial shade may actually be a bonus, since shade (especially afternoon shade) will protect plants from searing summer heat. You'll still want a spot with well-drained soil that's away from play areas and traffic and protected from prevailing winds. In hot southern areas, access to water is even more important than it is in cooler regions.

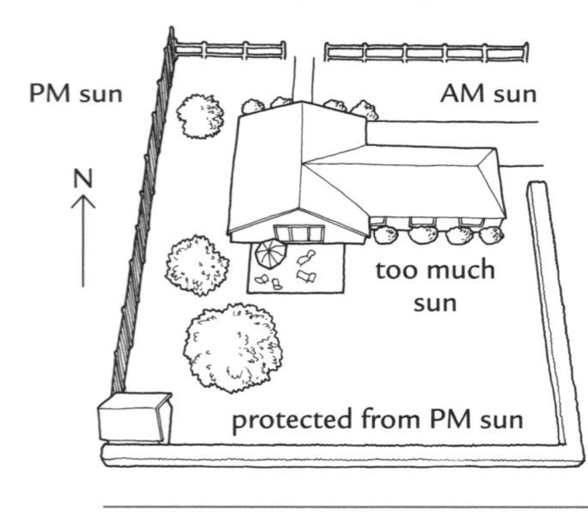

Q **Since my yard is tiny and the only sunny spot is on my deck, I'll have to grow vegetables in containers on the deck. If that will work, what are the best vegetables to try?**

A Vegetables make great container plants, and you can locate containers anywhere there is a patch of sun – on a deck or terrace, alongside a garage, or even along the driveway. Keep in mind that the larger the container the better the results. Fill containers with a purchased potting mix or make a batch of your own mix. For 12"–18"/30.5–45.7 cm containers, consider beans, broccoli, Brussels sprouts, cabbage, bush-type cucumbers, eggplant, peas, peppers, Swiss chard, and dwarf tomatoes. If you're using tubs or really large pots, you can plant dwarf or bush-type muskmelons, squash, or watermelons as well as full-size tomatoes. Beets, lettuce, radishes, spinach, and all sorts of salad greens will do fine in 10"–12"/25.4–30.5 cm pots. You can even combine crops in a large pot: Plant dwarf tomatoes with a ground cover or lettuce or other greens, for example, or even combine edible flowers with a mix of salad crops.

SEE ALSO: *For potting soil recipes, page 31.*

Q My grandparents always planted their garden in straight rows with paths in between, but they lived on a farm and had much more space than I have. Is there another way to organize my garden so I can fit in more plants?

Straight, single-crop rows with paths in between make laying out the garden a simple, straightforward matter. It's a very practical system if you use a tiller or tractor to prepare the soil. However, it isn't the most space-efficient system, since you'll end up with as much ground devoted to pathways as to crops. Instead, consider creating either wide rows or beds to use space more efficiently.

WIDE ROWS

Crops grown in wide rows are arranged with two, three, or more rows of crops planted close together without pathways in between. Fairly wide paths run between each set of closely spaced rows to provide access for weeding and harvesting. The number of plants in a single wide row varies according to how far the gardener can reach. For example, it's easy to reach across several rows of lettuce to harvest, but larger plants like cabbage are probably best planted two abreast so that you don't need to reach too far into the row.

BEDS

These are similar to wide rows, but the plants are arranged in bands rather than rows. Creating planting beds is the most space-efficient way to organize a garden, since only about one-third of the space is devoted to pathways and two-thirds to crops. Beds make it easier to concentrate soil-improvement, feeding, and watering in areas where plants will be growing, instead

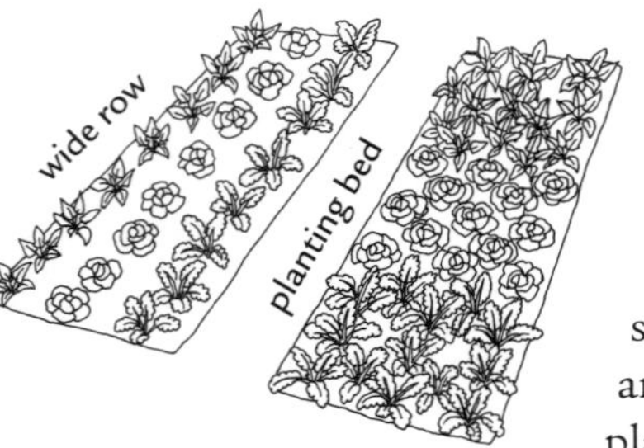

of on pathways. Beds can be raised, with the soil surface several inches above the surrounding area, or created so their surface is level with the surrounding soil surface or even below it.

Starting Seeds Indoors

Q **Why go to the trouble of starting seeds myself when I can buy transplants everywhere in spring?**

A Starting your own plants from seeds gives you greater control over what you grow, since you don't have to settle for what is usually a very limited local selection of transplants. Starting plants from seed is also a great way to experiment with unusual and/or heirloom vegetables. Raising your own seedlings is very enjoyable, and a great many gardeners look forward to filling pots and sowing seeds every year.

Another reason to grow your own is to ensure that you have a supply of healthy, vigorous transplants, and that can be an important issue if you don't have local suppliers who grow their own plants. However, if you can't grow vigorous transplants yourself due to lack of a good setup or lack of time, then don't do it at all. Spindly, home-raised vegetable seedlings are usually a big disappointment, producing little or no harvest.

Q **Is it difficult to start vegetable transplants from seed? What do I need?**

A Growing your own vegetable transplants is relatively easy. You'll need seed-starting mix, pots, and labels, along with the following:

- **WORKSPACE ESSENTIALS.** You'll need an indoor area where it's okay for things to get a bit dirty and possibly wet. For starters, look for a cool but heated space where it doesn't matter that there's a bit of soil on the floor. You'll need an old table or unused countertop for filling containers with soil and for growing seedlings. If you have a table that doesn't have a waterproof top, cover it with a sheet of plastic or a tarp to avoid damaging it.
- **GOOD LIGHT.** You don't need to have a greenhouse to grow great transplants, but you do need a source of bright light. Without it, you will never be able to raise healthy, stocky transplants.
- **HEAT FOR SEEDS AND SEEDLINGS.** You need to be able to regulate the temperature in your seed-starting area, but seedlings are happiest in fairly cool conditions. For cold-tolerant crops like cabbage and broccoli, temperatures between 50–60°F/10–15.5°C are fine. Keep seedlings of heat-loving plants between 65–75°F/18.3–23.8°C. Temperatures can be 10 degrees cooler at night.

Let There Be Light

LIGHT IS AN ESSENTIAL INGREDIENT for any seed-starting effort. If you have a greenhouse or cold frame, great, but there are other options. For example, you can set up a seed-starting area on a cool but heated sunporch, placing your flats on heat mats especially designed for warming soil to stimulate seed germination (they're available from garden centers and mail order suppliers). Many gardeners simply find a spot in a spare room or their basement where they can install a bank of fluorescent lights. Don't bother buying specially made lights for growing plants or invest in a more expensive system until you're sure you'll be doing lots of seed starting; ordinary shop lights are fine for most seed-starting efforts. Position the lights no more than 2"–4"/5–10 cm above the leaves of the seedlings (suspend lights from S-hooks and chains, so you can adjust the height of the lights as the plants grow) and give seedlings 16 hours of light per day. Use a timer to turn lights on and off automatically.

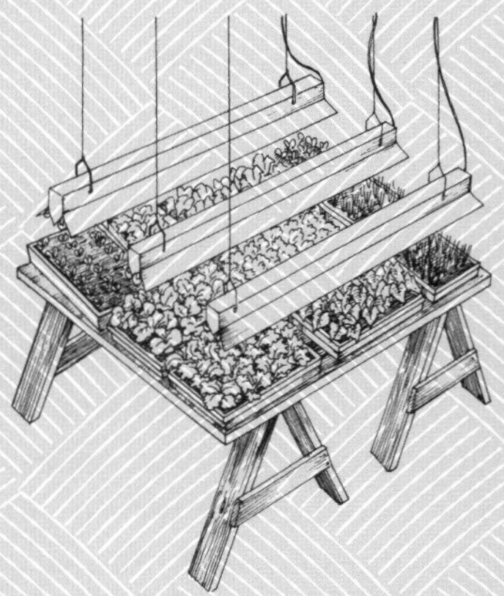

Shop lights provide supplemental light for seedlings.

Q I've never started transplants from seeds before but want to try it this year. What are easy, foolproof crops for a beginner to try?

A Some of the easiest transplants for home gardeners to grow are broccoli, Brussels sprouts, cabbage, cauliflower, leeks, lettuce, okra, onions, peppers, and tomatoes.

Q The instructions on seed packets refer to starting seeds or transplanting seedlings a certain number of weeks before the last frost date. What is this?

A Gardeners mark the growing season according to the last spring and first fall frost dates for their area. The last spring frost date is the average date when temperatures dip below freezing for a particular area. It is a useful benchmark for timing when to start seeds so transplants will be ready to move to the garden at the proper time. The last spring frost date is also useful for timing transplanting: Cold-tolerant crops like cabbage can be transplanted to the garden several weeks before the last spring frost, whereas heat-loving plants like peppers shouldn't be moved outdoors until several weeks after it. The first fall frost date is the date when temperatures typically dip below freezing for the first time. It is used to time sowing and planting for fall crops.

Keep in mind that these dates are based on averages, and the last spring or first fall frost in your garden in any given year may occur before or after the published dates for your area. Check the Internet or your local Cooperative Extension Service for information on your area.

Q What if I can't start my seeds at the right time? We're going to be away for the first 3 weeks in March, but our frost date is May 8.

A Sowing and transplanting schedules are recommendations, and you don't need to treat them like hard-and-fast rules. It's more important to start seeds when you have time to care for them properly than to start them on a particular calendar date. For example, even though sowing seeds indoors 6 to 8 weeks before the last frost may be the recommended schedule for tomatoes, they can also be sown 4 or 5 weeks before if your schedule is crazy earlier in the season. The same goes for transplanting: The ranges listed in this book and on seed packets are guidelines most often geared toward the earliest transplant date. Crops that thrive in warm temperatures will do just fine if transplanted a little bit late; cool-season crops like peas can be moved earlier, especially if you can protect them from unusually cold weather.

Q **Is it a good idea to start early and grow extra-big transplants?**

A In most cases, you're far better off if you don't try to get a head start on the schedule, because larger transplants aren't necessarily better. They're more likely to be spindly or potbound. Smaller, stockier transplants grown according to recommended schedules will generally outperform them in the garden because they experience far fewer problems with transplant shock than large plants do.

SEE ALSO: *For more on repotting seedlings, page 39; for more on transplanting problems, pages 50–55.*

Q **How can I tell if leftover seed is still good? I have some half-full seed packets that are two or three years old.**

A Seeds that are a year old will still germinate well provided they haven't been stored badly (in a hot, humid place, for example). Bean, pea, squash, and pumpkin seeds last three years if properly stored, while pepper and tomato seeds last four. Cabbage seed can be stored successfully for five years. You can plant stored seed and see how it performs or test it for germination before going ahead with a full-scale planting.

Here's how to do a germination test:

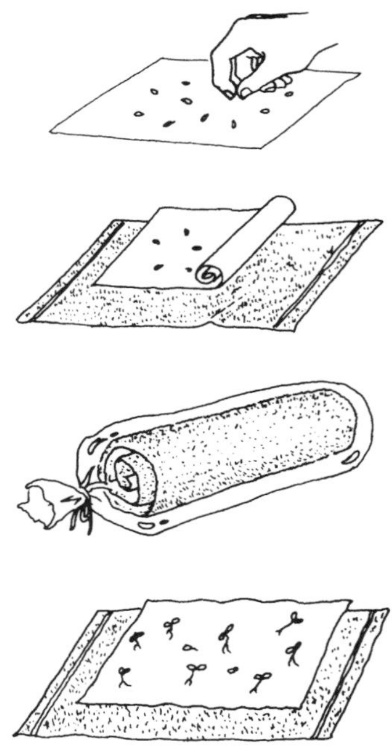

1. Write the name of the cultivar on a paper towel, and then moisten the paper towel and place ten seeds on it.
2. Fold or roll up the towel.
3. Place the rolled towel in a plastic bag and seal it with a twist-tie. Place the bag in a warm (70°F/21.1°C) spot.
4. Check daily to see if there are signs of sprouting. To determine the germination percentage, divide the number of seeds that sprout by the number that you started with.

If you don't want to discard the sprouted seeds, you can try planting them in moistened potting medium to produce transplants.

Q **A friend of mine has some seeds he saved from his garden last year that he'll give me. Are they okay to use?**

A That depends on what he saved and how he saved it. Seeds saved from hybrids – cultivated varieties that are the result of crossing two distinct parents – will not "come true" from seed. This means that the plants that grow from the seeds may not exhibit any of the fruit or foliage characteristics their parents featured. For this reason, they will probably yield disappointing results in your garden. If your friend grows heirloom and open-pollinated cultivars and saves seed from plants that did well in his garden, they're a good choice, since they will come true.

The other concern about saved seed is how it was stored. For best germination, seed needs to be stored in a cool, dry, dark place. While you can try to germinate seeds that have been stored in other conditions, germination will probably be poor, and you're far better off spending your time and effort on new seeds.

Soil Mixes for Starting Seeds

A "PART" CAN BE A CONTAINER of any size, from a clean cottage-cheese container to a large bucket. Even if you need a considerable amount of mix, however, make several small batches and then mix them together in a larger container. Otherwise, it's difficult to blend the ingredients. Use your hands or a trowel to mix everything together. Be sure to wear a dust mask to avoid inhaling any of the dusty ingredients these mixes contain.

Note that recipes made without compost don't contain any nutrients, so you will have to begin feeding seedlings with dilute organic fertilizer as soon as seedlings produce their first true leaves.

SOILLESS MIX

2 parts peat moss
1 part vermiculite
1 part perlite

EASY-MIX RECIPE

1 part vermiculite
1 part perlite
1 part milled sphagnum moss, peat moss, or screened compost

AMENDED POTTING MIX

2 parts commercial potting soil
1 part perlite
1 part screened compost or peat moss

SEE ALSO: *For more on feeding seedlings, page 38.*

Pots, Mixes, and Other Supplies

What kind of supplies do I need to start seeds?

You don't need many supplies. For indoor sowing, in addition to seeds, you'll need pots, labels to keep track of what's planted where, and seed-starting mix. Since most seeds germinate fastest with a little bottom heat, a heat mat is a good investment. They're available from garden suppliers. You also can set seed flats on top of a refrigerator or in another spot that radiates mild heat. Keep in mind that in most cases you want to warm the soil to about 70°F/21.1°C, so you want a spot that's warm, not hot.

Do I have to buy seed-starting mix? What about garden soil for starting seedlings?

While your crops eventually will be perfectly happy growing in garden soil, it isn't suitable for germinating seeds or growing seedlings indoors. Specially mixed potting soils and seed-starting mixes yield far better results because they are relatively sterile and minimize problems with diseases and pests. They also hold water well and provide ideal growing conditions for seedlings.

Q **I always have trouble trying to moisten dry potting soil, and seed-starting mix is even worse. The water just seems to roll off the surface. What's the secret?**

A The night before you plan to sow seeds, plant, or transplant, dump the mix into a 5-gallon/8.9 L bucket – the type that drywall compound comes in is fine, but wash out the bucket thoroughly first – or a clean garbage can. Then add water. You'll need about 1 gallon (3.8 L) of water for every 2 gallons/7.6 L of mix. By the next day the mix should have soaked up all the water and should have the moistness of a damp sponge. If the mix is sopping wet, just add more dry ingredients and stir until they're absorbed. If it's still on the dry side (test a handful; if you squeeze, some moisture should come out of the mix but not much), add more water. If you want to plant the same day, use hot water. Wait until it cools down, then stir, and all the mix should be wet.

Q **I hate buying pots! Do I have to buy new ones, or can I use recycled coffee cups or something else?**

A New containers are an option, but there are others. Smaller (2½"–3"/6.4–7.6 cm) pots that annuals or perennials come in are fine, and you can also reuse cell packs. For best results, wash previously used pots thoroughly and soak them in a 10 percent bleach solution

Containers for seed-starting

(1 part bleach to 9 parts water) to kill any disease organisms they may harbor.

You also can grow great seedlings in all kinds of recycled containers, provided they're clean and you punch a hole in the bottom of each one so water can drain out of the potting mix. Consider using coffee cups, yogurt containers, cottage-cheese containers, and sawed-off milk cartons or bottles. One thing to keep in mind, though: Your seedlings will be easier to care for if they're all in the same kind of container. That's because they'll all have the same soil volume and drainage and will need watering at similar times.

What about using peat pots? That way, you don't end up with all the plastic pots to throw away.

A Peat pots are a good option, too. Just be sure to tear the top edge off the pot when you transplant it into the garden, because if it sticks above the soil surface it will wick water out of the area around the seedling, forming a barrier that's hard for roots to penetrate. Just toss the torn pot edges onto the soil or into the compost.

Seed-Handling Secrets

Q What's the best way to sow seeds in pots?

A Fill the pots with premoistened medium to within about ½"/1.3 cm of the top, then sprinkle three or four seeds per pot. (Once seedlings are up, you'll thin to the most vigorous seedling in each pot.) Press the seeds onto the soil surface, and cover them lightly with moistened mix. Covering to a depth equal to the width of the seed (this isn't very much!) is a good general guideline. Just press tiny seeds onto the soil surface. Keep the medium evenly moist.

If you need a few dozen plants of a particular crop for your garden, consider sowing more seeds per pot or sow into small trays or flats. Then transplant seedlings into individual pots when they have at least one true leaf. (To sow more than one cultivar in a single flat, make short furrows and sow along them.) Be sure to mark each pot, flat, or furrow with a label that lists the crop name and the date it was sown.

Transplanting a seedling

Q Do I need to keep my seedlings warm to get them to grow well?

A Actually, once seedlings have germinated, they grow best if they're kept on the cool side, although seeds germinate best if they are in warm soil, between 75–85°F/23.8–29.4°C. The best way to do this is to provide bottom heat, either by placing pots on the top of a refrigerator or other warm spot, or better yet, by using a heat mat designed for germinating seedlings. Move pots off heat mats once seedlings have appeared, and then aim for an air temperature of about 60–70°F/15.5–21.1°C, and 10 degrees cooler at night. Keep cold-weather-loving crops like cabbages slightly cooler – 50–65°F/10–18.3°C. Seedlings that are kept too warm tend to be spindly, and while ones kept on the cool side will be smaller and slower growing, they will be stockier and make better transplant candidates.

Q Do I really have to thin my seedlings? There's something about throwing away all those baby plants that I just hate.

A Overcrowded seedlings don't make the best candidates for producing high yields, so steel yourself and thin your seedlings. Think of yourself as being kind to the plant you are leaving rather than cruel to the ones you're removing, if that helps. Overcrowded seedlings devote a considerable amount of energy to stretching for light or competing for nutrients, and thinning directs that energy toward producing healthy roots, short stocky stems, and vigorous roots.

The easiest way to thin is simply to snip off extra seedlings with scissors; this method minimizes disruption to the remaining plant. If you can't bear thinning, you can sow several seeds per pot and then when each seedling has at least one true leaf, carefully uproot and separate them, then plant each one in its own individual pot. If you end up with more transplants than you have room for, share the extras with friends and neighbors who garden, or offer them to a local community garden.

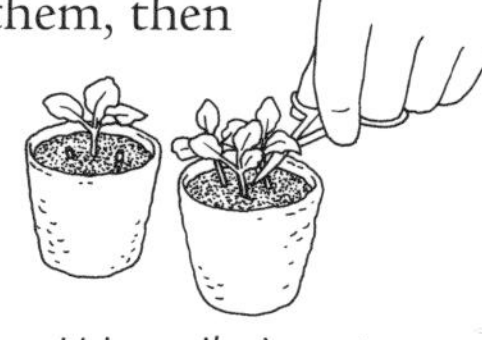

Using nail scissors to thin seedlings

Q What's the best way to water? I accidentally flooded my pots, and I think some of the seeds washed away.

A A fast, efficient way to deliver water to your seedlings is to set pots in a tray of water and let the water soak up from the bottom. Watering seedlings from the bottom keeps even the smallest seeds in place, and it also helps prevent damping off, which rots the stems just at the soil line. To bottom water, place individual pots or entire flats in a shallow tray or larger flat that holds water, then let the water soak up to the soil surface. If you don't have time to bottom water, use a small container so you can easily tip a small amount of water into each pot. Or use a watering can with a rose that sprinkles. Use room-temperature water to avoid shocking your seedlings.

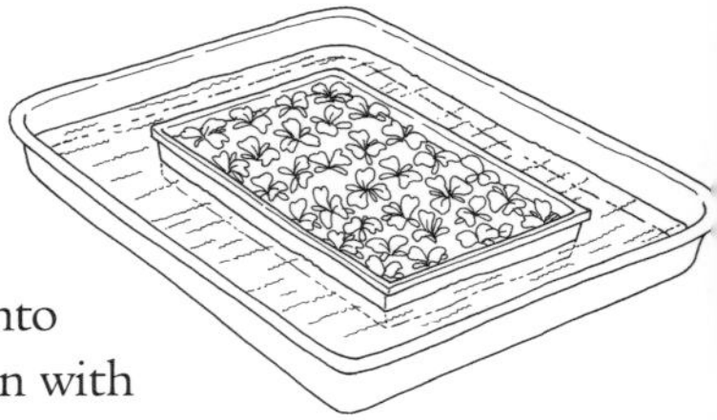

Bottom watering a flat of seedlings

SEE ALSO: *For more on damping-off, pages 40–41 and 156.*

Q What's the best way to feed the seedlings?

A If you're germinating seedlings in a mix that doesn't contain any nutrients – one with peat and vermiculite, for example – feed them once a week after germination. Water with a weak fertilizer solution: Mix fish emulsion or other balanced organic fertilizer at half the strength recommended on the bottle. Weak compost tea is also effective. After the first 3 weeks, feed with full-strength fertilizer every 2 weeks. If you are growing seeds and seedlings in a certified organic potting mix or a homemade mix that contains compost, you probably don't need to fertilize at all.

SEE ALSO: *For details about compost tea, pages 120–121.*

Q **I bought seedlings this year, but they already seem too big for their pots. They're growing in little cell packs, and I can't move them outside for another week or two. What should I do?**

A You're right to be concerned about seedlings that seem too big for their pots. Chances are they're becoming potbound, which means that the plant's roots have filled all the space available in the pot. When this happens, the plants can become stressed, and they won't perform as well as plants whose growth is unchecked. The best thing you can do is to repot your seedlings, putting each one into its own 2"–3"/5–7.6 cm pot (choose a pot that provides about 25 percent more root space than the seedlings have right now). This goes for purchased seedlings as well as homegrown seedlings that have gotten a bit too large for their cell packs or pots. The plants benefit from the extra root room, even if they receive only a week of extra time for growing and hardening off before being moved to the garden. True, repotting is extra work, but it allows seedlings to continue growing without interruption, which means better transplant success and better yields once plants are in the garden. If you can't plant outdoors on schedule and don't have time to repot, water with a half-strength dilution of liquid fertilizer.

Repotted seedling

Q My seedlings wilted today while I was away at work. How do I tell when it's time to water, *before* my plants are really suffering?

A Expert gardeners use a few different techniques. Lift a dry pot in your hand, then water it and lift it again. You should be able to tell the difference in the weight, since wet pots are heavier than dry ones. Or lift an entire flat of pots to judge the weight. (Either way, this technique underscores the value of using all the same pots for starting seeds, since they'll all weigh the same when wet and dry.) Another option is to stick a finger into the soil in a pot. It's okay if the surface is slightly dry, but the soil should be moist just under the surface. Keep in mind that seedlings in warm, dry portions of your house will need watering more often than ones in cooler, more humid areas.

Q The seedlings in two of my pots fell over last night. The tops look okay, but the stems are dark right at the soil line. Is there anything I can do to save them?

A If the stems are rotted at the base, just where the stem enters the soil, your seedlings have been felled by a disease called damping-off and can't be saved. Remove the afflicted pots and discard the potting medium. To prevent the problem from spreading to more pots, eliminate crowding by spreading out pots and thinning seedlings. A small fan will help improve air circulation, but avoid pointing it directly at seedlings. Disinfect the pots with a 10 percent bleach solution (1 part bleach, 9 parts water) before you reuse them. You may want to try a pasteurized seed-starting mix if the problem recurs. Pasteurizing ensures that the mix is free of pathogens that can cause damping-off.

SEE ALSO: *For more on damping-off, page 156.*

Q **My seedlings are pretty tall, and they look stringy, not stocky. What did I do wrong?**

A Insufficient light is probably the culprit. Suspend fluorescent lights 2"–4"/5–10 cm above the seedlings and keep them on for 14 to 16 hours per day. If you're using a windowsill, consider supplementing the light your seedlings receive by adding artificial light. High temperatures can also cause stringy seedlings, so move yours to a cooler spot to slow down growth. Directing a fan on your seedlings also helps keep them stocky (although this won't improve them if insufficient light is the culprit). Strangely enough, brushing plant leaves lightly with a cardboard wrapping-paper tube or a broom handle has a similar effect. Brush for 1½ minutes twice a day for best results.

Q **I have room for only one shop light inside, and that's not enough space for all the seedlings I want to start. I can't afford a greenhouse, either. Is there another option?**

A A cold frame may be just the ticket for increasing your seed-starting capacity. It's basically a bottomless box with a glass or Plexiglas top. Cold frames are great for starting seedlings of cool-weather crops like cabbages, and they're also useful for hardening off seedlings that are on their way to the garden. You can purchase premade cold frames from many nursery catalogs, but they're easy to make (search the Internet for plans with details on how to build them). Because a cold frame lid traps solar heat inside, the temperature inside the frame can build up quickly on sunny days. You can release excess heat by propping open the lid manually, but it's worth your money to invest in a solar-powered vent opener, which will open the lid and ventilate the seedlings automatically for you.

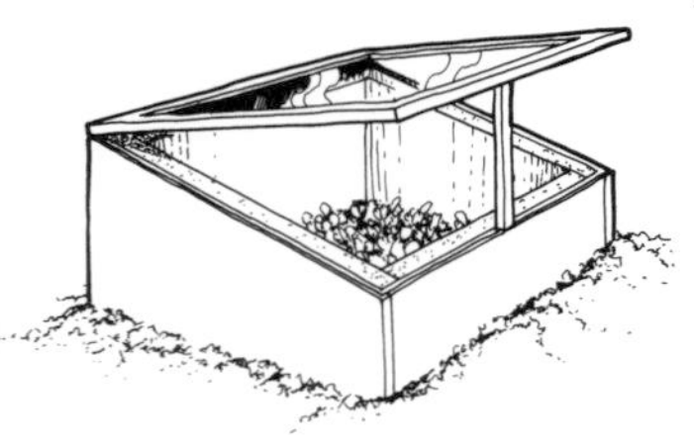

Venting a cold frame

SEE ALSO: *For an explanation of hardening off, page 54.*

Planting Outdoors

Q What do I need to do to prepare my garden soil so I can sow seeds?

A Soil that's rich in organic matter is perfect for sowing seeds, so use the recommendations in chapter 2 to amend your soil as necessary. To prepare an ideal seedbed for sowing, rake the soil smooth and break up any clods of soil. Remove any rocks and weeds.

Q After preparing my soil, do I just "plunk in" the seeds? Are there tips to make things easier?

A For larger seeds, plunking them in is just what you do. The traditional way to plant a straight row of seeds is to put a stake at each end of the row and run a string between the stakes. Then use a corner of your hoe to make a shallow furrow. An even easier method is to simply lay the handle of your hoe on the soil where you want the seeds to grow, and press it down to make a straight, perfect furrow in a single step.

Using a hoe handle to make furrows

Once the furrow is made, just place the seeds at the proper spacing, then use your hand or hoe blade to cover them lightly with soil. If you're sowing in wide rows or are sowing a crop such as lettuce, which has small seeds, lightly scatter the seeds over the top of the bed or sprinkle them along the furrows.

Q **I always end up with seeds that are too crowded or with all the seeds on one side of the bed. How can I spread them out more evenly?**

A To space out large seeds, try using a board with marks on it or notches cut out of it every 3"/7.6 cm. Use the notches to place seeds at their proper spacing. For tiny seed, try mixing it with a bit of builder's sand, then broadcast seed and sand together. There also are a variety of mechanical seeders available that help you sow seed and also reduce the need to thin out excess seedlings, from inexpensive handheld seeders to mechanical devices you push along the row to dig a furrow, seed, and cover all in one pass.

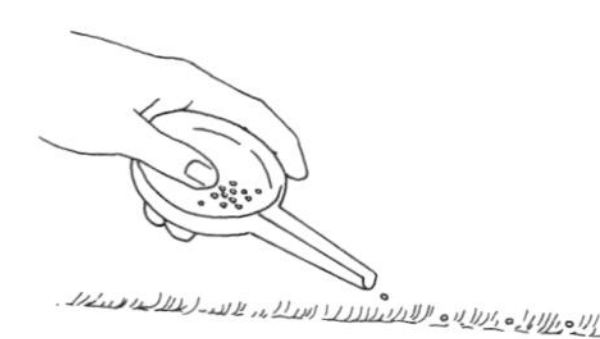

Handheld seeder for sowing small seeds

Q Is there any other way to space out seeds?

A You can make your own seed tapes. This is a great activity for late winter or early spring when there's not much you can do outside in the garden.

1. Rip off a 5'/1.5 m-long section of connected paper towels and cut lengthwise strips ¾"/1.9 cm wide.
2. Dissolve a tablespoon of cornstarch in a cup of water. Heat it until it boils, stir constantly to prevent lumps, and let it cool.
3. In a plastic sandwich bag, combine 1–2 teaspoons/4.9–9.9 ml of cooled cornstarch solution with ¼ teaspoon/1.2 ml of seeds.
4. Lay out a strip of paper toweling, and on it write the name of the crop you're sowing.
5. Cut a tiny hole in one corner of the plastic bag, and squeeze out tiny droplets of the solution along a strip of toweling. Space the drops according to the spacing of the crop you're growing.

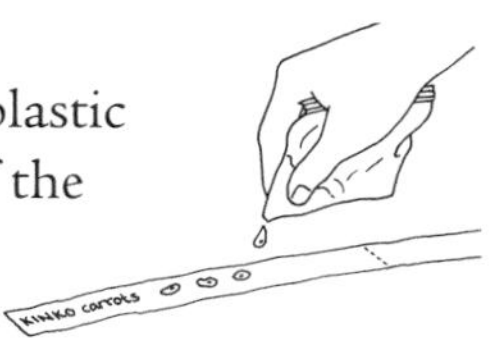

Making a seed tape

6. Let the paper dry, then roll it up and store it in a plastic bag in a cool, dry place.
7. When it's time to plant, just unroll your homemade seed tape in a furrow and cover it with soil.

Super-Simple Staking and Trellising

THE BEST TIME TO SET UP SUPPORTS for vegetable crops is before or at planting time. When they have support, pole beans, peas, and tomatoes will produce a better-quality crop that's also easier to pick. String trellises and free-standing teepees are fun and easy to set up.

String Trellises

String trellises with simple teepees as the end supports work well for supporting pole beans. Use three bamboo poles or 6'/1.8 m-long garden stakes for each teepee. Place another pole across the top that runs from one teepee to the other. Run strings between the outside legs of the tee-

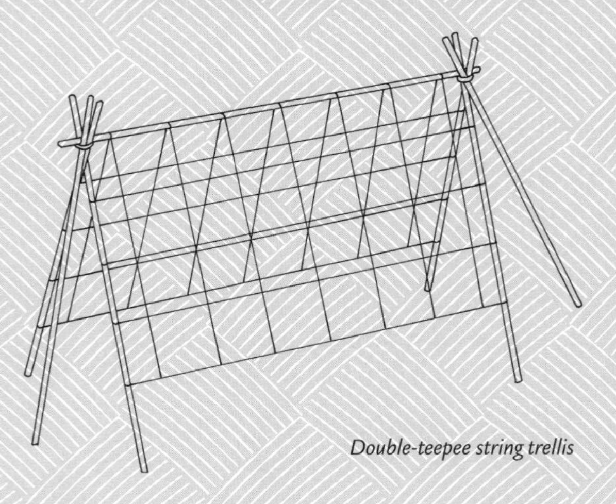

Double-teepee string trellis

pee. Then tie strings vertically from the top pole down to the strings that run across the bottom. Plant transplants or seeds at the bottom of each vertical string. At the end of the season, cut down all the strings; roll them up, plants and all; and add them to the compost pile.

Freestanding Teepees

Teepees are a great option for trellising pole beans as well as cucumbers and peas, all of which either climb by twining or clasping supports with tendrils. They're easy to make, inexpensive, and quite handsome. Make them from bamboo poles, 1"x2"/2.5x5 cm wooden stakes, or even saplings. Use five or more poles that are about 8'/2.4 m long and tie the tops together with heavy twine. Add twine between poles for extra support. Be sure to stick the base of each pole 4"–6"/10–15.2 cm into the soil so the teepee is sturdy.

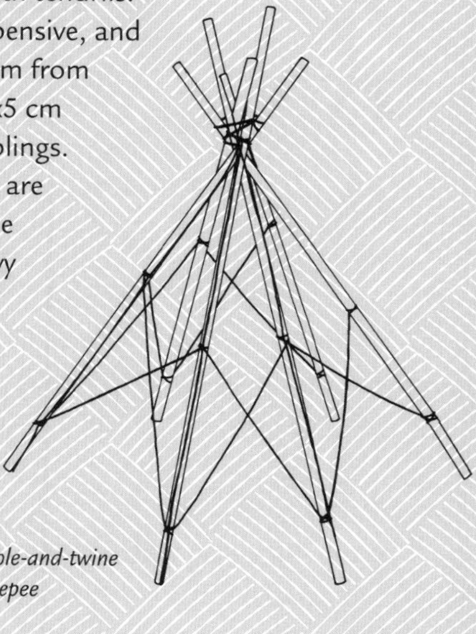

Pole-and-twine teepee

Q I'm ready to plant my garden and will be growing a few things that need staking or trellising. Do I plant first or put up the trellises first?

A While it is possible to gently insert a small stake next to a new transplant without damaging it, you definitely want to install trellises before you sow seed or move transplants. Otherwise, it's far too easy to crush baby plants, break off branches, or damage roots. If plants aren't in the picture yet, once you've installed supports it's easy to fluff up the soil and add a bit of extra compost to repair any damage caused by stepping on the soil by mistake.

Q Do I need to water the garden after I've sown seeds?

A If you are planting in spring, the soil usually is moist enough for seeds to germinate without much supplemental watering. But don't just think of sowing as a springtime activity! Ideally, you'll be planting new batches of seed throughout the season, from spring to fall, to keep the garden producing and to spread out the harvest. For best results whenever you sow, give seeds a little extra TLC, and you'll be rewarded by bumper crops later on. Consider the following:

- **COVER NEWLY SOWN SEEDS** with potting mix instead of garden soil, then cover the sown area with floating row covers. Potting mix is lighter and less prone to crusting than garden soil, and it will let seedlings break through to the surface more easily. Floating row covers protect seedlings from wind, pests, and other problems.

- **IF THE SOIL IS DRY,** water the row at planting time and sprinkle the area regularly to keep it evenly moist but not wet. In summer you may need to sprinkle newly sown seeds daily or every other day. Try placing a full watering can in view as a reminder. If you forget to water and the soil dries out once seeds have begun to germinate, the seedlings can die.
- **ONCE SEEDLINGS ARE UP** and growing, check them frequently, and water as necessary to keep the soil evenly moist.

Q What other care do seedlings need?

A Thin plants to their final spacing when they have a few sets of true leaves, either by cutting them off or pulling them up. If you pull up the extra seedlings, be sure to gently press down the soil around the remaining seedlings. It's also a good idea to cover sown seedbeds with floating row covers (see pages 134–136) to help protect emerging plants from all types of insect pests. See chapter 4 for more on preventing problems with pests.

Dealing with Transplants

Q **I don't want to bother with seeds this year, so how do I make sure I buy healthy transplants?**

A First, you're better off buying transplants from a garden center than from a grocery store or big-box store, where they may or may not get adequate watering or other care. Look for bushy, compact plants that have healthy green leaves. Check the roots, too, by gently dumping a plant out of its pot while holding the top of the rootball between your fingers. Avoid plants that show any of the warning signs of poor quality, as described on page 52.

If you decide to buy larger plants, pick off any fruits that have already started forming. This redirects the plants' energy into producing roots, which it will need for the long haul. If the nursery or garden center you usually shop at only offers seedlings in market packs, and you don't want to grow six plants of a single cultivar, try one of these options:

- **SHOP AT A LOCAL FARMERS' MARKET** in spring. Local growers often offer vegetable seedlings for sale.
- **SHOP FOR SEEDLINGS ONLINE.** There are Internet companies that sell single transplants.
- **BUY MARKET PACKS** of all the cultivars you want to grow, and share excess seedlings with friends and neighbors. Or see if a local community gardening

group, garden club, or food pantry would be able to use the extras.

- **ASK IF THE NURSERY WILL LET YOU "SWITCH OUT"** cultivars in a market pack.
- **BUY ALL THE CULTIVARS YOU WANT** to grow, and toss the extra plants on the compost pile.

Q **I bought plants growing in 4"x6"/10x15.2 cm plastic containers with eight plants in each container. How should I transplant them?**

A A few days before you're ready to transplant, water them, then use a sharp knife to cut between the individual plants. Don't take them out of the containers; just leave them where they are. This technique, called blocking, encourages roots to branch so the plants will be ready to go into the garden. It will be easy to slip the individual plants free of the container on planting day.

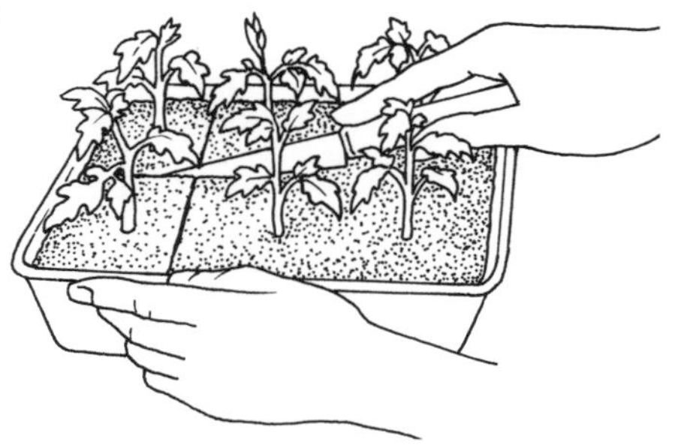

Blocking a container of transplants

DON'T BUY ME!

Before you buy, check each and every six pack for these warning signals. If you see any of them, it's buyer beware!

- **OVERGROWN PLANTS** that are very tall but whose roots are still contained in tiny pots
- **PLANTS THAT ARE POTBOUND,** with loads of roots circling the rootball
- **DRIED-OUT ROOTBALLS** or soggy rootballs with dark roots
- **SICKLY LOOKING,** yellow, or purplish leaves
- **CRISPY, DEAD LEAVES** or signs that the plants have been allowed to dry out and wilt between waterings
- **SIGNS OF BUG INFESTATIONS:** Put on your reading glasses if you need them to spot tiny pests like aphids. Also look for webs on the uppermost leaves and stem tips, yellow spots on foliage, a sticky coating on leaves that may be covered by sooty mold, or clouds of insects that fly up when disturbed.

Q **What's the best way to transplant my veggie starts? Will they need special care right after planting?**

A Once you've hardened off your plants as described on page 54, water them thoroughly on the day they're going to go into the garden. Starting at one end of the row, begin digging holes and setting plants in place. Make each planting hole about the same depth as but slightly wider than the transplant's soil ball, and firm the soil gently around each plant when you set it in the ground. Leave a shallow depression around each transplant, so water can collect. If the soil is at all dry or the weather is sunny (transplanting on a cloudy or rainy cool day is best), water each plant as you go. Especially if the weather is sunny, provide shade to protect transplants until they've adjusted. Upturned bushel baskets, pieces of lattice propped along the row, or burlap draped over supports are all easy ways to provide a bit of shade. If you haven't been watering each plant as it went into the ground, be sure to water the entire row thoroughly once you're finished. It's also a good idea to install a cutworm collar around each seedling as you plant.

SEE ALSO: *For more on cutworms, page 157.*

Getting Your Transplants to the Garden

SEEDLINGS THAT HAVE BEEN PROTECTED INDOORS aren't ready for the rigors of the garden just because the last frost date has passed. Drying winds, intense sun, variations in soil moisture, and other extreme conditions cause a condition called transplant shock, which leads to wilted and even dead seedlings. Before you move homegrown veggies (or purchased transplants) to the garden, be sure to harden them off by gradually exposing them to the outdoors. Hardening off helps toughen plants so they can handle the vagaries of weather outdoors. Set the seedlings outdoors in the following sequence:

DAY 1. In a spot with bright light, but not direct sun, for an hour or so.

DAY 2. In the same spot for about 3 hours.

DAY 3. In a partly sunny spot for about 5 hours.

DAY 4. In a partly sunny spot for the day.

DAY 5. In the morning and leave them out for the day and overnight.

Protect your seedlings from animal pests throughout this process. When they're fully hardened, transplant, ideally on a day when the weather is cloudy, overcast, or even rainy.

Q **The calendar says it's time to start planting, but it still seems pretty chilly in the morning. What can I do to protect my seedlings from the cold?**

A Preheating the soil by covering it with black plastic mulch is a great way to improve conditions in the garden and get plants growing on time in spring. Floating row covers (pages 134–136) provide a bit of protection for transplants but not more than a couple of degrees. For more protection, cut the bottoms from milk jugs and place them over transplants (remove the caps during the day for ventilation), or place wire hoops over the rows and cover them with ventilated clear plastic. You can even use paper bags or fold hats out of newspaper and place them over seedlings for protection during an unexpected cold snap.

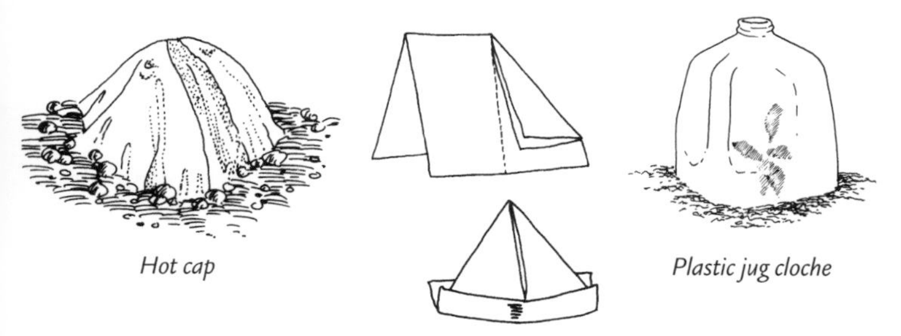

Hot cap

Plastic jug cloche

Newspaper hat: fold corners to center and bottom flaps up

SEE ALSO: *For more on plastic mulch, pages 105–106.*

Garden Scheduling

Q As I begin to read about individual vegetables, I am overwhelmed by the number of different dates and schedules. How do I keep track of what to plant when?

A One of the simplest systems is to jot a schedule down on a calendar, preferably one that you use every day so you'll see reminders regularly. First, list the crops you want to grow on a sheet of paper or in a garden notebook. Next, determine your average last spring frost date, by calling your local Cooperative Extension Service office or checking the Internet.

Start your planting schedule with the first crop on your list. Check the seed packet(s) or the sowing and transplanting recommendations in Part Two to determine how you are going to grow it. Let's use tomatoes as an example. The seeds need to be started indoors 6 to 8 weeks before the last spring frost date and transplanted out once the weather warms up. To determine when to sow seeds, count back 6 to 8 weeks from your frost date, then jot a note, such as "sow tomatoes," on your calendar. Make a similar note for the recommended transplant date, 2 weeks after the last frost date.

Repeat the process for each crop you are planning to grow. If you end up with too many crops to sow or transplant on a particular date, simply move some of them to another date that works for you. The end result is an organized plan of attack for your spring gardening activities.

Q **I live in central Florida, and it's just too hot in the summertime to garden — both for me and for most of the vegetables I grow. Should I just let everything die and wait for cooler weather?**

A Many gardeners in hot climates simply split their growing season in half. They grow crops in spring and early summer, and then again from fall to winter. You can let everything die out and start over once the weather is a bit cooler, since plants that have been stressed by the heat and disease likely won't produce as well as fresh new transplants. If you do decide to replant everything, it's best to pull out or cut down the plants from your spring garden (especially if they're diseased) and take steps to protect the soil from the blazing summer sun. Either plant a cover crop, or cover the soil with a layer of mulch to protect it until you can replant. If your crops such as tomatoes and peppers don't seem stressed by the midsummer heat, prune them back, sidedress with compost, and water them deeply to give them a jump start for the second half of the season.

SEE ALSO: *For cover crops, pages 68–69.*

Cool Season, Warm Season

DEPENDING ON THE TEMPERATURES they prefer, vegetables fall into two general groups: warm season or cool season. Warm-season plants, such as tomatoes, peppers, eggplants, and beans, thrive in hot summertime weather, are started around the same time in spring, and are planted out on or around the last spring frost date. (In southern zones, where summers are hot, they're often grown in spring and early summer, then again in fall and early winter.) While none tolerate cold weather, they don't share everything in common. Beans can be moved to the garden when the soil is 55°F/12.7°C, but peppers or eggplant require a minimum of 60°F/15.5°C.

Cool-weather vegetables – cabbage, broccoli, lettuce, kale, and spinach – are the plants to grow in spring and fall. Start in spring for an early summer crop or in late summer for fall harvest. (In mild climates, grow over winter.) While temperatures in the 60s and 70s/15.5–26.1°C are ideal, they also adapt to cooler temperatures and can be grown under plastic tunnels or other season-extending devices.

COOL-SEASON CROPS		WARM-SEASON CROPS	
Beets	Lettuces	Beans	Squash
Broccoli	Peas	Eggplant	Sweet Potatoes
Cabbage	Radishes	Melons	
Carrots	Spinach	Okra	Tomatoes
Cauliflower		Peppers	

Succession Planting and Interplanting

Q I had a nice lettuce crop this year, but the weather is too hot for another lettuce planting now. I don't want to just pull it up and leave the space empty. What should I plant next?

A Following one crop with another is called succession planting, and it's a great way to increase the harvest from your vegetable garden without making the garden any bigger. You can follow a crop of spring lettuce with heat-loving tomatoes, peppers, or eggplants. Bush beans are another option. Late in the season, follow these warm-weather crops with cool-season greens such as lettuce or spinach.

Q I live in Helena, Montana, and our growing season is really short. Is it even possible to do succession plantings?

A Gardeners in Helena (Zone 4) have about 95 frost-free days in the growing season. Add the number of days to maturity together for the crops you want to grow to see if your season is long enough. In areas where the season is short, you probably have time for only two crops – peas followed by a fall crop of lettuce, for example. Gardeners in Zone 5 have a little more time and can probably fit in three crops – lettuce followed by tomatoes, followed by kale in fall, for example. In contrast, gardeners in Picayune, Mississippi (Zone 8 or 9), who have approximately 221 frost-free days in which to grow, can produce a succession of crops from late winter to late fall.

Keep in mind that as fall approaches, plants grow more slowly than they do in spring. They may be as much as 2 to 3 weeks later than the days-to-maturity indicated on the seed packet. (On the other hand, if fall weather is warm, they might beat the days-to-maturity by a week.) To make sure there's enough time for a harvest, add 2 weeks to the days to maturity for fall crops to compensate for declining light and cooler temperatures later in the growing season.

For extra insurance in fall, plan on installing season-extension devices over late crops: Hoops covered with polyethylene give good protection, but be sure to vent or remove them during the day when temperatures are warmer. You can also wrap polyethylene around tomato cages or cover crops with floating row covers to protect them.

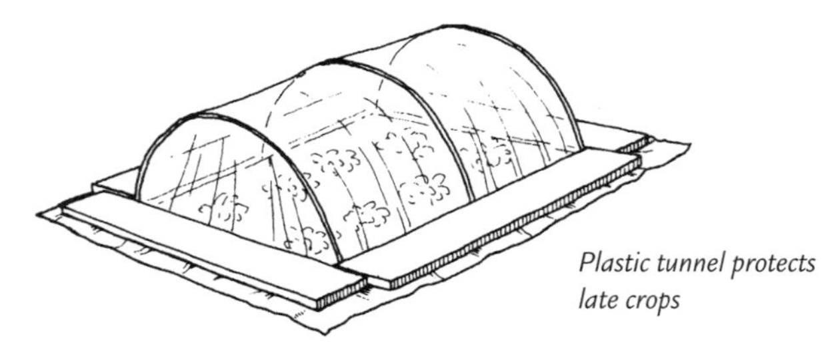

Plastic tunnel protects late crops

SEE ALSO: *For more on zones, page 170.*

Q **I've spaced out my cabbage and broccoli plants, but there's a lot of unplanted soil between them. Can I use it to grow other plants?**

A Interplanting – planting a fast-growing crop in between a slower-growing one – is an excellent way to use that unplanted space. It also boosts yields without expanding your garden. To use this technique, first plant a slower-growing, longer-season crop, such as onions, leeks, peppers, tomatoes, Brussels sprouts, or eggplant, using the standard recommended spacing. Then fill the space in between the slower-growing plants with fast-to-mature crops such as leaf lettuce, radishes, beets, bush beans, or spinach. The fast-growing crops will be ready for harvest by the time the slower-growing ones have grown large enough to need all the space.

Onions interplanted with lettuce

Crop Rotation

Q How does rotating crops help my garden?

A Rotating crops makes it easier to maintain soil fertility, because some crops are heavy feeders and others are not. Also, different crops remove different amounts of the various minor nutrients, such as iron and magnesium, from the soil. So by rotating crops, you'll make the most efficient use of the nutrient reservoir in your soil.

Is there a really simple crop-rotation plan I can follow?

A Yes. To keep the soil fertile, pay attention to how each crop affects the soil. Crops can be heavy feeders, light feeders, or soil builders. Heavy feeders include tomatoes, broccoli, cabbage, corn, lettuce and other leafy vegetables, eggplant, and beets. Alternate heavy feeders with either light feeders or soil builders. Light feeders include garlic, onions, peppers, potatoes, radishes, rutabagas, sweet potatoes, Swiss chard, and turnips. Soil builders include peas, beans, and cover crops like clover.

Q **My garden is tiny, so I don't have many places where I can plant different crops. Will my garden fail if I don't rotate crops?**

A No, it won't, especially if you add plenty of compost in spring and/or fall to ensure that nutrients used up by heavy-feeding crops like corn or tomatoes are replaced. You may also want to consider planting some living mulches or green manures to add additional organic matter and nutrients. Try sowing legumes such as dwarf white clover or hairy vetch around tomatoes, for example, or plant these crops immediately after pulling up your tomatoes for the year. Till the residue into the soil in spring.

SEE ALSO: *For more information on living mulches and green manures, pages 68–69.*

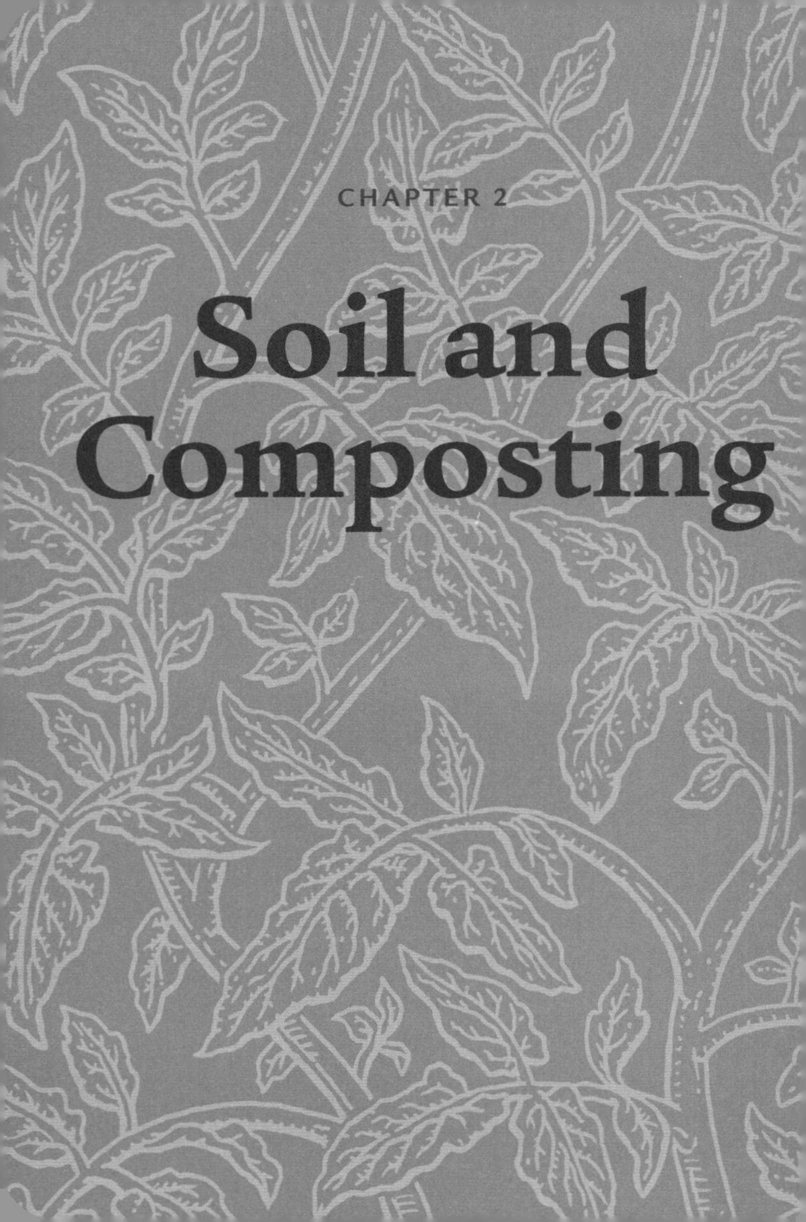

CHAPTER 2

Soil and Composting

Great Soil for Great Gardens

Q I heard someone on a radio gardening show talking about soil care and how important it is to take care of your soil's "microherd." Just what does that mean?

A Soil isn't just an inanimate substance that supports plant roots; it's actually a complex community of living things that successful gardeners actively cultivate. Organisms in the soil – its microherd – break down compost and other organic matter slowly, releasing nutrients to plants. They're the basis for the process that organic gardeners swear by: "Feed the soil, and let the soil feed the plants." Earthworms are one component of a soil's microherd, but it contains many other organisms, including insects, bacteria, fungi, and other microscopic organisms, both good and bad. Gardeners care for soil and its microherd by adding compost, manure, and other organic matter. A large, active microherd speeds the breakdown of organic matter and also helps decrease problems with plant diseases and pests. The more organic matter a soil contains – and the more different types of organic materials you add to your soil – the larger and more active its microherd will be. And the more active the microherd, the more nutrients there are that are available to plants.

Soils rich in organic matter have good tilth, meaning they have a loose, crumbly structure and are easy to dig or work. (The microherd helps form this crumbly structure that's so desired by gardeners.) Ideal planting soils drain well, because they have plenty of large spaces, or pores, that hold air that plant roots need to grow. Organic matter – especially humus, the end product of the decomposition of compost and other organic matter – also holds moisture in the soil, which is essential to plants as well as the microherd.

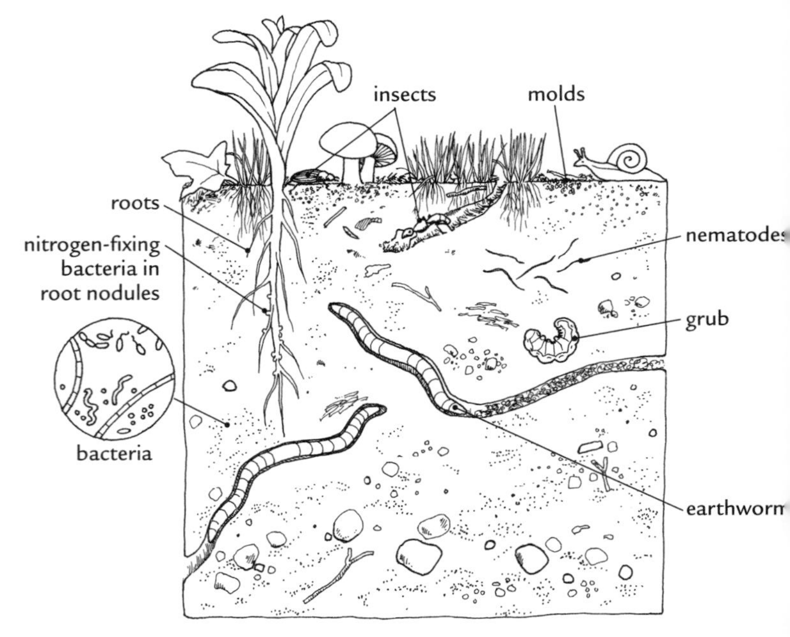

The Soil Microherd

Q **Why is it important to know whether my soil is clayey or sandy?**

A You need to know because it will affect when and how you plant and water your garden.

- Clay soil is very heavy when wet. It holds water and nutrients but stays wet and cool for a long time in spring, so you may have to plant your crops later than the standard recommended time. When it's dry, the soil can be as hard as cement, and naturally, plant roots don't fare too well in those conditions!
- Sandy soil is gritty and doesn't hold together well; water drains through it quickly. It's easy to plant in sandy soil, because it warms up and dries out quickly in spring, but it requires more frequent watering, and more added organic matter to keep crops from suffering nutrient stress.
- Loamy soil, which contains a relatively equal mix of clay, sand, and silt, is ideal for vegetable gardening.

Grab a handful of soil and rub it between your palms. Clay soil has a sticky texture, and you can form a long "worm" of soil easily. Sandy soil is gritty and won't stick together at all. Loamy soil clings together, but clumps break apart easily with a little pressure from your thumb.

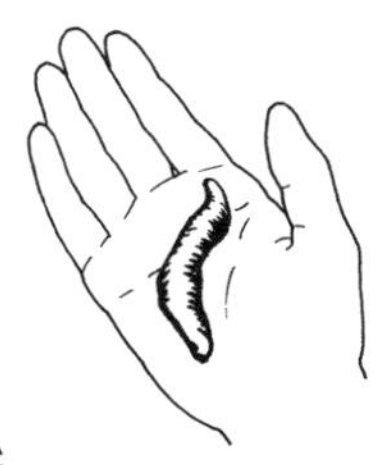

A "worm" of clay soil

Keep It Covered

COVER CROPS — also called green manures — offer one of the easiest ways to improve your soil. They not only add essential organic matter to the soil; they also reduce erosion, improve compacted soil, outcompete weeds, encourage beneficial insects, and pull nutrients up from lower soil layers. Tilling or digging a cover crop into the soil also encourages robust populations of beneficial soil microbes, which reduces pests and diseases. In fact, they are one of the biggest undiscovered secrets to a great garden, plus they're easy to plant and grow.

Sow cold-tolerant crops in early spring or fall, heat-tolerant ones in summer. Sow about 1 cup per 50 square feet/4.5 square meters; read seed package instructions for more exact rates. Simply broadcast the seed over the soil and rake it in. Water the area gently after sowing, unless rain is expected.

Here's how to put cover crops to work in your garden:

- **PROTECT THE SOIL.** Cover crops to sow in spring or fall include crimson clover, hairy vetch, oats, ryegrass, and kale. Try buckwheat, red clover, Sudan grass, or sweet clover in spring and summer.
- **TAKE A SUMMER BREAK.** In the South, summertime temperatures make gardening difficult. Sow a heat-

tolerant cover crop such as Sudan grass, cowpeas, or buckwheat until you begin to garden again in fall.

- **USE A KILLED COVER.** You don't necessarily have to dig in a cover crop: Sow crops in late summer or fall that are killed by winter cold, then plant your crops through the remains of the crop when the next season starts. Try this with hairy vetch or annual ryegrass (from Zone 5 north).
- **PLANT SMALL BLOCKS.** Don't wait until your entire garden is empty. Sow cover crops as small blocks and patches of soil become available.
- **DIG IN.** Be sure to dig in cover crops before they go to seed, self-sow, and become weedy. No more than a week after they begin to flower, cut them down, using a mower or string trimmer.
- **PLANT AGAIN AND AGAIN.** If you are leaving part of your garden fallow for a season or are improving new soil for next year, dig in one cover crop and plant another.
- **GROW SOME MULCH.** Use cover crops as living mulches to protect soil and reduce weed problems: 4 or 5 weeks after planting your main crop, sow seed of crops such as crimson clover, dwarf white clover, or annual ryegrass.

Q When and how can I add organic matter to my garden?

A Try to add organic matter every time you plant, dig, or till. Here's a basic plan that will improve any soil, from clay to sand:

- **ADD BEFORE YOU PLANT.** When preparing a new garden bed, spread a thick layer of compost, well-rotted manure, or other organic matter. Then add a new layer of organic matter every spring after that. See the next page for help determining how much organic matter you'll need.
- **APPLY MULCH.** Once the soil warms up and crops are in place and growing, spread a layer of organic mulch, such as straw, dried grass clippings, or chopped leaves.
- **DIG IN AT SEASON'S END.** Once a particular crop is finished, dig the mulch and crop residue into the soil (unless it is diseased).
- **PLANT A COVER CROP.** Once you've pulled out a crop at season's end, sow an annual cover crop like red clover or hairy vetch to protect the soil over winter, control weeds, and add more organic matter. Dig it into the soil a few weeks before planting in spring.

Q **I'm preparing a new garden bed this spring. How thick a layer of organic matter should I spread over it before I start planting?**

A The amount of organic matter you should add depends on where you live, what kind of soil you're starting with, and also how you garden. In the North, a 1"–2"/2.5–5 cm layer is sufficient. After the first year, add at least 1"/2.5 cm per year in the spring. Since organic matter is used up much more quickly in southern gardens because of the hot, humid weather, start with a 3"–4"/7.6–10.2 cm layer. In subsequent years, add 2"–3"/5–7.6 cm per year. No matter where you live, if you are dealing with heavy clay soil or sandy soil or if you are planning on gardening intensively, add twice the standard recommended amounts for your area.

Q **What will happen if I just prepare a bed and plant a vegetable crop without adding any extra organic matter?**

A One of the most straightforward ways to answer this question is to try it. Follow the bed preparation steps on pages 78–79, but skip the step of adding organic matter. Wait a couple of weeks to let the soil settle, then start planting. As your crops grow, monitor how vigorous they are, and at the end of the season, evaluate your harvest. If plants aren't doing well, mulch with compost and consider supplementing with organic fertilizers. You may get satisfactory results from a single crop, but keep in mind that you'll need to add more organic matter before you plant the next one, because each crop uses up lots of nutrients in the soil.

SEE ALSO: *For a year-round approach to improving garden soil, page 71.*

I have horrible soil and am very close to giving up on gardening. Is there any hope?

A Raised beds are a terrific solution if horrible soil is your lot in life. Whether you have pure clay or only an inch of soil over bedrock, you can make framed raised beds and fill them with purchased topsoil mixed with compost to create perfect growing conditions. See page 82 to learn how to make this kind of raised bed.

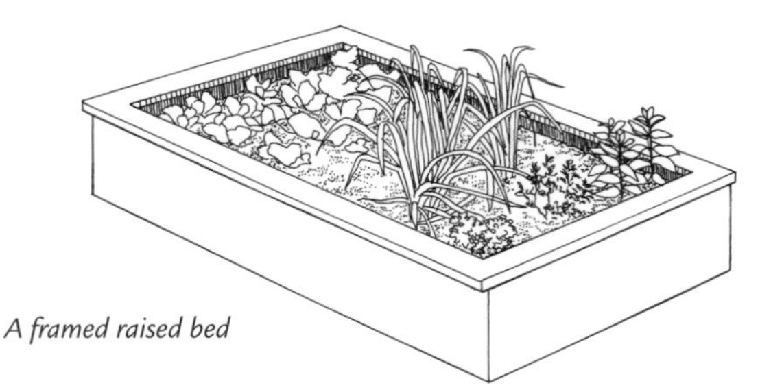

A framed raised bed

EARTHWORMS

If you have loads of earthworms, you probably have rich, healthy soil. Earthworms tunnel through soil looking for organic matter to ingest, and in the process they aerate the soil, making it looser and easier for roots to penetrate. They also bring organic matter from the soil surface down into your plants' root zones.

It's easy to check how healthy your soil's earthworm population is. First make sure your soil is moist and relatively warm. (You won't find earthworms in dry soil or if the weather is too cold or too hot, since they tunnel down deep to escape extreme conditions.) Dig a 1'/⅓ m-wide, 10"/25.4 cm-deep hole. Count the number of worms in the soil removed from the hole. If you have more than ten, your soil is in great shape; six to ten, it's pretty good but would benefit from more organic matter. If you find fewer than six earthworms, your soil has low organic matter levels, poor soil drainage, or a pH level that is either too acid or too alkaline.

I want to have a really great garden. What are the big soil-care mistakes I should try to avoid?

There are a few basic rules all gardeners should follow. First, develop the habit of adding organic matter every chance you get. In addition:

- **DON'T WORK SOIL WHEN IT'S TOO WET.** Squeeze a handful in your hand; if it forms a tight ball, it's too wet. The handful should crumble easily before you dig, as shown on page 77.
- **DON'T WORK SOIL WHEN IT'S TOO DRY.** Digging dusty-dry soil will pulverize it and destroy its texture. Water dry soil deeply before you work it.
- **DON'T LEAVE IT BARE TOO LONG.** Direct sunlight dries out soil fast, and your soil microherd will die out without moisture. Bare soil erodes when it rains, and it's an invitation to weed problems. Except for short periods when you're trying to warm the soil, keep it covered with mulch, veggie crops, or cover crops.
- **KEEP OFF!** Once you've prepared the soil for planting, don't walk on it. Half the volume of soil should be pore space occupied by air and water. Walking on soil compresses the pores and makes the soil less hospitable to plant roots.

DRAINAGE DILEMMAS

If your soil is soppy for days after a rainstorm or stays wet for a long time in spring, you need to do something to improve drainage. Vegetables need soil that is moist and rich but that drains well, because, in addition to water, roots need air in the soil to grow well. If you're gardening on a low-lying spot, look around your property for a higher sunny spot with better drainage. You could try regrading the site to improve drainage, but this can be a large-scale, expensive project. Installing drainage tile is a project for professionals, too.

Other problems that can cause poor drainage include heavy clay soil and/or compacted soil. Adding sand to clay soil isn't a practical solution, because it would take several tons to improve the top 6"/15.2 cm of soil.

The best solution is to build raised beds on the site and fill them with improved soil. If possible, loosen the soil at the site and add plenty of organic matter to it before you build the beds.

Soil Management Basics

Q Do I have to get my soil tested?

A There are good gardeners who have their soil tested regularly and equally good gardeners who have never had it done. If your plants don't seem to be growing as well as they should or you suspect your soil's pH is out of the best range for vegetables (6.5 to 7.0), testing your soil will help you adjust nutrient levels and pH. On the other hand, if everything seems to be growing well, and it doesn't bother you that you don't know your exact pH, don't worry too much about it. If you do decide to have your soil tested, follow the directions for collecting the sample carefully. Also, ask for organic recommendations for correcting nutrient deficiencies.

Many local Cooperative Extension Service offices provide soil-testing services. Contact your local office to find out where to pick up a kit. They are sometimes available through the office itself but also may be available at the local library. Commercial soil-testing labs are another excellent option. Finally, you can also purchase a home soil-test kit to test for pH as well as nutrient levels.

SEE ALSO: *For more information on pH, page 413.*

Is It Ready Yet?

PLANTING INSTRUCTIONS for peas and other crops say to sow "as early as the soil can be worked in spring," so it's helpful to know how to test whether your soil is "ready to work." Grab a handful of soil from the bed you want to plant and squeeze it tightly. It will probably form a clod or clump. Press on the clod with your thumb: If it breaks apart easily with gentle pressure, the moisture level is right for digging. If it doesn't break apart, it's too wet to dig, so wait a few days. If your soil won't form a clod at all, it's too dry, so water it deeply, and test it again. For early spring crops, the soil also has to be warm enough for seed to germinate. (The range of temperatures at which seed will germinate varies from crop to crop.) A soil thermometer will tell you exactly what the temperature is, or you can use other seed-sowing guidelines, such as the number of weeks before the last spring frost date, to determine whether it should be warm enough to plant.

Too wet

Just right

Too dry

Q **My husband and I have picked out our garden site. What do we need to do next to get it ready for planting?**

A Prepare the soil well before it's time to plant: Ideally, a full season ahead – in fall for spring planting, for example. If you can't do that, dig a new garden in spring once the soil is dry enough to work, as explained on page 77. For fabulous results, mark off the site with stakes, then follow these steps:

1. **REMOVE GRASS AND WEEDS.** Slice off lawn grass with a sharp spade, or rent a sod cutter to remove it. (Cut pieces of sod can be put upside-down on a compost heap; lift and reposition them if any continue to grow. They'll break down into terrific compost in a few months to a year.)

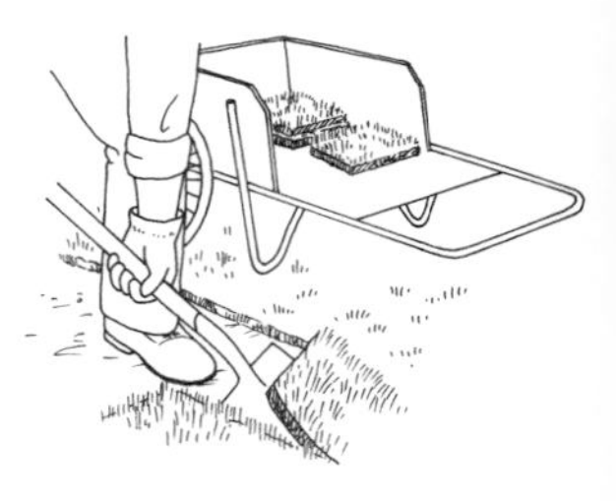

2. **SPREAD ORGANIC MATTER.** Spread a 3"–4"/7.6–10.2 cm layer of organic matter over the site and dig or till it into the soil. You can use compost, well-rotted manure, grass clippings,

chopped leaves, or any combination of organic matter that's at hand. If you decide to use grass clippings, chopped leaves, or other rough organic matter, wait several weeks for it to break down before planting the bed.

3. **MULCH.** Apply a light layer of compost or other organic mulch to help prevent rain from beating down the soil clods and wind from blowing soil away until you're ready to plant the bed. If you need to prewarm the soil for spring crops, cover it with plastic mulch, as described on pages 105–106.

4. **RAKE IT SMOOTH.** On planting day pull back the covering of organic mulch and rake the surface of the bed smooth. Break up large clods of soil as needed, but don't try to break up every clump of dirt. Ideally, you want the surface to be covered with small, loose clumps.

If you prefer not to dig to create garden beds, try one of the other bed-preparation methods described on pages 82–84.

Q I've got a tiller to break up my soil. How often should I use it?

A Tillers are great back-saving devices, but use them too much and you'll actually destroy your soil. While dirt doesn't seem like something you could destroy, tilling it too often (or working it when it's too wet or too dry) breaks down both small and large clods until the soil is essentially dust. Soil clods, called crumbs or aggregates, affect how water and air move through soil and how available both are to roots. They also are important for the health of earthworms and other beneficial soil organisms. When preparing a new garden or incorporating a new layer of organic matter, try to accomplish the job with a single pass of the tiller. Avoid using a tiller for everyday weeding or routine soil cultivation, to avoid breaking down smaller soil aggregates. A good rule to follow is never to till your soil without adding more organic matter to it.

SEE ALSO: *For more about soil structure, page 414.*

Can I create a vegetable garden on a site that's covered with bindweed or poison ivy?

A To kill a stubborn woody weed like poison ivy, cut it back to the ground and cover the whole site tightly with a layer of black plastic for up to a year. Then remove the plastic, and cover the site with a thick layer of newspapers topped by mulch, as shown on page 82.

Raised Beds

Q Do raised beds have to be a certain size or shape for growing vegetables?

A Raised beds can be any shape you like, although rectangular is traditional. The simplest raised beds are freestanding, meaning they are created by simply hoeing up soil to create a bed that's higher than the surrounding soil. Freestanding beds are a good option if you aren't sure exactly how your garden is going to be laid out. You'll need to maintain them by periodically hoeing up soil, compost, and mulch that have spread from the beds out into the pathways.

Make the beds narrow enough that you can easily reach the center of the bed from the sides – from 3'/.9 m to perhaps 5'/1.5 m wide – so you can tend plants without stepping on the soil. It's best to create ones that aren't too long, too. Otherwise it's tempting to walk across them if you need to move from one row to another, and you'll compact the soil in the process.

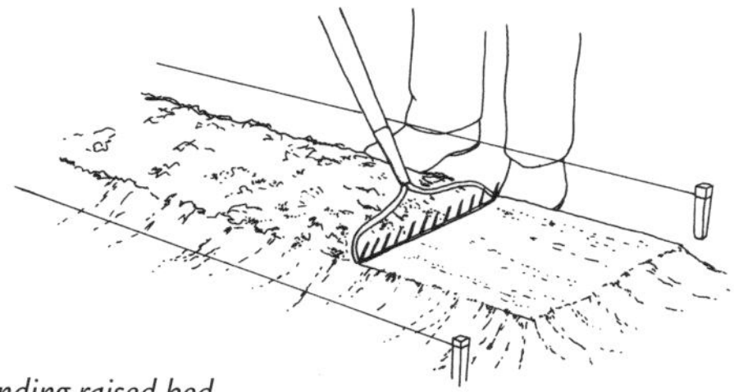

Making a freestanding raised bed

Q **I don't have any gardening beds prepared. Are raised beds the quickest way to make them?**

A Yes, even if you have a site that's currently covered by lawn, you can build a raised bed right on top of the sod and be ready to plant in as little as a weekend. To do this, mark off the site and cover the grass with a thick layer of overlapped newspapers or corrugated cardboard. (Weight down the paper or cardboard with shovels full of topsoil as you spread it or soak it with the hose; otherwise the wind will blow it away.) Then frame the site with landscape ties or 2×6s/38×140 mm, laying the sides over the edge of the paper or cardboard to discourage grass from growing up into the garden. Use stakes to hold the frame in place. Fill the garden with a mix of purchased topsoil and compost. Mound the soil mix several inches above the outer frame, then water it thoroughly to help it settle. Let the soil dry for a day or so before planting.

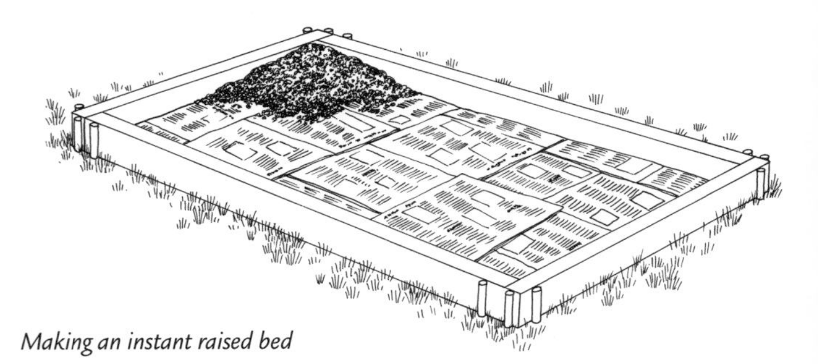

Making an instant raised bed

Q **What are the other options for framing in permanent raised beds?**

A If you don't want to use landscape ties, consider framing raised beds with boards that are connected by wood screws at the ends and staked in place along their length. You also can purchase corners for beds that hold the boards or landscape ties in place (they're available from mail-order garden suppliers). For a more formal look, consider framing beds with stone or brick.

Q **I plan to enlarge my vegetable garden quite a bit next season. Is there anything I can do to eliminate having to dig up the lawn by hand?**

A If you're not itching to plant tomorrow, you can use no-dig methods to create great garden beds. Here's how:

1. If you haven't had rain recently, water the site thoroughly – you'll want to soak the soil to a depth of at least 6"/15.2 cm.
2. Cut down all the vegetation on the site as close to the soil surface as possible.
3. Cover the site with either large pieces of cardboard or a thick layer of overlapping newspaper, eight to ten sheets thick. (Do your

covering on a windless day, and have a pile of soil or mulch to dump on each sheet as you spread it.)

4. Once you've got cardboard or newspaper in place, cover it with thick layers of any other mulch you can find – chopped leaves, compost, weeds (that have not gone to seed), plant residue, grass clippings, you name it. Add layers of well-rotted manure, too, along with other materials such as upside-down chunks of sod, topsoil, straw, and spoiled hay. You can cover the site in sections, as organic matter becomes available.

5. Consider adding a layer of topsoil over all the mulch. Ideally, you want to pile a minimum of about 6"/15.2 cm of the stuff, but 10"–12"/25.4–30.5 cm is better. Then wait.

6. Sow the bed with a cover crop, such as rye or oats, in late summer or early fall.

7. In spring, plant directly into the mulch (including the remains of the cover crop).

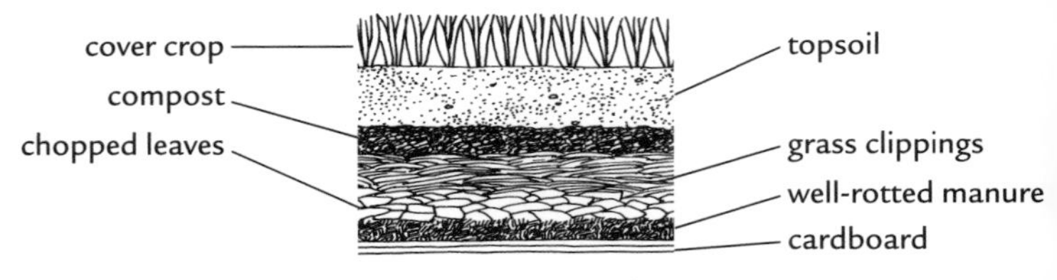

Making a no-dig bed

Q **I live in Arizona. Are raised beds the best option for me?**

A Actually, in dry climates such as the Southwest, ground-level or even sunken beds often are a better option, since preserving soil moisture is so important. To create a sunken bed, dig the soil to at least a shovel blade's depth and remove caliche layers, which are hardened calcium carbonate cemented together with other soil particles. In soil, caliche is either a dense, light-colored layer or it appears as white- or creamy-colored lumps mixed into the soil. Layers of caliche can vary from a couple of inches to several feet, and you may encounter more than one layer of it. Removing caliche is hard work, requiring the use of a mattock or a heavy-duty pick, but you'll only have to do it once. Amend the remaining soil with compost. The surface of the prepared soil should be several inches below the pathways, and beds should be rimmed with soil or framing so that water stays on the beds, where you want it. Crops growing in sunken beds also receive some wind protection because they're slightly below the surrounding soil surface.

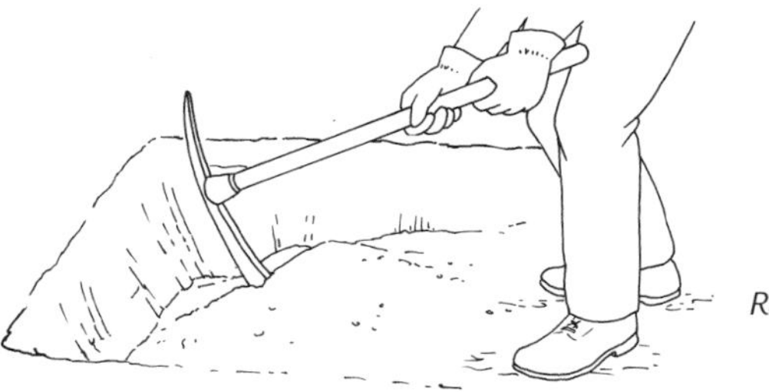

Removing caliche

SOIL MIXES FOR CONTAINERS

If you have little space for your veggie growing, or very poor soil, you can still have a garden: Try growing in containers.

For topnotch harvests from vegetables grown in containers, you'll need to start with a good soil mix. For a variety of reasons, soil dug from your yard isn't suitable for filling pots. Instead, you can create a soil mix that includes purchased topsoil, or you can blend a soilless potting mix.

SOIL-BASED POTTING MIX

2 parts purchased topsoil
1 part screened compost
1 part peat moss
1 part perlite
1 part vermiculite

Note: If the topsoil is very sandy, add 1 additional part compost.

SOILLESS POTTING MIX

2 parts vermiculite
2 parts peat moss
3 parts screened compost
1 part perlite
1 part builder's sand

Q **What's the best way to make hills? I've frequently seen melons and squash grown in them.**

A Hills offer warm, well-drained soil and are ideal for many crops, especially melons, watermelons, squash, and pumpkins. To build hills, use a hoe to mound soil up 1'/.3 m high and 2'–3'/.6 to .9 m wide. Work at least two shovelfuls of finished compost into the soil in each hill. To give plants an extra boost, before pulling up soil to make a hill, first dig a hole that's 1'/.3 m deep and 1'–2'/.3–.6 m across, then fill the bottom with compost, well-rotted manure, or a mixture of the two. Create a hill on top of that. As the plants become established, their roots will penetrate this cache of superamended soil for extra nutrients and water.

Making Compost

Q **What is compost?**

A Often called "gardener's gold," compost is the decomposed remains of organic matter – such as leaves, kitchen scraps, and other garden remains – produced in a pile or a specially designed structure. Compost is a valuable soil amendment that will improve soil structure and provide nutrition for plants.

Q Do I have to make compost to have a good garden?

A You can purchase bagged compost at your local garden center, but the quality varies, so it pays to read the label and/or open the bag and look at the compost before you buy. The best bagged composts smell woodsy or earthy, and they're moist but neither too wet nor too dry. They should have a granular texture and be dark brown or nearly black in color. Ground-up or shredded bark isn't compost – it's mulch – so don't pay compost prices for it. If you're buying manure-based compost, make sure it isn't gooey and wet and that it doesn't smell like ammonia or other unpleasant substances. (If you buy some that does, just dump the bag on your compost pile and let it finish composting.)

Many municipalities have large-scale composting operations that offer compost free or for a small fee. While these can be a great source for organic matter, municipal composting operations take in a wide range of materials that you may not want to add to your garden, including weed seeds, diseased plant parts, and grass clippings that contain herbicide residue. Compost made from leaves collected in fall is a better bet than that made from yard waste, so ask about the source of the materials used. Also, it's a good idea to ask friends and neighbors if they've used it and whether they've experienced any weed, disease, or other problems after adding it to their gardens.

Q What kind of setup do I need to make compost?

A To start a compost pile, select a level spot that is convenient to your garden. While flower gardeners try to keep their composting operations out of sight, vegetable gardeners find it's most convenient to make their compost right in the garden or right next to it. (It is best to look for a spot that is shielded from neighbors' yards.) Stash a bale of straw next to your pile so you can easily cover up kitchen scraps whenever you bring them out.

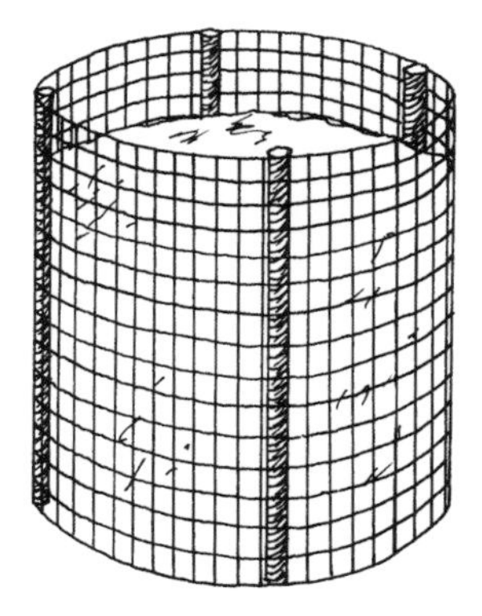

Compost bin made from stakes and wire mesh fencing

You can compost in an open pile or contain your composting operation in a cage, bin, or other structure, either purchased or homemade. A structure makes your composting area look neater, helps keep the materials evenly moist, promotes faster decomposition, and discourages animals from rooting around in the pile. For fast, efficient composting, plan on a pile or enclosure that is 3'–4'/.9–1.2 m square. Two enclosures are best so you can fill up the second one while materials in the first are breaking down.

Q What goes into a compost pile?

A The main ingredients in most gardeners' compost piles are trimmings and clippings from the garden, including weeds, grass clippings, and leaves. In addition, add kitchen scraps, sod (place it upside down), wood shavings, manure, spoiled hay, and shredded newspaper – even the guck from cleaning out gutters. Droppings from rabbits, guinea pigs, and other small rodents make great compost, along with their spoiled bedding.

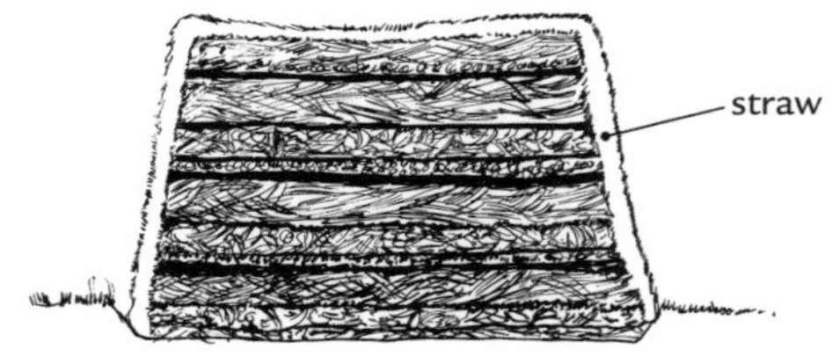

A layered compost pile covered with straw

Q Is there anything I should not add to my compost pile?

A Don't add cat or dog droppings to the pile, because they can spread disease. Avoid adding plant parts that show signs of disease, weeds that have gone to seed, and roots of perennial weeds unless you leave them in the sun to make sure they're very, very dead. (The length of time it takes for the sun to kill weeds varies: Plants with fleshy, succulent stems or fleshy taproots may take several days to die, while plants with less succulent leaves or finer fibrous roots will die within a couple of hours.) Also don't add meat, bones, or cooking fat to your compost pile.

Q I've got two neighbors. One just piles up his clippings, and the other one is always digging through them and moving them around. Which is the better way to make compost?

A Your neighbors are using two different composting systems: cold composting and hot composting. Both yield compost, but hot composting produces it faster than the cold method. To cold compost, simply toss ingredients in a pile or other enclosure, and then wait a year or two for them to break down. Turning the pile, which means moving the materials from one spot to another to mix them up, is optional, although tackling this task once or twice a year will speed up the decomposition process.

Hot composting takes more time and energy to prepare but produces finished compost in about 3 months. It also lets you produce more compost per year in the same amount of space. Hot composting gets its name because all the microorganisms busily breaking down materials generate heat within the pile.

Composting on the Move

IF YOU'RE BUILDING A NEW GARDEN BED or improving the soil in an existing one, start a new pile right on the site where you'll be working. That way, you won't have to move finished compost to the site. Trench composting is another supereasy way to keep your compost where you use it. Dig a trench 1'–2'/.3 to .7 m wide and up to 1'/.3 m deep. Pile the excess soil alongside it. Then, as kitchen scraps and other compostables become available, simply dump them in a section of the trench. Spread out the material in a layer no deeper than about 4"/10.2 cm, and don't pack it down. Top that with 2"–3"/5–7.6 cm of soil, and place a board on top (to keep out animals). Continue layering until the trench is nearly filled, then cover with 3"–4"/7.6–10.2 cm of soil. Plant directly into this soil topping. Earthworms and other soil organisms will gradually decompose the organic matter below and spread the benefits throughout the bed.

Trench composting

Q **Apparently, building a pile for cold composting is easy — just throw yard waste in a pile and leave it alone. But how do I build a pile for hot composting?**

A To build a pile for hot composting, it's best to stockpile materials and build the pile all at once. You need to build a pile that is 3'–4'/.9–1.2 m square and at least 3'/.9 m tall; otherwise it won't heat up and break down the materials quickly. You can pile the organic matter in layers or just mix it all together. Chopping up or shredding leaves or other large materials speeds up the composting process but isn't essential. As you pile up materials, spray them with water periodically unless they're very wet. The finished pile should feel lightly moist to the touch, like a damp sponge. The pile will heat up in a day or two. Once it begins to cool off, usually after a few weeks, turn it by dumping the materials into a new pile next to the old one. This aerates the materials. Add water if materials in the pile seem dry. Let the pile heat up again, and turn it again in another few weeks once pile temperatures cool off, or use the compost if it is finished.

Cut woody material into pieces before composting

Q **I need bins or something to contain my compost, but I'm not handy. What can I buy or make without having to use any tools?**

A Ordinary wood pallets make a fine composting system. Wire them together at the corners – either drill holes for the wire or simply wire the corners together. You can make a single bin with three pallets and use a fourth bin or a sheet of lattice for a front to keep pets out of the compost. Add additional bins by wiring on another back and side to the end of the first bin. You can also make a round compost bin with a 10-foot (3 m)-long length of 4'/1.2 m-tall welded wire fencing. Fasten the ends with wire ties or pieces of wire.

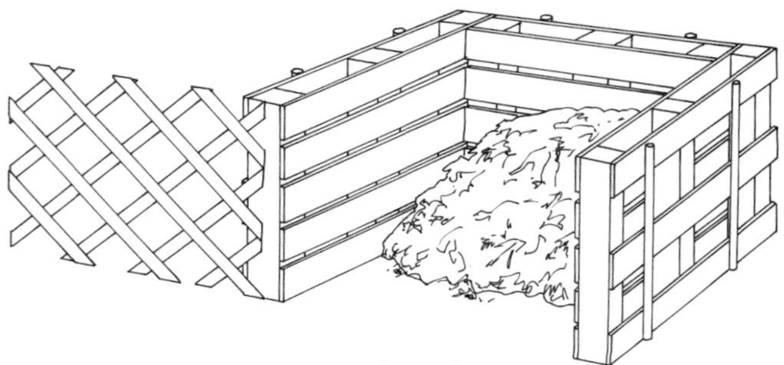

Wooden pallet compost enclosure with lattice door

SEE ALSO: *For an illustration of a round bin, page 89.*

Q I want to make lots of compost. I don't think I can collect enough organic matter in my own yard. Where else can I get some?

A Devoted composters are very creative when it comes to finding compost ingredients. Here are a few suggestions:

- **PICK UP BAGGED LEAVES** and grass clippings set out for trash collection.
- **CONTACT A LOCAL STABLE** for manure and spoiled hay or bedding.
- **ASK YOUR LOCAL GROCERY STORE** what they do with spoiled produce. (Some composters hit the dumpsters behind grocery stores for cast-off produce – really!)
- **COFFEE GROUNDS** make great compost. Ask at a local coffee house or restaurant if you can provide a bucket to collect them. (You'll be far from the first composter who does this, so don't be shy. Set up a regular schedule for collecting and replacing the bucket.)
- **CHECK WITH FACTORIES** in your area for locally available, compost-safe materials like sawdust.
- **CHECK OUT LOCAL FARMERS' MARKETS** to see if you can collect leaves, vegetable discards, and/or spoiled produce.

Q What does finished compost look like?

A Finished compost is dark and crumbly, and the original ingredients are mostly unrecognizable. It's fine if there are still some lumps in it, especially if you plan to work it into the soil. If you don't want lumps, sift the compost before using it. To sift compost, staple ½"/1.3 cm mesh screen to a square wood frame (2'–3'/.6–.9 m on all sides is fine). Place the screen over a garden cart or wheelbarrow and add a shovelful of compost on top. Gently sift the compost through, and break up the larger lumps as you sift. Return any large lumps or pieces of plants to the compost pile for further decomposition.

My last compost pile smelled bad, and the one before it just sat there! What am I doing wrong?

A To build a compost pile that breaks down quickly and doesn't smell, you need to pay attention to the quantities of the materials you use, plus how moist the materials are. Ideally, you need 2 or 3 parts high-carbon materials with 1 part high-nitrogen materials. Here's a simple way to remember which is which: High-carbon materials usually are brown and dry, and high-nitrogen ones are green and moist. Two materials that don't fit this rule are kitchen scraps and manure: Both are high in nitrogen, so use them as green and moist ingredients.

If your compost pile isn't performing up to par, try one of these tactics to revive it.

- **ADD AIR.** Turning a compost pile by forking material from one place to another is one way to give microorganisms the air they need to decompose organic matter, and that helps keep the pile smelling good. It's hard work (and good exercise!), but passive ventilation is an easier way to get much-needed air into your pile. The three methods shown here – a bundle of cornstalks, a perforated plastic pipe, and a tube formed from wire mesh fencing – all ensure airflow deep into the pile, where it can be in short supply. Select the ventilation method that's most convenient for you, and incorporate two to three in your pile as you build it. If you have a pile that's already built but needs ventilation, jam a pry bar or a spade down through the center of the pile to make enough room to jam in sections of perforated pipe.

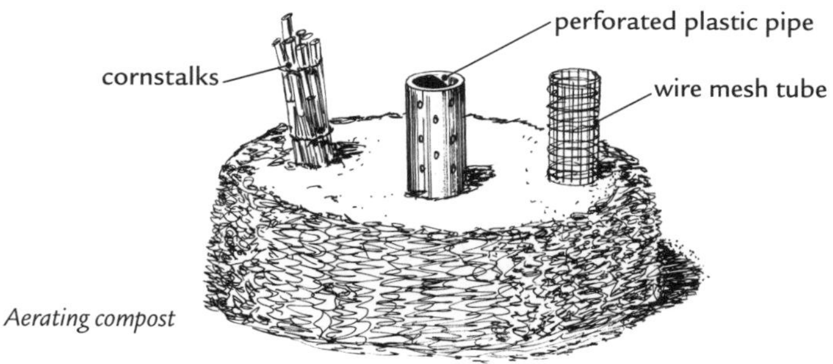

Aerating compost

- **ADD CARBON.** If you go overboard with the high-nitrogen ingredients, your pile may turn smelly. If that is the problem, turning the pile and adding more high-carbon materials (brown and dry; ingredients like chopped leaves, spoiled hay, dried grass, or sawdust) will correct it.
- **STOP THE FLOOD.** Even if you have a good balance of materials in your pile, if it's too wet, a compost pile can turn smelly and slimy. (The smell is caused by anaerobic bacteria that thrive when there isn't enough oxygen at the center of a wet, compacted pile.) Gardeners in rainy climates, such as the Pacific Northwest, may want to construct a roof over their compost piles, since conditions that are too wet are commonplace there. In other areas, use a tarp over the pile in rainy weather to keep it from getting drenched.
- **REBUILD IT.** To fix a smelly, too-wet pile, first put on old clothes and gather a few bushels of coarse, dry materials such as leaves, clean straw, grasses, cornstalks, or even twiggy brush. Lay down a layer of cornstalks or a mix of twiggy brush and straw, then fork on a layer of the soggy compost. Continue alternating layers of coarse, dry materials and wet compost. Cover the finished pile so that rain won't saturate it again.

CHAPTER 3

Caring for the Garden

Watering Wisely

Q It rains fairly regularly most summers here in Iowa. Can I just let Mother Nature take care of watering my garden?

A Maybe. If your garden gets between 1"–2"/2.5–5.0 cm of rain a week all summer long, it will probably produce a bumper harvest. To keep track, install a rain gauge somewhere in your yard. However, if periods of rainy weather are interspersed with dry spells that last long enough to cause your plants to wilt, your crops will be damaged and won't bear as well. For best results, mulch your garden and have a plan for how you are going to deliver enough water to avoid water stress throughout the season.

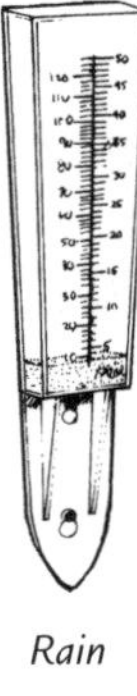

Rain gauge

Q Are there general guidelines for how much and when to water?

A One-size-fits-all watering recommendations aren't the best way to decide when to water. In Southern California and the arid Southwest, where no rain falls for months at a time, it's best to water every day or every other day to maintain soil moisture. Elsewhere, watering once, twice, or three times a week, depending on rainfall, is best.

Use the following guidelines to determine the schedule that works best for your garden:

- **USE A RAIN GAUGE** and water whenever rainfall is less than 1"/2.5 cm of water per week. Keep in mind that 1"/2.5 cm of water may be fine for a plant in early summer, but in midsummer that same plant will be larger, and temperatures will be hotter, so it will need up to 2"/5.0 cm, depending on the size of the plant, where you live, and your soil.
- **TO CHECK THE AMOUNT OF MOISTURE** in your soil, 2 days after a good rain, pull back the mulch and dig a 6"/15.2 cm-deep hole in the soil. If you can make a ball from a small handful of soil from the bottom of the hole, plenty of moisture is available. Refill the hole, then wait and test it again in a few days.

Q Do some crops need watering more often than others?

A Yes. Cucumbers can turn bitter and radishes hot-tasting if they don't receive enough water. In general, regular watering is important from the time plants begin flowering through harvest. There is such a thing as too much watering: Although tomatoes thrive with frequent watering, heavily watered plants tend to produce blander-tasting fruit than ones that are watered less often.

Q **I sprinkle my garden with the hose every evening, but my plants still wilt. What am I doing wrong?**

A Frequent watering isn't necessarily good for plants, since it encourages shallow roots that dry out quickly. For best results, get in the habit of watering long enough for the soil several inches down to get wet, rather than just the top inch or so. If you're not sure whether you've watered long enough, dig a small hole to check how much moisture has percolated down into the soil. Another simple way to determine how much water your sprinkling has delivered is to place empty cans (tuna or cat-food cans are ideal for this) in the area you are watering. When you think the sprinklers have delivered enough water, check the cans to see how much really fell on the ground. (Applying 1"/2.5 cm of water will wet the soil several inches/cm deep.) You'll probably have to run the sprinklers for considerably longer than you would expect.

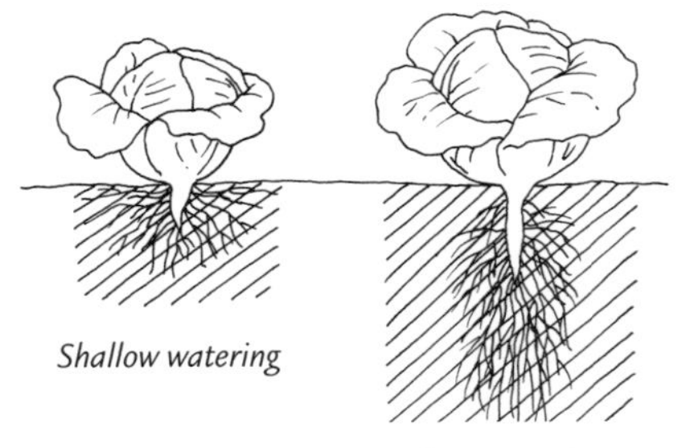

Shallow watering

Deep watering

WATERING PRINCIPLES

Although 1"/2.5 cm per week is a standard watering recommendation, sometimes you'll need to apply more than that, sometimes less. Keep the following guidelines in mind to make sure you're providing enough — but not too much — water.

Crops need less water than the "average" when:

- The soil surface is covered with organic mulch.
- The soil has been amended with compost.
- The weather is cool and humid.

Crops need more water than the "average" when:

- They're growing in sandy soil.
- They're growing in raised beds.
- They're growing in containers (as often as once or twice a day, especially in hot weather).
- They're exposed to wind — especially dry wind.
- The weather is warm and dry.

Q **Watering my garden by hand is tiresome and time consuming. Are there more time-efficient ways to water than standing there holding a hose?**

A Steer away from overhead sprinklers, since a large percentage of the water they deliver evaporates before it hits the soil. Instead, try one of the following methods:

- **FOR A LOW-TECH VERSION OF DRIP IRRIGATION,** use a sharp nail or an awl to poke a couple of tiny holes in the bottom of several 1-gallon/3.8 L plastic jugs. Set one jug next to each plant you want to water. Fill each jug with water, which will seep out right where you want it. Be sure to make small holes, since you want water to drip, not flow, out.

Holes in jug release water slowly

- **SOAKER HOSES, ALSO CALLED LEAKY PIPE,** offer an easy, efficient way to deliver water to thirsty plants. Lay soaker hoses along each row or snake them through wide beds or rows. To water, connect your garden hose to the end of each soaker hose in turn. Be sure you adjust the water pressure to the right level. The object is for

Properly adjusted soaker hose

water to drip slowly out along the length of the hose; if the pressure is too high, water will squirt out the top of the hose. You'll need to leave the water flowing for 1 to 2 hours and then transfer the garden hose to the next soaker hose.

- **CUSTOM-DESIGNED DRIP IRRIGATION SYSTEMS** are the ultimate in efficient watering. You can design your own drip system or have an expert design it for you. They're more expensive than soaker hoses but are practical for cutting water bills.

Much Ado About Mulch

Q I've never used plastic mulch before but want to try it this season. What are the benefits? I live in Vermont.

A Plastic mulch helps warm up the soil in spring, an important benefit for gardeners where the growing season is short and an early start is essential to success. Black plastic warms up the soil by about 10°F/-12.2°C. Clear plastic warms it even more – up to 18°F/-7.7°C – although it encourages weed growth underneath it. Keep in mind that plastic mulch doesn't benefit the soil like organic mulch does. Plan on adding organic matter before or at the end of the season.

For the maximum warming benefit, put down plastic mulch about 2 weeks before you're ready to plant. Plan your watering system before you install the plastic mulch. The easiest way to water is to install a soaker hose, then cover it with the plastic. Otherwise, hand water at the base of the plant so that water can seep through the hole cut in the plastic at planting time. Rake the soil surface as smooth as you can, removing all stones and clods, and wet it well before you lay the plastic. Even contact between the soil and plastic is important for good heat transfer to the soil.

1. Unroll the plastic mulch along the row, and weight down the edges with soil to prevent it from blowing and to seal in heat.
2. Cut an X or small square in the plastic for each plant.
3. Plant through the holes.

Remove plastic mulch at the end of the season before mulching the soil for winter or planting a cover crop. Or, use a plastic mulch that's biodegradable, which should break down on its own during the course of the growing season.

Q **I have sandy soil and want to pick the best mulch to help keep my soil moist. What should I use?**

A Fine-textured mulches such as rotted sawdust or grass clippings are the best choices for holding moisture in sandy soil. Since fine-textured mulches can form a dense layer that excludes water and air, use only a thin layer – up to 2"/5 cm – and replenish it regularly.

Q **I never seem to have enough mulch! I know I can buy straw, but what else can I use?**

A Consider using any of the following: grass clippings, chopped leaves, rotted sawdust, shredded newspaper, weeds (provided they haven't gone to seed), hay from soybeans or other legumes, spoiled hay, and wood chips. If you have any food-processing companies in your area, ask about the availability of crop residue, such as ground-up corncobs or seed hulls. While one of these types may be easiest or most accessible for you, keep in mind that it's a good idea to use as many types of mulch as you can. Because different kinds of mulch stimulate different kinds of soil organisms as they decay, contributing to the richness of the microherd.

Q How much mulch should I use?

A The ideal thickness of the layer depends on the type of mulch. If you're using coarse-textured mulch like straw, you can put down a layer as much as 8"/20.3 cm thick. Use less – no more than 4"/10.2 cm – for finer-textured materials such as composted wood chips (uncomposted wood chips and bark chunks are best used on pathways), and no more than 2"/5 cm grass clippings, which pack down densely.

A well-mulched bed

Q Is there ever any reason that I shouldn't mulch my garden?

A Wait until seeds are up and seedlings are established and growing before mulching. If you live in an area with cool summers, or where spring is slow in coming and the soil remains cool, mulch may keep the soil too cool for optimum plant growth, especially for warm-season crops such as peppers or eggplants. In areas with wet, humid summers, mulch can stay damp too long and promote pests, such as earwigs and slugs.

Q **Do I have to continue adding mulch all season, or is once enough?**

A For mulch to do its work – to retain moisture and keep down weeds – you'll want to add to your mulch layer as it decomposes and becomes too thin to be effective. An 8"/20.3 cm-deep layer of straw, leaves, and/or spoiled hay will settle into a thinner blanket fairly quickly but will still remain effective for quite some time. Add more mulch once you notice a few weed seedlings emerging through the mulch or if the soil doesn't seem to be holding moisture as well as it was. Also, cover your soil with mulch (or a cover crop) in fall to protect it from wind and rain as well as to add organic matter over the winter.

Managing Weeds

Q **I hate weeding! What can I do from the start to minimize the time I have to spend on this gardening chore?**

A Up-front weed prevention will really cut down on weeding headaches in years to come. Try the following techniques:

- **REMOVE ROOTS.** Dig up and discard roots of perennial weeds and grass when you prepare soil.

◆ **CONSIDER SMOTHERING.** Instead of digging up soil, consider making a deep layer of mulch to smother weeds. This technique works best on seedling perennial weeds as well as annuals, but you'll need to take tougher steps to control such thugs as thistles and tough grasses.

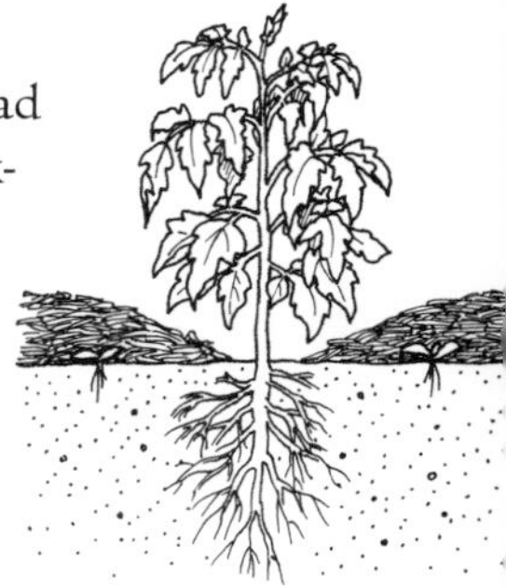

Deep mulch smothers weeds.

◆ **MULCH, MULCH, MULCH.** Covering the soil surface discourages weed seeds from sprouting. Mulch established crops with up to 8"/20.3 cm of coarse mulch, such as weed-free straw. When using finer mulches, such as grass clippings, use less, about 2"/5 cm. Finer mulches can pack down too much, which holds in soil moisture, but also causes rainfall to run off without soaking in. Weed seedlings that sprout beneath deep mulch will die without emerging; if a few weeds do poke through shallow mulch, they'll be easy to hand pull.

Spread grass clippings thinly for best results.

◆ **PICK THE FLOWERS.** Even if you don't have time to pull up weeds, pull off and dispose of their flowers before they form seeds. Pull off seedheads that you see as well. Toss flowers and seedheads in the trash, not on the compost pile. This prevents seedlings in years to come.

SEE ALSO: *For more techniques for controlling stubborn weeds, page 114.*

Q **I do weed my garden, but it isn't my favorite activity. Is there any way to make it go faster?**

A Combine preventive measures such as mulching with the suggestions listed below to dispatch weeds in a hurry.

- **TRY THE TWO-FISTED GRAB.** You can pull twice as many small weeds if you learn to use both hands at the same time and grab weeds between your thumb and forefinger with a pinching motion.
- **GET 'EM WHILE THEY'RE SMALL.** Frequent, short weeding sessions are the best way to stay on top of weeds. Not only does this eliminate a long, tiring weeding session, it also lets you dispatch weeds while they're still small and easy to eliminate. Seedling weeds can be quickly pulled by hand or chopped off with a hoe. Large weeds are another matter: They're tougher to eliminate because of deeper, more established roots and larger top growth.
- **WEED WET.** Weeding goes faster and easier when the soil is moist than when the soil is dry.

◆ **ARM YOURSELF.** A hoe is a great tool for chopping the tops off a great many weeds. For deep-rooted weeds such as dock and dandelions, use a dandelion fork, also called an asparagus knife. Follow the taproot down with the blade of the dandelion fork, and rock it back and forth a few times to loosen and dislodge it.

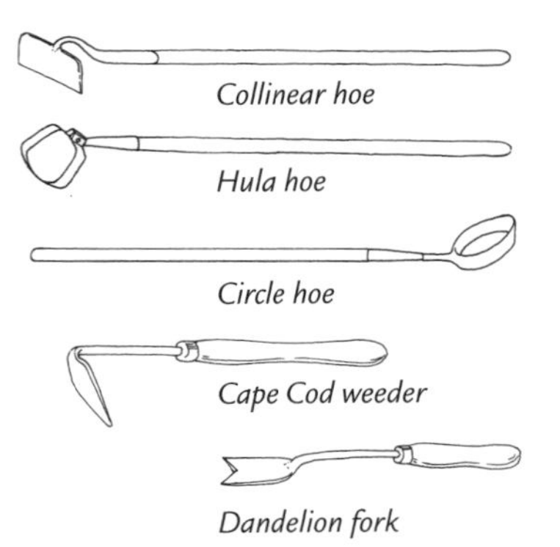

◆ **THUMBS UP WHILE HOEING.** To turn your hoe into an effective tool for weed control, use it to slice the tops off weeds just under the soil surface. For best results with this technique, you'll need to hold your hoe differently from the way most gardeners do. Instead of gripping the handle with thumbs pointing down toward the blade, and bending over while you hoe the soil, try using a "thumbs up" grip," which is easier

"Thumbs up" weeding

on your back and more effective. Hold the hoe with your thumbs pointing up on the handle, and pull it toward you using your arms, not your back.

- **SHARPEN YOUR ARSENAL.** Keep hoes and other weeding equipment nice and sharp (you can sharpen blades with a metal file). A sharp blade will cut through weed roots with less effort, making the job easier and quicker for you.

Q **I just pull up weeds without really looking at them. Do I need to pay attention to what I pull?**

A While you don't need to know each weed by name, it does help to know whether you're dealing with weeds that don't spread too much or you're fighting really serious thugs. Annual weeds, along with fibrous-rooted perennial weeds, are pretty easy to control, since they are easy to pull. Watch out for the thugs, though, since they're deep rooted and many of them spread by underground stems called rhizomes. Dig them out or use smothering techniques to bring them under control as quickly as possible. Also keep in mind that tilling, unfortunately, is an effective propagation technique for rhizomatous weeds: Chop the roots up into little pieces with a tiller, and you have effectively created a thicket of them.

- **TAPROOTED WEEDS.** Deep-rooted weeds like dandelions and dock grow back quickly if you don't dig them out or smother them.

Dock

- **RHIZOMATOUS GRASSES.** Quack grass and other grass species that travel by underground rhizomes can travel far and wide. They're especially problematic if they invade crowns of perennial vegetables like asparagus.

Quack grass

- **RHIZOMATOUS PERENNIALS.** Thistles and bindweed are two of the worst perennial invaders, and they're difficult to dig because their roots are brittle and break off when you pull them. The pieces left in the ground resprout.

Bindweed

Q **Can weeds go into the compost pile?**

A Weeds that have not yet gone to seed are great candidates for the compost pile, and they also make fine mulch if you leave them wherever you've pulled them up. But don't dispose of weeds that have flowered and gone to seed this way, or you'll be planting new weeds to pull up next year. Perennial weeds are notorious resprouters, so discard them in the trash or spread them in the sun until they're completely dead before using them as mulch.

Q **We've got tons of grass coming up in our garden. Is there any way to get it under control?**

A Determined weeds, such as grass – especially tough rhizomatous grasses – can be a real headache. In planted sections of the garden, lay down a layer of up to eight sheets of newspaper and top it with a heavy mulch such as wood chips to hold down the newspaper. Cover pathways with sheets of cardboard, again held in place with heavy mulch. Be sure to overlap the edges of the newspaper or cardboard. If you use soaker hoses or a drip system to water, just cover them up with the mulch, and this system will preserve even more soil moisture. Otherwise, when watering, make sure that the water soaks down through the paper to reach the soil.

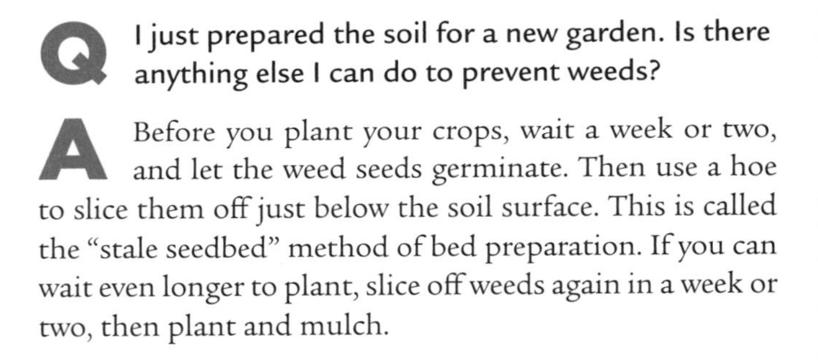

Q **I just prepared the soil for a new garden. Is there anything else I can do to prevent weeds?**

A Before you plant your crops, wait a week or two, and let the weed seeds germinate. Then use a hoe to slice them off just below the soil surface. This is called the "stale seedbed" method of bed preparation. If you can wait even longer to plant, slice off weeds again in a week or two, then plant and mulch.

Training and Other Tasks

Q **My tomatoes are top-heavy, and I'm afraid the cages will blow over during the next storm. What should I do?**

A Drive sturdy stakes into the soil around the outside of each cage and wire the cage to the stakes for extra support. For sturdy supports, use 3'/.9 m-long or longer stakes and drive them at least 1'/.3 m into the soil.

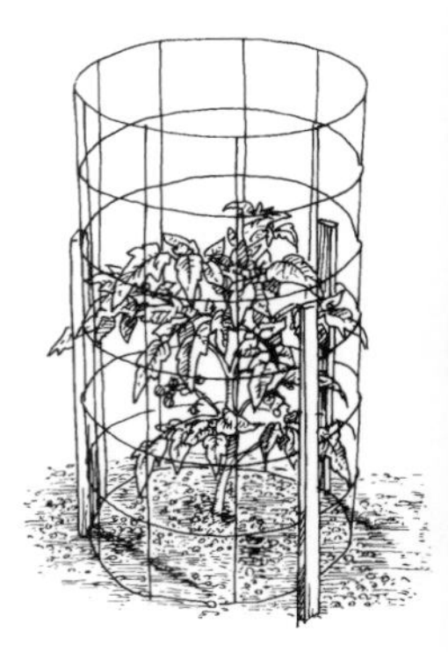

Stake reinforcing tomato cage

Q **I'm using stakes to keep a couple of plants upright, mostly tomatoes and peppers. What can I use to tie them in place?**

A You should use soft string, yarn, or another material that won't bruise the stems. Other options include strips of cotton T-shirts, panty hose, sheeting, or flannel.

Q **Some of my broccoli and tomato plants have flopped over! Can I prop them back up?**

A If your plants have already grown halfway to the next town, leave them alone and harvest wherever the stems have flopped. Trussing up already-overgrown plants such as tomatoes or pole beans is a lost cause, and you're likely to do more damage than good. If plants are still small, get in the habit of attending to new growth by tucking stems back into cages or around trellises, tying them when necessary, when they are still small. Use the same guideline for other plants that can flop, such as broccoli, Brussels sprouts, and peppers. Try to install stakes or cages while they are small enough that you can do it without damaging plants.

Keeping Up with the Garden

ONCE YOUR GARDEN IS PLANTED AND GROWING, keep up with watering and weeds, but don't neglect the following chores, either.

- **PRUNE AND TRAIN.** Redirect stems while they're still small to keep them inside cages and on trellises.
- **THIN CROPS.** Root vegetables like beets and radishes, as well as lettuce and other greens, need to be thinned to their proper spacing in order to produce the best crop. Also thin other late crops that you've direct seeded.
- **HILL UP SOIL.** Use a hoe to shore up soil along the edges of raised beds that aren't contained by landscape ties. Also hill soil up over crops like potatoes.
- **PROTECT FRUIT.** Slip pieces of board or shingles under pumpkins, watermelons, winter squash, and melons to keep them clean and dry.
- **WATCH FOR PESTS AND DISEASES.** Cultivate the habit of checking for signs of problems and dealing with them before they get out of hand.

SEE ALSO: *For more on pest and disease problems, chapter 4.*

Feeding Fundamentals

Q How often do I need to feed my garden?

A Actually, if you prepared your soil well and added a generous amount of compost, your plants probably will grow just fine without additional feeding. Too much fertilizer is just as bad as too little, since soil that is too rich, especially in nitrogen, yields lanky plants that produce less fruit than they would otherwise. Don't feed your plants during the season unless they show signs that they need it, like stunted or yellowed leaves, spindly growth, general lack of vigor, and weak stems.

Q If I decide that my plants need a fertilizer boost, what should I use?

A One of the handiest fertilizers to use is compost. Spread a layer of compost around plants and water it in to give them a quick boost. Watering with compost tea provides another effective fertilizer boost. You can make your own compost tea (see pages 120–121) or purchase it. Purchased organic fertilizers such as fish emulsion or kelp extract are also effective. There also are various bagged dry organic fertilizer blends available. Read the labels carefully, and apply them according to package directions.

Q How do I make compost tea?

A You'll need finished compost, a 5-gallon/18.9 L bucket full of water, a burlap bag, and some string to make this simple recipe. Place two shovelfuls of compost in the burlap bag, and tie it shut. (You can also use a large square of burlap tied shut.) Place the burlap-encased compost in the water, and leave it to soak for a few days to let it brew. Then remove the bag, and dilute the resulting brew with water until it is the color of weak tea. Dump the wet compost in your garden or back on the compost pile.

Aerated compost tea is another option, and compost brewers are available in catalogs and at garden centers. Proponents claim that compost tea prepared using optimum oxygen levels contains more beneficial aerobic microorganisms and compounds than tea prepared using more conventional methods.

Making compost tea in a bucket

To make manure tea, brew two shovelfuls of well-rotted (composted) manure in water for a few days to make manure tea. Be sure to dilute it with water before using it: Manure tea is quite a bit stronger (and darker) than compost tea and will burn crops if not diluted. It, too, should be the color of weak tea when diluted. Do not use manure tea on a crop that is to be harvested soon, since it is not safe to consume. After applying it, wait at least 90 days to harvest if the edible portion of the crop does not come in contact with the soil (tomatoes, peppers, beans, for example). If the edible portion of the crop does come in contact with the soil, wait at least 120 days (onions, potatoes, lettuce, for example).

Both manure and compost teas are great for giving crops a quick fix of nutrients. You can fill up a watering can and use it to feed plants weekly or every other week. Sprinkle diluted compost or manure tea directly on plant leaves for foliar feeding, or use either one for watering.

Q How should I put fertilizer on my garden?

A That depends on what kind of fertilizer you are applying and when you are putting it down. If you are applying soil amendments early in the season, before the garden is planted, put them directly where the rows will be and work them into the soil. Manures, wood ashes, blood meal, and other dry fertilizers can be applied this way. During the season, top-dress with organic fertilizers by spreading them across the entire bed. Pull back the mulch, sprinkle on the fertilizer and work it into the top couple of inches of soil, then remulch. (Read package directions, and don't overfeed.)

Sidedressing is probably the easiest alternative during the growing season, since it puts fertilizers near the most actively developing roots. To sidedress, spread a band of fertilizer along the row, just outside the dripline of the plants. Work it into the top few inches of soil.

I grow lots of my vegetables in containers. What's the best way to feed them?

A Weekly watering with compost tea, or with a dilute solution of fish emulsion, should keep container crops growing well. For best results, dilute commercial fertilizers such as fish emulsion to half the recommended dosage, and water twice as often.

Harvesting Hints

Q I didn't pick snap peas for about a week, and now they're all woody. Which crops do I need to check daily, and which ones can wait a few days?

A While you want to pick every crop at the peak of freshness, it's important to hurry some crops from garden to table more quickly than others. Snap peas are just one of the crops you need to watch carefully and pick daily to catch them at the peak of ripeness. Others that fall into this category include sweet corn and cucumbers, as well as summer squash and zucchini, which are best picked when they are still very small and tender. Also watch broccoli and cauliflower closely, and harvest when the flower heads are still dense and firm.

Crops that are a little more patient – so you can pick them every few days – include cabbage, lettuce and other greens, peppers, melons, and tomatoes. Finally, carrots, onions, potatoes, winter squash, and dry beans can be left for a few weeks until you have time to harvest, but don't wait too long, or even these crops will lose quality.

Q **Is it better to harvest in the morning or the evening, or does it make any difference?**

A The best time to pick produce is in the morning, after the dew has dried off it, because leaves and fruit have the highest water content then, and they're also coolest. On cooler or cloudy days you can pick anytime, because the sun won't have warmed up and dried out your produce. If a bad storm is predicted, you may want to pick leaf lettuce and other tender greens whenever you can to prevent damage from pounding rain. Since high winds also can damage crops, consider picking or at least protecting crops (reinforcing stakes and covering smaller plants with buckets are two options) if you have time before the windstorm hits.

HANDLE WITH CARE

When picking produce, whether you're using your hands, a knife, or clippers, it's a good idea to hold onto the plant with one hand while you pull or cut the fruit with the other. This helps prevent damage to the plant, since tugging or twisting on it often damages branches and dislodges roots.

Are there basic tools or supplies I should have on hand for harvesting?

A You don't need anything high tech to harvest, but a few simple tools will make picking easier. You'll also need a container to carry produce.

- **SCISSORS OR CLIPPERS.** Use sharp garden snips, scissors, or clippers to cut peppers and okra. You can pinch peas and beans off plants, but scissors or snips work great for detaching them as well. Larger vegetables, such as winter squash, require full-size clippers. Scissors or clippers also work for harvesting leaf lettuce and other greens.
- **KNIFE.** Cut heads of broccoli, cabbage, cauliflower, and lettuce with a sharp knife. You can also use a knife to harvest winter squash.

- **DIGGING IMPLEMENTS.** To harvest carrots, potatoes, turnips, and other root crops, you'll need a fork, a spade, or a shovel.
- **OTHER EQUIPMENT.** For some crops – specifically, squash and okra – you'll want to wear long sleeves and gloves, since both crops can cause a skin rash.

Q It's midsummer, my garden is out of control, and I'm overwhelmed! What should I do?

A The best approach depends to some extent on where you live. If it's August and you're in one of the northern zones where the first fall frost date comes in mid-September, you may want to just let it be and harvest what you can. Pull up spent crops and mulch empty beds heavily to get them ready for winter. Or plant them with fast-maturing crops like radishes and leaf lettuce or cold-tolerant crops like kale and spinach. In warmer zones, where frost may be 3 or more months away, you have time to pull up plants that are past their prime, cut back overgrown ones like tomatoes, and start again. In fact, many warm-season gardeners say they have two gardening seasons, not one. To start a new fall garden, till under the entire plot or cut back plants you can save. Add compost or sidedress rows with well-rotted manure or another organic fertilizer, then start planting fall crops.

Q What do I need to do to prepare my garden for winter?

A Once you've picked most of the produce left in your garden, take time to clean up the beds. Time spent cleaning up in fall makes getting the garden ready to plant in spring that much easier.

- **REMOVE PLANTS.** Cut down or pull up plants and add them to the compost pile. Don't compost diseased plant matter or weeds that have gone to seed: Discard these in the trash.
- **CLEAN UP.** Pick up stakes, labels, boards or shingles used under melons and pumpkins, and any other items that have been left out over the summer. Pick up plastic mulch if you used it, as well as floating row covers Discard the mulch, but hose off row covers and hang them to dry if they're in good enough shape to use for another season.
- **CLEAN UP AND SHARPEN TOOLS.** Wipe on a light coat of mineral oil to protect metal parts.
- **COVER YOUR SOIL.** Don't leave soil uncovered over winter. Protect it with a deep layer of straw or plant a cover crop.

CHAPTER 4

Pests, Diseases, and Other Problems

Organic Gardening 101

What steps should I take to begin growing my vegetables organically?

A First, stop using chemical pesticides and fungicides. When you garden organically, you won't ever use those products, and even approved "organic" pesticides will be your last resort. There are lots of effective pest-control methods that don't involve spraying, but you can also try homemade sprays using such ingredients as baking soda and dishwashing liquid. These may solve all, or nearly all, your pest problems. More and more organic products are available at garden centers these days, so this switchover is a lot easier than it once was.

Keep in mind, though, that there also are homemade remedies that will eliminate problems, and there are effective preventive steps to take long before you bring out a sprayer. The following tips and techniques are a key part of avoiding pest and disease problems in an organic garden, but read on in this chapter for more options.

- **BUILD HEALTHY SOIL** by applying compost, mulch, and natural fertilizers. See Chapter 2 for details on soil building.
- **ASK EXPERTS** as well as friends and neighbors who garden which pests and diseases pose the biggest pro-

blems in your area. Find out how they control these problems organically.

- **WALK THROUGH YOUR GARDEN DAILY** – or every other day at minimum – to check for pests as well as signs of diseases or other problems. Catching problems early allows you to step in and correct a problem before it becomes severe.

- **KEEP PLANTS WELL WATERED AND FERTILIZE REGULARLY** if you suspect your soil is not yet up to par. Plants that are healthy and growing vigorously are far less subject to problems than ones that are struggling.

SEE ALSO: *For homemade spray, page 145.*

Q What are some easy organic controls that are good to use for most crops?

A The smart way to deal with pest problems is to avoid allowing pest or disease organisms to invade your crops in the first place. Here are some techniques to try:

- **PLANT RESISTANT AND TOLERANT CROPS.** Crops with built-in resistance or tolerance to disease stack the deck in your favor. You'll see these characteristics listed in descriptions on seed packets and catalogs.

- **INSPECT TRANSPLANTS CAREFULLY** at the garden center. Don't buy any that have insect infestations or obvious signs of disease. Stocky, healthy-looking plants are your best bet for producing bumper crops.

- **USE ROW COVERS.** These prevent pests from ever reaching your crops so you don't have to spray at all.
- **USE CUTWORM COLLARS WITH TRANSPLANTS.** These prevent cutworms from cutting down transplants altogether.
- **PICK OFF AND DISPOSE OF DISEASED LEAVES** during daily inspection tours. Signs of disease include spotting or yellowing.
- **ENCOURAGE BENEFICIAL INSECT** by planting some annuals and perennials with daisylike flowers.
- **DON'T WORK IN THE GARDEN WHEN PLANT LEAVES ARE WET.** Wet conditions make it easy for you to transport fungus spores and other disease-causing organisms from plant to plant on your hands and clothes.
- **HANDLE PLANTS CAREFULLY.** Bruised leaves and torn stems give pests and diseases easy access to plants.

SEE ALSO: *For information on how to use row covers, page 135; for details about cutworm collars, page 157; for suggestions for beneficial insects, pages 138–139.*

Q As I walk around my garden every day, what should I look for specifically?

A During daily inspection tours, start by looking at your plants as a whole. Are they stunted, wilted, or deformed? Have seedlings fallen over or disappeared? Have branches died? Also look closely for such symptoms as webby stem tips, curled or blackened growth, and leaves that have spots or are distorted, sticky, curled, tunneled, or chewed. All are common pest or disease symptoms. Be sure to check out the undersides of leaves and inside flower blossoms, both of which are places pests commonly hide. Don't forget to examine the soil around the plants, since pests such as cucumber beetles frequently hide there as well.

Aphids

Leafminer tunneling

SEE ALSO: *To find out what's causing the problem and how to handle it, pages 146–162.*

Q **If purchased sprays aren't the only thing organic gardeners use to control pests, what other techniques are effective?**

A There are several levels of acceptable organic controls, and purchased or homemade sprays usually are the last resort when dealing with an insect or disease problem.

- **CULTURAL CONTROLS** are the first line of defense against pests and diseases. These include techniques like growing resistant or tolerant crops and keeping plants healthy and well watered. Cleaning up and discarding diseased plants is another cultural control that reduces the problems you'll encounter in future years.
- **BIOLOGICAL CONTROLS** are another type of very effective controls. Birds, along with beneficial insects that feast on pests, are two examples of biological controls. You also can purchase biological controls, including *Bacillus thuringiensis* (Bt), a popular microbial insecticide that infects and kills many types of caterpillars, beetles, and other pests. Spinosad is another, relatively new biological control that is effective against caterpillars, thrips, and a variety of other insects. It is also the active ingredient in new organic fire-ant baits.
- **PHYSICAL CONTROLS** include floating row covers, cutworm collars, and other barriers that block insects from reaching plants or discourage them from feeding,

such as kaolin clay (a natural mineral substance used in a wide variety of products, including toothpaste) and wood ashes. Blasting aphids and other small pests off plants with a stream of water also is an effective physical control. Handpicking, trapping, and pulling and destroying infested or infected plants or plant parts are other effective physical-control options.

HANDPICKING HOW-TO

The easiest way to handpick insects is to tap them into a bucket or large-mouthed jar of soapy water, where they'll sink to the bottom and drown. For best results, do your handpicking in the early morning when insects are still a bit cold. They move more slowly then, making them easier to catch.

For fast-moving bugs, try a different strategy. It may come as something of a surprise, but a small, cordless, handheld vacuum cleaner is a great tool for sucking up speedy pests. Just suck them up, then dump them into a bucket of soapy water.

Q **My neighbor covers some of the beds in his garden with what look like white sheets. He calls them floating row covers. What are they for?**

A Floating row covers are sheets of lightweight, spunbonded polyester or polypropylene that gardeners use to protect crops from pest damage as well as from cold injury. The covers are available in two different weights: lightweight for use as an insect barrier and heavyweight that provides frost protection to about 28°F/–2.2°C. (You can also double up lighter-weight covers to protect plants from the cold; each sheet provides 2 to 4 degrees of protection.) The fabric allows sun, water, and air to reach plants, but at the same time, floating row covers are one of the most effective tools for preventing damage from such leaf-chewing pests as flea beetles and caterpillars. They're also handy for sheltering any type of vegetable crop if the weather gets a little too nippy. They provide protection from wind, thereby maintaining seedbed moisture and also helping prevent the soil from crusting, so seedlings can emerge more easily. You can buy row covers in various widths and lengths; one common size is 6' × 9'/1.8 × 2.7 m, which covers a 3'–4'/.9 to 1.2 m-wide bed, or you can buy rolls up to 50'/15.2 m long and cut them to fit as needed.

Q How do I install row covers, and what else do I need to know to use them?

A Installing row covers is easy: Simply lay the covers over the garden bed (do this on a windless day if possible). If you're using only a single layer of lightweight row cover, you can lay it directly over the plants; for double layers or heavier-weight frost-protection covers, it's a good idea to install hoops to keep the covers up off the plants. To prevent insects from crawling under the covers to reach your plants, bury the edges of the cover with a mound of soil all the way around the outside of the bed. Or use wire staples (sold for this purpose) to hold down the edges. For best results with staples, fold over the edge of the row cover and pierce both layers. Keep in mind that row covers prevent pollinating insects such as bees from reaching crops, so if you're growing plants that aren't self-pollinating, you'll need to remove the row covers once flowers appear. Also, weeds thrive in the protected conditions under row covers, so you will have to take off the covers regularly to weed.

Soil secures row cover edges

Garden Helpers

Q Insects give me the creeps. I'd like to get rid of *all* the bugs in my garden, but I've heard that's not a good idea. Why not?

A Lots of people share your dislike of creepy crawly things, but if you want a successful garden, it's important to tolerate insects, even if you can't learn to like them. Entomologists estimate that about 90 percent of insects are beneficial. The best-known beneficial insects are lady beetles, which feed on pests like aphids and spider mites, and honeybees, which pollinate crops and are essential if your melons are going to produce fruit without your intervention, for example.

Widespread spraying kills these beneficial insects right along with the pests. Insects that prey on caterpillars and grubs include yellow jackets, hornets, ground beetles, tachinid flies, and many true bugs. Dragonflies aren't usually mistaken for garden pests, but here's a good reason to encourage them to visit your yard: They eat mouthfuls of gnats and mosquitoes as they fly! So try to focus on the good things insects can do in your yard and garden, and design your garden to encourage them to stay around.

Don't worry that insects will overtake your garden. The more types of insects you encourage in your garden, the better the chances that beneficial species will keep the pests in check. You'll still want to monitor populations of pest insects in your garden by walking along the rows and looking for problems. Once you spot a problem – aphids or spider mites that have built up on a particular crop, for example – check to see if lady beetles or other beneficials are moving in to dispatch them. If not, take steps to correct the problem.

SEE ALSO: *For more on defensive steps to take, pages 146–162.*

THE WATER CURE

One of the most effective controls for aphids and spider mites is to simply blast them off your plants with a hose. Pests like aphids appear first in the garden, but it takes populations of beneficial predators a bit longer to build up and take care of these pests. Blasting pests off plants with water may seem like a stopgap measure, but by the time the pests have regrouped, the predators will be in place and able to keep them under control.

How do I attract so-called beneficial insects to my garden?

Try these tactics to encourage "beneficials" to make your garden their home:

- **ALLOW SOME WEEDS.** Leave a weedy patch alongside your garden, or leave a few weeds along the rows. These provide shelter and an alternative food source for beneficials.
- **PLANT SOME FLOWERS.** Including companion plants that provide nectar and pollen is a great way to encourage beneficial insects.
- **CONSIDER PERMANENT PATHWAYS.** Beneficials can hide in mulched pathways or nearby mulched flower beds during times when you are harvesting or spraying in the vegetable garden.
- **MAKE A BUG BATH.** Insects need water, too! Fill a shallow dish with stones and water to give beneficials a safe place to drink.

"Bug bath" for beneficial insects

Flowers for Beneficials

BENEFICIAL INSECTS ATTACK PESTS in a variety of ways. Some adults attack and eat pests directly, while others simply lay their eggs on insect pests and let their larvae do the damage after they hatch.

Braconid wasps are one example of this latter lifecycle: The adult wasps feed on nectar, not insects. However, when it's time for them to lay eggs, they'll seek out tomato hornworms for depositing their eggs. The braconid larvae feed on the hornworm, and then emerge and spin cocoons on the outside of the worm. If, during one of your garden-inspection tours, you see a large green caterpillar, usually on a tomato plant, covered with tiny white cocoons that look like grains of rice, don't kill it! Move it off the tomato plant and then leave it be. From the little cocoons will emerge adult wasps that will attack other caterpillars.

Some gardeners practice a technique known as companion planting, and grow flowers not only to beautify their yards, but also to attract beneficial insects whose larvae attack pests. Aster-family plants (Asteraceae) like daisies, asters, and yarrows (*Achillea* spp.) are a rich source of nectar for adult braconid wasps and many other beneficial insects. Members of the mint family (Lamiaceae), such as mints (*Mentha* spp.) and catmints (*Nepeta* spp.), also are good choices, as are plants in the carrot family (Apiaceae), including dill (*Anethum graveolens*), fennel (*Foeniculum vulgare*), and parsley (*Petroselinum crispum*).

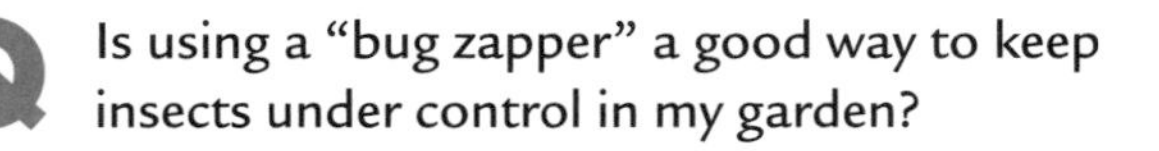

Q **Is using a "bug zapper" a good way to keep insects under control in my garden?**

A Actually, bug zappers (light traps that use an ultraviolet light) kill as many beneficial insects as they do pests, so they're not a very effective way to control pests. If you're growing sweet corn, though, a light trap located out in the corn patch helps control adults of corn earworms, European corn borers, and fall armyworms. To minimize damage to beneficials, put the light trap on a timer and run it between 11:00 P.M. and 3:00 A.M.

Q **Are there any creatures besides beneficial insects that help control insect pests?**

A Insect-eating birds are beneficial, and bats are tremendous insect consumers. A full-size toad can gobble about three thousand slugs and other insects a month, and frogs make good garden hunters as well. Even in suburban neighborhoods, a backyard water garden can attract or support frogs and toads. Be sure to incorporate a shallow soaking area, no more than a couple inches deep so toads have access to water. Soaking areas can be freestanding, away from a conventional pond. Just dig

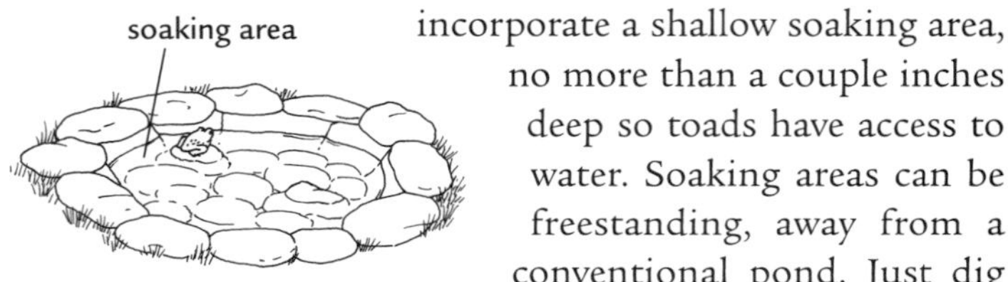

River rocks cover pond liner

BENEFICIAL BIRDS

While crows have been known to walk along corn rows, pulling up seedlings and eating the seeds, for the most part birds are beneficial garden visitors. When they have babies to feed, bluebirds, wrens, and other songbirds consume a tremendous number of insects (admittedly, pest and beneficial alike). So make an effort to attract birds to your yard. Install a birdbath, and give it a weekly cleaning; use an electric de-icer to keep the water unfrozen all winter long. If you've had insect pest problems in a particular bed, you may want to leave that bed unmulched for a few weeks after harvest and lightly turn the soil to bring up larvae and pupae for the birds to eat. Plant native shrubs and trees to provide food and nesting sites. Since birds such as chickadees spend their time in winter feeding on aphid eggs and other "potential" insects, you may want to institute a program to encourage them to stay year-round.

out a shallow depression, cover it with a piece of rubber pond liner, then hide the liner with a layer of rounded river rock. Your soaking area will provide a safe watering hole for birds, beneficials, and other wildlife, including toads. Be sure to flush it out with a hose and replace the water every few days. Other beneficial creatures to encourage are spiders and snakes.

Last Resorts: Organic Sprays and Dusts

What kinds of safe, organically acceptable insecticides do garden centers offer?

A Organically acceptable chemical controls are the last resort, the final line of defense for organic gardeners. These include soap sprays, along with stronger pesticides derived from plants or other naturally occurring substances. Look for products that say "organic" on the label. Neem, pyrethrins, rotenone, and spinosad (technically a biological control) are some of the botanical insecticides you'll find. Products may contain more than one organically acceptable pesticide. There also are organic fungicides, including various sulfur sprays and dusts, as well as products that contain *Bacillus subtilis*. While organic sprays and dusts tend to be less harmful to the environment than synthetic controls, they should be used as a last resort only after other controls fail.

Q Why are organic controls better than regular garden sprays?

A One reason is that they biodegrade quickly. Pyrethrins, for example, are persistent for only a few hours in sunlight when temperatures are above 50°F/10°C. Neem lasts 3 to 7 days on plants and a few weeks in the soil. Rotenone is effective against a wide spectrum of insects, including caterpillars, flies, and beetles. It has a short lifetime in the environment, but it is extremely toxic to fish. Keep in mind that all of these pesticides are toxic to beneficial insects such as lady beetles, and even though they are organically acceptable, you should follow label directions very carefully when using them. Also label your pesticide sprayer so you don't mistakenly use it to apply fertilizer.

Q How do soap sprays kill insects? I've heard that they can damage plants, too.

A Available at garden centers, soap sprays (nontoxic to humans) are very effective for killing slow-moving, soft-bodied pests like aphids, spider mites, whiteflies, and thrips. They're not very effective for controlling hard-bodied pests like beetles. To make a soap spray more effective, add ½ cup/118.3 ml rubbing or isopropyl alcohol to 1 quart/.95 l of spray.

Soap sprays can cause the leaves of some plants to turn

brown, especially if the weather is hot and/or humid. For this reason, it's best to spray on an overcast day and avoid using soap sprays when temperatures exceed 80°F/26.6°C. To determine which of your crops could be damaged, mix up a batch of soap spray and spray it on a leaf or two of each crop you are growing. (Be sure to mark the leaves you have sprayed with yarn, string, or ribbon.) Check for damage after 2 days, and make a list of the crops that the spray damaged. Store this list with your spraying equipment so you know what plants to not spray. Still, if you need to spray a crop that may be damaged by your soap spray, try this trick: 3 hours after spraying, hose off the plant's leaves. The soap will have taken care of the pests, and removing the remnants of the spray helps avoid the damage.

Are there organic spray products besides insecticidal soap?

A Horticultural oil, long used to control a wide variety of pests in orchards and on woody ornamentals during the dormant season, also can play a role in the food garden. Look for highly refined oils (viscosity of 60 or more), and read the label very carefully to determine the *growing season dilution.* (You'll see that there's a separate dilution for use on dormant plants in wintertime, when the spray can be stronger.) To make horticultural oil more effective, after diluting it, add a squirt of liquid dish soap.

Since oil sprays can be poisonous to plants, before spraying be sure to test oil sprays on a leaf of your plant, then wait 24 hours before spraying. Horticultural oils are effective for killing aphids, spider mites, caterpillars, and other soft-bodied pests. They also prevent some fungus diseases, yet they don't persist very long in the environment and are relatively harmless to beneficials.

Horticultural oils are a petroleum product, but newer oil sprays depend on plant oils to control pests. Some also are useful for controlling powdery mildew and other plant diseases. Clove, mint, rosemary, and cinnamon oils have all demonstrated insecticidal properties: Formulations of these oils, alone and in combination, are available from companies that sell organic gardening products.

Q Is there a homemade spray I can use to fight insect pests?

A Soap-and-oil spray is the easiest homemade spray to make and is very effective for controlling a wide range of pests. Start by mixing a concentrate solution to keep on hand by combining 1 cup/.24 L of vegetable oil and 1 tablespoon/14.8 ml of liquid dish soap. To dilute this mixture to use in your garden, combine 2 teaspoons/9.86 ml of the concentrate with 1 cup/.24 L of water. Put the mixture in a hand sprayer and spray it on infested plants. Be sure to wet both tops and undersides of leaves.

Q What products can be used to control diseases?

A Farmers and gardeners have used sulfur and copper sprays to fight plant diseases for a century or more. Many products that contain sulfur and copper are acceptable for organic gardens, but check out some of the newer disease control products, too. Fungicidal soaps are one option, as well as sprays based on potassium bicarbonate as the active ingredient. There are even products that harness the fungus-fighting power of a naturally occurring soil bacterium called *Bacillus subtilis.*

Symptoms and Solutions

If I see a pest or damage in the garden, how do I decide what to do about it?

A First, don't simply assume that a nearby insect did the damage, unless you see it feeding. The insect or insects you see may be innocent or may be beneficials that have already dispatched the pest. Use the pages that follow to identify what's attacking your plants. It's helpful to have a garden insect guide handy, too, so you can identify any unfamiliar insects you encounter.

SEE ALSO: *For garden insect guide suggestions, Appendix.*

Damaged Leaves and Stem Tips

Q The leaves and/or stem tips of my vegetable plants are curled up and distorted. What's causing this problem?

A Several pests, along with one disease, can cause curled or distorted leaves. Some of them are listed below.

APHIDS AND LEAFHOPPERS

Aphids are tiny pear-shaped insects found in dense clusters. They may be white, green, black, gray, or pink; they excrete sticky honeydew on leaves. Leafhoppers are wedge-shaped insects that jump and fly in all directions when startled. Their nymphs lack wings.

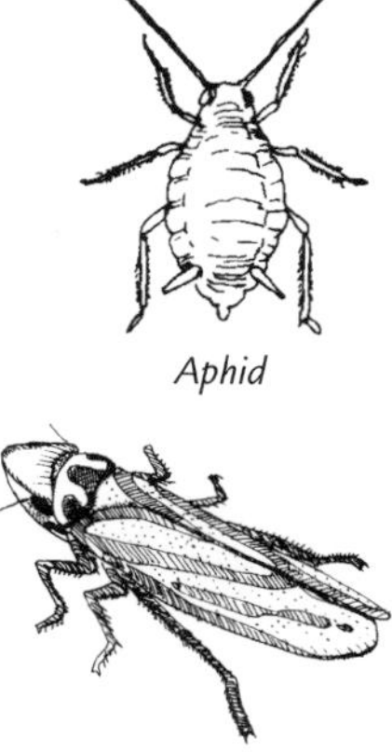

Aphid

Leafhopper

CONTROLS: Blast aphids and leafhopper nymphs with a strong stream of water; attract beneficial insects; use insecticidal soap. As a last resort, spray neem or pyrethrins.

ASTER YELLOWS

Leafhoppers spread this disease, which causes curled, stunted leaves and dwarf plants. Pull up any infected plants you see, for there is no cure.

TARNISHED PLANT BUGS

Both the ¼"/6.35 mm-long light green to brown adults and the yellow-green nymphs suck plant juices and cause leaves, stems, flowers, and fruit to become distorted and drop. Several other closely related insects cause this problem.

Tarnished plant bug

CONTROLS: Cover plants with floating row covers (hand pollinate flowers, as necessary); attract beneficial insects. As a last resort, spray insecticidal soap or pyrethrins.

SPIDER MITES

Look closely for webbing on the stem tips and for clusters of tiny (1/50"/.5 mm) eight-legged mites.

CONTROLS: Wash mites off plants with water; spray insecticidal soap. Use neem as a last resort.

Spider mite

Q **Light green patches developed on my squash and pumpkin plants; then the leaves and stem tips died. What caused that?**

A Squash bugs have been feeding on your plants. Both the adults (½"/12.7 mm-long brown-black insects) and the whitish green juveniles suck plant juices. Infested plants won't produce fruit.

Squash bug

CONTROLS: Handpick the insects from underneath the leaves or lay boards on garden rows to trap them: The insects will hide under the boards and can be handpicked. Floating row covers will keep these pests away from plants, but you'll need to hand-pollinate the flowers to get fruit. As a last resort, spray squash bugs with insecticidal soap, pyrethrins, or neem.

Q **There are spots on the leaves of my vegetable plants. What could have caused them?**

A Lots of small yellow spots are one of the early signs of a spider mite infestation, so look closely for webs to identify these tiny pests. Several other pests and diseases can cause this problem, including tarnished plant bugs, whose feeding eventually results in wilted leaves and stem tips. Other causes can include any of the following:

THRIPS

These pests rasp leaves and cause silver streaks or speckling on the leaves and flowers. In severe cases, they can stunt plants. **CONTROLS:** Encourage beneficial insects; spray insecticidal soap, pyrethrin, neem, or spinosad.

Thrips

RUST

This fungal disease causes yellow or white spots on the tops of leaves and orange ones beneath the foliage.

CONTROLS: Ensure good air circulation by spacing out crops; do not wet leaves when watering plants; dust plants with sulfur powder as a preventive or to keep a mild infection in check.

FOLIAGE DISEASES

Many different plant diseases begin as spots on the leaves. One example is downy mildew, which causes yellow spots on the tops of the leaves and corresponding cottony blotches on the undersides that are white, gray, or tan. Unfortunately, it can be difficult to identify which specific disease is infecting your plants.

CONTROLS: One way to avoid many foliage diseases is to plant resistant or tolerant cultivars. Picking off afflicted leaves or pruning off infected growth are other effective tactics. Pruning to increase air circulation can reduce problems with many diseases. But if plants become moderately to severely infected, pull them up and be sure to dispose of them in the trash, not the compost pile.

SEE ALSO: *For information about spider mite infestation, page 147; for tarnished plant bugs, page 148.*

Holes in leaves

Q **Ugh! There are great big holes in the leaves of my plants! What do I do about them?**

A Large holes in leaves – or leaves that have been eaten away altogether – are one of the most common signs of a pest invasion. Here are some of the possible culprits:

SLUGS AND SNAILS

If you see slimy or shiny trails on the leaves, slugs or snails are the culprits. These pests hide under mulch, rocks, and other objects during the daytime and feed at night. They pose the biggest problem in wet weather.

CONTROLS: Trap these pests under boards, cabbage leaves, flowerpots, or other objects, then scrape them into a bucket of soapy water to dispatch them. Or lure them to containers filled with stale beer: Set containers with the lip at soil level so that slugs and snails are lured in and drown. Surrounding plants with a band of wood ashes discourages them as well, as long as you renew it frequently. Attracting birds, toads, and other beneficial animals to the garden also helps control slugs. Organic slug and snail bait also is available. The active ingredient is iron phosphate and Sluggo is one brand name to look for.

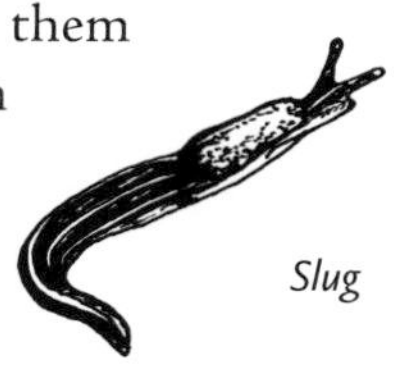

Slug

CATERPILLARS

Various caterpillars feast on vegetable foliage, chewing large holes in leaves or devouring leaves completely.

CONTROLS: All caterpillars can be controlled by hand-picking or by spraying with *Bacillus thuringiensis* (Bt). Attracting beneficial insects will decrease problems with caterpillars, and if you see any that seem to be sick (they'll be sluggish or yellowish in color, or have ricelike cocoons on them), leave them alone and let the disease or the parasitic wasp spread to other caterpillars. Spinosad is also effective against caterpillars.

CUCUMBER BEETLES

If you see ¼"/6.35 mm-long yellow and black beetles – either spotted or striped – cucumber beetles are eating your veggies. Both feed on a wide variety of vegetables, and both carry various diseases that cause plants to wilt and die suddenly.

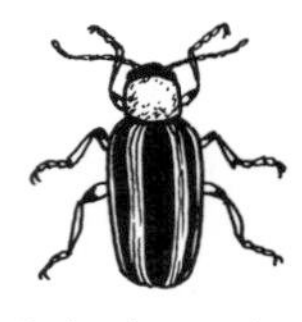

Striped cucumber beetle

CONTROL: Use floating row covers on seedlings, and hand-pollinate crops such as squash and melons that need it to produce fruit. Apply parasitic nematodes to the soil to control the beetles' larvae, and spray pyrethrin or rotenone to control the adults. Kaolin clay is also effective against cucumber beetles. Be sure to clean up the remains of crops and dispose of them in the trash, since these pests overwinter in them.

ANIMAL PESTS

Various animal pests can also chew leaves and plant parts, so don't overlook them. Deer may eat entire plants, but they also can browse off the tops of your vegetables. Crows have been known to pull up seedlings and consume them, and rabbits are eager to chomp away at all manner of vegetable plants.

CONTROLS: See pages 163–167 for information on controlling these pests.

Q **My bean plants have holes chewed in them, but the damage has a lacy look, since most of the leaf veins are still there. What insect could be causing such damage?**

A Mexican bean beetles are oval, yellow-brown pests that are ¼"/.64 cm long and have black spots on their hard wing covers. (Bean beetles look somewhat similar to lady beetles.) Both the adults and the bristly orange-yellow larvae feed from underneath the leaves, chewing holes and leaving a skeletonized pattern. The adults lay clusters of yellow-orange eggs shaped like grains of rice.

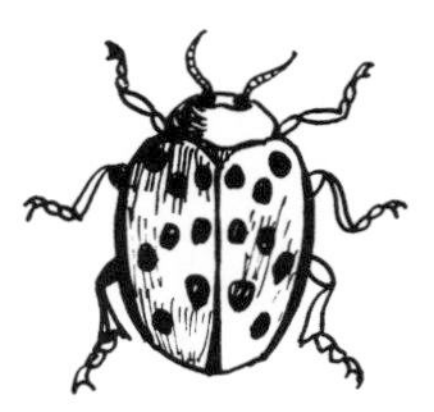

Mexican bean beetle

CONTROLS: Avoid the main generation of beetles by growing early-season bush beans; grow beans under floating row covers until the plants are large enough to tolerate any damage. Plant soybeans nearby to attract the beetles, then destroy the plants once they're infested; handpick adults and larvae daily and drop them in a jar of soapy water; attract beneficial insects. As a last resort, spray every week with insecticidal soap or neem, or rotenone. Kaolin clay is also effective against these beetles.

Q **The leaves on my eggplants and other vegetables are just covered with tiny holes. What pest might have caused them?**

A Look closely, and you'll see tiny, shiny black beetles that hop away whenever you disturb them. These are flea beetles, and they chew holes in leaves. They also spread diseases.

Flea beetles

CONTROL: Use floating row covers to protect seedlings and transplants early in the season. For later infestations, spray with spinosad; kaolin clay is also effective against flea beetles.

Getting the Best from Bt

BACILLUS THURINGIENSIS, or Bt, is a safe and effective control for caterpillars and beetle larvae, yet it doesn't harm beneficials. Unlike conventional insecticides, it is a toxin that is produced by a bacterium. Several subspecies are available, some for caterpillar control and others for beetle larvae, so read labels and make sure the one you purchase will control the pests that are eating your plants. Bt is available in several formulations: liquid concentrate, a powder that is mixed with water before spraying, and in dust or granular form.

Applying Bt correctly is a must if it is going to work properly, because the pests need to eat it as they munch on plant leaves. Spray it on both upper and lower leaf surfaces, and make sure to coat the stems. Be aware that it doesn't persist for long in the environment and degrades especially quickly in sunlight. Bt is most effective on young larvae and won't kill adults, so apply it as soon as you see caterpillars or beetle larvae. Reapply every 7 days to manage persistent populations of pests. Keep in mind that it will kill all caterpillars, including those of butterflies, so spray infested plants only, and never apply it to plants where butterfly larvae are feeding.

Whole Plant Problems

My seedlings fell over, but the tops still look okay. Can I prop them back up?

A Unfortunately, your seedlings are probably done for. If you take a close look at the base of the damaged seedlings, you'll discover what caused the problem:

DAMPING-OFF

If the base of the seedlings look dark, sunken, and/or soft and rotted, the problem is damping-off, a fungal disease.

CONTROL: For seedlings indoors, to prevent damping-off, disinfect pots with a 10 percent bleach solution (1 part bleach, 9 parts water). Also, use pasteurized seed-starting mix, water seedlings from the bottom, and run a small fan continuously to circulate air. Spray seedlings with compost tea once the first true leaves emerge.

If the problem is out in the garden, you'll want to take a different approach, since eliminating the fungus that causes damping-off isn't practical, and healthy soil contains loads of microorganisms that help control it. Improve soil drainage by working compost into the soil, check the soil temperature before you sow, and don't sow too early, when the soil is still too cool. Also, don't sow the seeds too deeply, because the longer the germinating seedlings are underground, the more susceptible they are. To be sure air can circulate, don't sow seeds too thickly. Finally, water plants in the morning so they dry out by nightfall, and try to keep the soil evenly moist but not sopping wet.

CUTWORMS

These chubby, 1"/2.5 cm-long brown or gray caterpillars live in the soil. Cutworms chew through the base of seedlings and transplants and also can eat them entirely.

CONTROLS: When transplanting, slip a cutworm collar over each seedling as you plant it. To make cutworm collars, cut 2"–3"/5–7.6 cm-long sections of cardboard tubing (toilet paper or paper-towel tubes are perfect). Push the collars into the soil around each plant; they'll provide protection until the plant is large enough that it's no longer of interest to the cutworms. Another cutworm control is to mix bran cereal with Btk *(Bacillus thuringiensis* var. *kurstaki)* and spread it around all the transplants. Or spread parasitic nematodes a week before transplanting. These are available from companies specializing in organic controls.

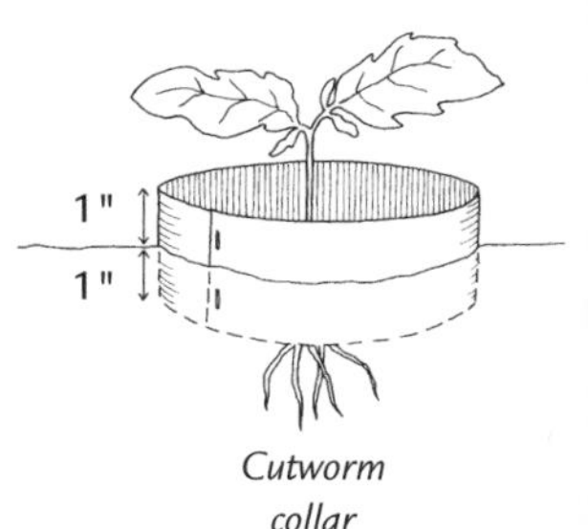

Cutworm collar

My transplants disappeared overnight! Where could they have gone?

A variety of pests play this unkind trick! Cutworms can eat seedlings and transplants entirely, instead of just cutting them down. Slugs and snails also can be quite voracious: Look for their slimy or silvery trails to see if these pests are the culprit. Armyworms are another pest that will consume plants entirely. They feed at night (as do cutworms, slugs, and snails) and hide in leaf litter or under rocks during the day. Look for greenish brown caterpillars with white stripes running along their backs.

Armyworm

CONTROLS: To help control any of these pests, take steps to attract beneficial insects, as well as toads and frogs to your landscape. Spray armyworms with Btk (*Bacillus thuringiensis* var. *kurstaki*). Use kaolin clay to discourage adults from laying eggs on target plants.

SEE ALSO: *For more slug and snail controls, page 151.*

Q **My squash plants died! First one branch seemed to wilt, then the entire plant wilted and died really quickly — almost overnight. What happened?**

A Both insects and diseases can cause this problem:

SQUASH VINE BORERS

These caterpillars tunnel into the stems of squash plants and eat out the centers of the stems, causing plants to wilt

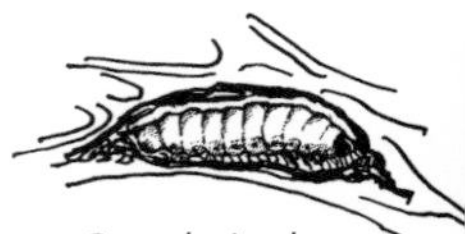
Squash vine borer

suddenly. The adults are greenish brown moths with red abdomens, but it's the white larvae, which have brown heads, that cause the damage.

CONTROLS: Cover plants with floating row covers, but uncover them when flowers appear so bees can reach them or hand-pollinate. Heap a shovelful of soil over leaf nodes at various intervals along the vines, and then water them to encourage root formation. Look for entry hole(s) at the base of the stem with frass (chewed plant material) coming out of the hole. Slit the vine lengthwise and carefully pull open the stem to reveal the borer. Crush borers as you find them. Close up the vine and cover the slit with about 1"/2.5 cm of moist soil. Water the spot with compost tea for a few weeks to encourage roots to form. You can also look for borers with a flashlight at night: Hold it next to the stems and look for silhouettes of the pests in the stems. Pierce them with a hatpin. Repeat this activity every 2 or 3 days until you don't see any borers.

WILT DISEASES

If you don't see an insect, suspect a wilt disease such as bacterial, fusarium, or verticillium wilt. These disease organisms gum up the internal transport system of the plants, blocking the flow of water to the top of the plant and causing it to collapse.

CONTROL: If you suspect a wilt disease, plant resistant cultivars in the future. Pull up afflicted plants and dispose of them in the garbage, not the compost pile.

Q **My cabbage plants started wilting during the middle of the day, but watering didn't seem to help them. Now they're really stunted looking. What should I do?**

You'll probably have to give up and try again. Here's what could be causing the problem:

CABBAGE MAGGOTS

Cabbage maggots (fly larvae) bore into the roots of cabbage, broccoli, and other cabbage-family plants. The damage they do to roots causes plants to wilt at midday, but their feeding also makes it easy for disease organisms to attack as well.

CONTROLS: Pull up and discard the roots of cabbage-family plants; don't add them to compost. Use floating row covers to prevent adults from laying eggs on transplants, and be sure to secure the edges of the covers with soil to keep adults out; spread parasitic nematodes along the row up to a week before planting. To stop females from laying eggs around the base of transplant stems, cut 5"/12.7 cm-wide circles or squares out of tar paper, scraps of rubber pond liner, or foam rubber. Make a slit to the center of the circle and

Cabbage maggot fly barrier

cut a very small opening to accommodate the plant's stem. Place these barriers around seedling stems.

CLUB ROOT

This fungus disease can cause these symptoms as well. Pull up an afflicted plant, and you'll find a gnarled mass of roots.

CONTROLS: Pull and destroy infected plants and discard them in the trash, not on the compost heap. To prevent this disease, raise the soil pH to 7.2, because the fungus that causes it requires neutral to acid conditions.

Q **Whenever I walk past my vegetable garden, clouds of tiny white insects fly up. Will they eventually cause a problem?**

A What you have in your garden are probably whiteflies, tiny insects with white wings that hide under leaves and fly up when disturbed. They suck plant sap and also excrete sticky honeydew, which supports the growth of sooty mold on the leaves. These insects also can spread viral diseases. Eventually their feeding will weaken plants.

CONTROLS: Inspect plants carefully at garden centers, since whiteflies are often carried home on purchased plants; attract beneficial insects; spray with insecticidal soap or neem.

Q **I don't see any insects on my leaves, but the leaves look like they've been dusted with talcum powder. What causes that?**

A Leaves that are dusted with white or gray are infected with powdery mildew, which also can cause distorted growth. Unlike many fungal diseases, which pose the biggest problem in cool, damp weather, powdery mildew is at its height in the garden when days are hot and nights are cool.

CONTROLS: Pick off individual leaves that are infected, prune to improve air circulation, or spray with sulfur. Ordinary baking soda (sodium bicarbonate) is effective as well but is best applied beginning 2 weeks before symptoms appear. Dilute 1 teaspoon/4.9 ml baking soda in 1 quart/.95 L of water. (Commercially available bicarbonate, potassium bicarbonate, is also used for this purpose.) Surprisingly, milk is another option you may want to try. Add 1–2 tablespoons/14.8–29.6 ml of milk to 1 cup/.24 L of water and spray on foliage; milk is best applied before symptoms appear as well.

Coping with Animal Pests

Q Something big is eating my vegetables! Whatever it is takes big chomping bites out of leaves or takes off entire tops of plants. I never see what it is, though, so how can I control a pest that I don't see?

A Most animal pests feed in very early morning or late in the evening, and it can be difficult to tell just what is damaging your crops. Look carefully during those times of day to see if you see pests like rabbits, groundhogs, deer, or birds feeding. Look for signs that each animal leaves, such as footprints, feces, and feeding patterns – deer chomp away at plants from the top, rabbits from the bottom, for example. Birds can peck at fruits and vegetables and will pull up seedlings, and larger pests can make plants disappear entirely, so it's important to figure out what you're dealing with.

Q I've got deer and rabbits eating me out of house and home! What should I do?

A For all land-bound pests, including rabbits and deer, fencing is the best option. The best time to erect a fence, though, is *before* the animals learn that you're cultivating tasty produce. Other controls give varying results. Some gardeners swear by them; others say they don't work at all. Pests faced with hunger and overpopulation are much more determined than ones that aren't, so deterrents will be less effective on desperate creatures. Nevertheless, try some of the following:

- **HANG BAGS OF FRAGRANT, HEAVILY PERFUMED SOAP** on stakes throughout your garden. (Place some close to the ground if you are trying to deter rabbits.) Leave paper wrappers in place and drill a hole through the bar. Mist the soap with water in early evening, just before deer begin to feed. Soap will keep pests at bay until they become accustomed to the fragrance.
- **HANG BAGS OF HUMAN HAIR** (you can collect this at beauty shops). Renew them frequently.
- **COMBINE 2½ GALLONS/9.5 L OF WATER WITH SIX EGGS** (don't include shells, which will clog the sprayer), then spray the mixture around the perimeter of your garden. Humans won't be able to detect the smell of the rotting eggs, but deer will. Reapply after a rainfall.
- **SPRINKLE A MIX** of half bone meal and half blood meal around plants (both of these substances are available at garden centers). Renew after a rainfall.
- **LIGHTS OR SPRINKLERS** that are activated by motion detectors also have been effective at controlling deer.

- **CAGING INDIVIDUAL PLANTS** or sections of your garden is quite effective. Try lightweight wood frames covered with chicken wire.

SEE ALSO: *For information on fencing, page 166.*

Q What about trapping pests? I have resident rabbits and groundhogs, but I don't want to kill them.

A You can use Havahart traps to capture pests and move them to another area, but in most cases other individuals will move in to the now-empty territory. Your relocated captives also won't necessarily fare well at their release site, so this often isn't a humane alternative to wildlife control. They're likely to be killed or driven away by other animals that already have laid claim to the territory. Finally, it's important to have a plan in mind in the event that you trap an unexpected pest, such as a raccoon, which might be rabid, or a skunk, which can be a trial to transport. If you do choose to move wildlife, make sure it is legal in your area, and release animals at least 1 mile/1.6 km away from your house – farther is better. For a long-term solution, fencing is more effective.

Q What kind of fence will keep all the local critters out of my garden?

A In a smaller garden – 60'×40'/18.3×12.2 m – a 3'/.9 m-tall fence will keep deer at bay, since they don't like to jump into a confined area. Ordinary snow fencing works fine for this purpose. If your garden is larger, for a single fence to be effective, it needs to be 8'/2.4 m tall to prevent deer from jumping over it. Or consider installing two shorter fences, which actually are quite effective because deer find it difficult to jump both fences. Try a 4'/1.2 m-tall chicken-wire or wire mesh fence with a single strand of electric fencing located 2½'/.76 m off the ground and 3 feet (.9 m) outside the first fence. (To prevent raccoons, use a three-strand electric fence, with strands separated 3"-4"/7.6–10.2 cm, and the lowest strand 3"/7.5 cm

Garden fence with underground extension

off the ground.) Electrified-netting portable fence, which comes in a roll with posts installed in the netting, is another easy solution for keeping a wide range of critters at bay. They're also easy to take down at the end of the season for garden cleanup.

Since rabbits and groundhogs tend to dig under fences, install the fence with an underground extension as shown, or dig a trench around the base of an existing fence and line it with chicken wire. Bend the lower edge of the the chicken wire out at a 90-degree angle. You can also reinforce an ordinary picket fence with chicken wire if rabbits are your primary pests: Attach a 2'–3'/.6 or .9 m-wide section to the base of the fence, and ideally, use it to line a trench dug along the base of the fence.

Q How can I stop birds from uprooting seedlings? Obviously, a fence isn't going to be effective.

A Covering plants with floating row covers or lightweight plastic netting is an effective way to keep birds away from your crops. Scare tactics work as well. Try suspending unwanted CDs, aluminum pie plates, or any other shiny materials that move in the breeze. For best effect, change their locations frequently. Moving a scarecrow around the garden also can be effective (and fun!). Rubber snakes, owl decoys, and bird-scaring balloons also help control pests.

PART 2

Crop by Crop

Secrets of Success with Your Favorite Vegetables

Fitting a diverse selection of crops into a garden and keeping them all happy and growing vigorously is a challenge. When you consider the care that each crop requires to grow well – from raising delicate seedlings to helping transplants adjust to the outdoors to preventing water stress and pest problems – it's very easy to get caught up in, and overwhelmed by, the details. When is it time to start the lettuce or broccoli seed? Is it too late to plant tomatoes? Will the peppers survive if they're moved outdoors now, or should I wait a week? What does a ripe eggplant look like? How do I grow a fall crop of kale or cabbage?

While experienced gardeners do keep track of many of the details for each crop, they're also aware of the similarities these crops share. For one, nearly all of them will grow in well-prepared garden soil that is rich in organic matter. So prepare the soil once for everybody, then plant.

In the pages that follow, you'll find information that will help you produce a topnotch harvest of the most popular vegetable crops. Each crop entry begins with tricks and tips for starting seedlings and moving transplants to the garden and then goes on to cover essential care during the growing season and how to harvest produce at its prime. You'll also find a list of essential Tips for Success that summarize the most important techniques for growing each crop like an expert. Problem Patrol guides you through the challenge of averting common pest, disease, and other problems you may encounter with each crop. To make information easy to find, crops that have the same growing requirements and that are grown on similar schedules are grouped together. For example, if you turn to page 210, you'll find the entry that covers broccoli, cabbage, cauliflower, and their relatives. For more information about USDA hardiness zones and to find out what zone you garden in, go to www.arborday.org/treeinfo/zonelookup.cfm or inquire at your Cooperative Extension Office.

As you gain experience with the crops featured here, you'll identify tricks that work well in your garden, schedules that make sense for you, and favorite ways to handle chores from trellising to pest prevention. That's one of the most enjoyable aspects of gardening: It's personal. Your garden is different from that of every other gardener, as is the way you take care of it. Enjoy the process!

Artichoke (*Cynara scolymus*)

SUNFLOWER FAMILY, ASTERACEA

TIPS FOR SUCCESS

- Plant in full sun but provide light shade where daytime temperatures exceed 80°F/26.6°C.
- Provide a long growing season with warm days and cool nights.
- Replace plants every 4 or 5 years; in cold climates, grow them as annuals.

Q Can I grow artichokes? Are they annuals or perennials? I live in southeastern Pennsylvania.

A Also called globe artichokes, these Mediterranean perennials can be grown as annuals in the Mid-Atlantic and some other parts of the country provided you select the right cultivars to grow, start them early, and protect them from cold spells. 'Imperial Star' is a good choice for annual cultivation. Start seeds indoors 8 to 12 weeks before the last spring frost, and grow them at temperatures between 60–70°F/15.5–21°C. The seedlings need to be exposed to cool temperatures – 50°F/10°C – for at least a week or 10 days in order to flower, so about 2 weeks before the last spring frost, move them to a cold frame or a spot where you can maintain cool temperatures. The plants won't grow during this cold treatment, but it is essential if they are to produce chokes. Watch the weather carefully, and bring them indoors if colder weather threatens, since artichokes don't tolerate cold snaps. Move them to the garden about 2 weeks after the last frost.

Although artichokes are hardy from Zone 8 south, they do not tolerate the heat and humidity of Southeast summers well. Outside Northern California they probably won't produce well when grown as perennials. Try 'Violetto' or 'Texas Hill' for areas with hot summers and warm winters.

How do I grow artichokes as perennials in Northern California?

A From seed, artichoke plants take 110 to 150 days to produce flower buds, which are the edible portion of the plant. Start seeds indoors 8 to 12 weeks before the last spring frost. For faster turnaround, start with divisions, which will begin producing buds about 100 days after planting. Plant seedlings or divisions with the crowns of the plant just above the soil surface; when growing them as annuals, plant them slightly deeper, and mulch with straw or floating row covers until the weather warms up. Space plants 3'/.9 m apart in rows 3'–4'/.9–1.2 m apart. For fat, fleshy flower buds, the soil should be evenly moist but not wet. In warm climates, add a 3"–4"/7.6–10.2 cm layer of compost or other mulch to keep the soil cool. Water monthly with fish emulsion in spring and summer. Plants tolerate drought but won't flower well in dry soil.

RIPE AND READY

Artichoke flower buds are ready for cutting when they are still green. The bracts (see Glossary) should be tight against the bud. To harvest, cut them with 2″–3″/5–7.6 cm of stem still attached. After harvesting the central stalk, which flowers first, cut it back to about 1′/.3 m to encourage side shoots and more flower buds to form.

Cutting an artichoke bud

Q What care do artichoke plants need at the end of the season?

A In late fall cut the plants to the ground and mulch them. Artichokes are seldom troubled by pests or diseases, but clumps do begin to lose vigor after 4 or 5 years. When that happens, dig the clumps and replace them in spring. In areas where artichokes are not hardy (Zone 7 north), try digging and potting up clumps 1 month before the last frost date. Overwinter them in a cool, frost-free place, and move them back to the garden after danger of frost has passed.

Asparagus (*Asparagus officinalis*)

LILY FAMILY, LILIACEAE

TIPS FOR SUCCESS

- At planting time, pay special attention to soil preparation, along with annual soil improvement, since plants will produce for 15 years or more.
- Choose all-male cultivars, which are two to three times more productive than conventional cultivars.
- Harvest spears daily once plants are in full production, twice a day if temperatures are in the 80s/26.6–31.6°C.

I live in northern Mississippi. Is asparagus a crop I can grow?

Yes, you can. Asparagus makes a great perennial crop for gardeners throughout much of the United States and southern Canada. The only areas where asparagus won't thrive are along the hot and humid Gulf Coast and in Florida. The plants require a dormant period so the crowns can rest before producing new growth for the next season. In California's Imperial Valley, where temperatures reach 115°F/46°C, heat and drought send plants into summer dormancy.

Q Where should I plant asparagus?

A Plant rows of asparagus alongside, but out of, the main vegetable garden. The perennial crowns and wide-spreading roots are easy to damage accidentally when tilling or replanting annual crops. Site plants along the west or north side of the garden so their ferny, 5"/1.5 m-tall foliage won't shade other crops. Raised beds are a good choice for asparagus, because they supply well-drained conditions and can be filled with rich soil. For best results start with certified disease-free, 1-year-old crowns, not seeds. Two-year-old crowns are more expensive and suffer more from transplant shock than 1-year-old crowns, so avoid them.

Q Which cultivars are best?

A Asparagus produces both male and female plants (such plants are said to be dioecious). Female plants spend a lot of energy producing berries and seeds. Since all-male hybrids don't produce seed, they bear more spears than old-fashioned dioecious cultivars. New hybrids also resist or tolerate rust and other common asparagus diseases. Planting them in well-drained soil eliminates most disease problems. Planting all-male plants also eliminates the need to weed out less-productive, self-sown seedlings.

Q What's the best way to plant asparagus crowns?

A Well-cared-for asparagus can produce for 15 to 20 years, and good soil preparation pays off. Ideally, have your soil tested, and adjust the pH if necessary before you buy plants. Prepare the soil in fall for spring planting by working in a good dose of compost and well-rotted manure. It's also important to plant crowns as soon after you purchase them as possible. (Store them in slightly moist sphagnum moss if you can't plant immediately.) In spring dig a 6"–7"/15.2–17.8 cm-deep trench with a slight mound at the bottom that runs down the center. Spread a handful each of bonemeal and wood ashes where each crown will go, then top that with a 1"/2.5 cm layer of compost. Soak asparagus crowns in compost tea for about 15 minutes before planting. Space out the crowns – just lay them on their sides, without spreading out the roots – 1½'/.45 m apart in rows 3'–4'/.9–1.2 m apart. At first, cover them with just 2"/5 cm of soil. Gradually cover them with more soil as the shoots emerge, until the trench is full. The bed should stay moist but not wet.

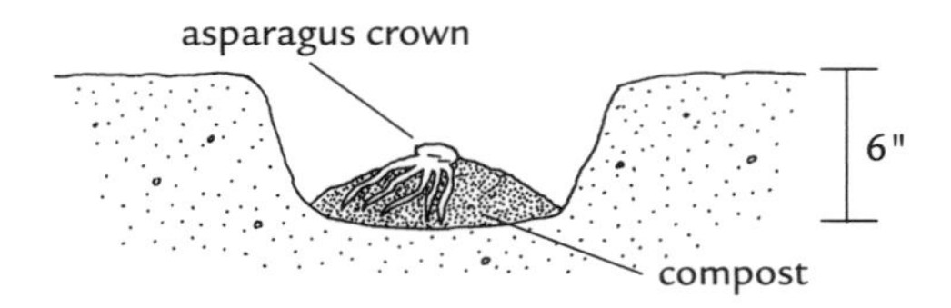

Q My asparagus crowns never came up. What happened?

A Be sure the soil has warmed to 50°F/10°C before planting, because crowns won't grow in cold – or wet – soil, which also exposes the plants to diseases. Plant in raised beds if your soil tends to be damp.

Care through the Season

Q What do asparagus plants need to stay healthy?

A Asparagus crowns grow up toward the soil surface each year, and this results in smaller, less-tender spears. Prevent this by mounding 1"–2"/2.5–5.0 cm of soil up over the rows each spring. Add a layer of compost at the same time to enrich the soil. Adjust soil pH if necessary. Keep the soil evenly moist during the harvesting season, and cover beds with several inches of weed-free straw, chopped leaves, or grass clippings once the harvest has finished.

SEE ALSO: *For more about pH, page 413.*

Do I need to be careful about weeding my asparagus patch?

A Weeds can easily overrun an asparagus bed and cut productivity, so it's very important to stay ahead of them. Keep the rows mulched, and pull weeds as regularly as you can. Pull carefully, or just cut weeds off at the soil surface during the harvest season to avoid damaging

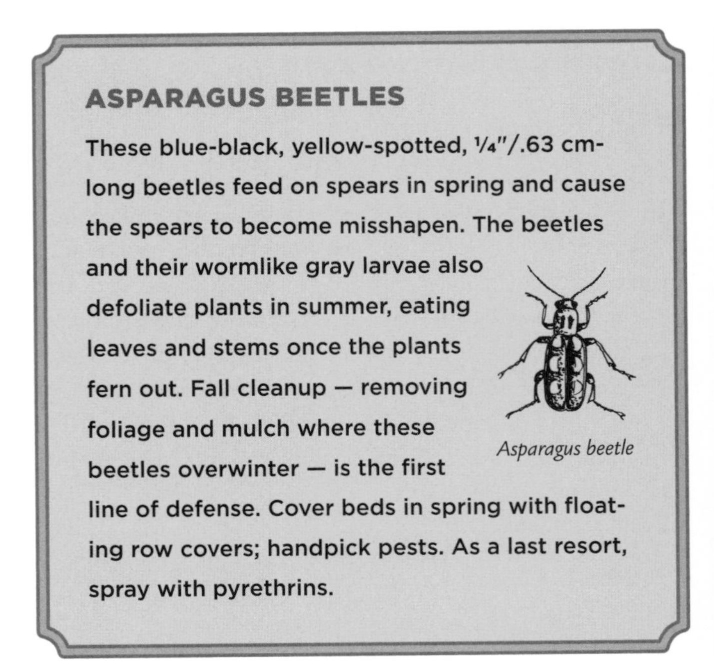

ASPARAGUS BEETLES

These blue-black, yellow-spotted, ¼"/.63 cm-long beetles feed on spears in spring and cause the spears to become misshapen. The beetles and their wormlike gray larvae also defoliate plants in summer, eating leaves and stems once the plants fern out. Fall cleanup — removing foliage and mulch where these beetles overwinter — is the first line of defense. Cover beds in spring with floating row covers; handpick pests. As a last resort, spray with pyrethrins.

Asparagus beetle

emerging spears. In fall, cut down the asparagus foliage after it has yellowed, then cultivate shallowly to eliminate annual weeds. Don't dig deeper than 2"–3"/5–7.6 cm, since the crowns are at most 6"/15.2 cm down. One option for dealing with weedy, self-sown asparagus seedlings is to dig up female plants (the ones that produce berries) and replace them with male ones, which bear more and don't self-sow.

Gathering the Harvest

Q **The first spears have come up in my new asparagus beds! Can I cut them?**

A Resist the temptation to harvest from newly planted asparagus. The first year, don't pick at all: Let the spears "fern out" so they can produce energy to support root growth. The second year, pick no more than two or three of the thickest spears from each crown. Let the rest go. The third year, harvest all the spears for about 4 weeks. The fourth year, once plants are fully established, harvest for 8 to as much as 12 weeks. Stop harvesting when more than half of the spears are less than the thickness of a pencil.

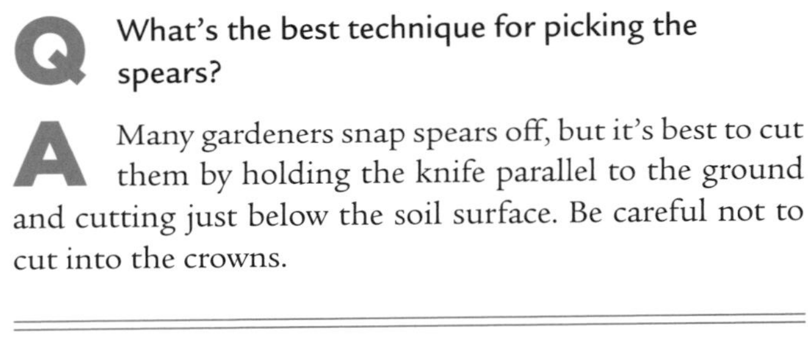

What's the best technique for picking the spears?

Many gardeners snap spears off, but it's best to cut them by holding the knife parallel to the ground and cutting just below the soil surface. Be careful not to cut into the crowns.

How do I tell when the spears are tender and ready to pick?

Look at the tips of the spears. Tight tips will be tender; loose ones may have turned woody. Pick spears every 2 or 3 days — daily or even twice a day if temperatures are above about 85°F/29.4°C.

ASPARAGUS STORAGE SECRET

Plunge cut asparagus spears into ice water right away to cool them down, then store them upright in the refrigerator in jars with 1"–2"/2.5–5 cm of water in the bottom. Loosely cover the spears with a plastic bag. They will keep for a week or more at 35°F/1.7°C.

Q **My family loves white asparagus. How do I grow that?**

A It's easy to produce this gourmet treat. Start with any green asparagus, and use a hoe to mound loose soil up over the rows. Mix the soil with compost if it seems heavy, since a light, loose covering is best. Pile the soil up over the emerging spears, and continue adding more until they're ready for harvest, to keep them in the dark. Gently remove the soil to harvest.

Q **We never have enough asparagus. Is there any way to spread out the harvest?**

A If you have plenty of gardening space, plant twice as many asparagus crowns as you need for your household. You're going to designate half the plants for spring harvest, and half for fall. In spring, harvest spears as you normally would from the spring half of the bed. Let plants in the other half of the bed "fern out"; then in late July cut down their foliage. Water the bed deeply if the weather has been dry. The plants will produce new spears that can be harvested into the fall. Mulch the soil with chopped leaves or another light mulch so a crust doesn't form that would be too hard for the spears to break through.

To keep the plants vigorous if you use this method, be consistent and always harvest spears in the spring bed in spring and the fall bed in fall. A fall-harvest schedule is harder on plants than traditional spring harvest, because because fall harvest puts stress on the crowns just before winter arrives. For this reason, fall-harvested plants may need to be replaced before spring-harvested ones will.

Perennial Companions

Are there other perennial vegetables I can plant near asparagus?

Although used more like a fruit than a vegetable, rhubarb *(Rheum rhabarbarum)* is another popular perennial crop. Plantings will last 20 years and, like asparagus, can be hard to fit into a bed with other vegetables. Instead, site rhubarb alongside your vegetable garden, where it won't suffer root or crown damage when you till or dig your garden.

How do I grow rhubarb?

Plants need full sun to light shade and deeply prepared soil that's well drained and rich in organic matter. Rhubarb grows best in areas with cool summers – summer highs averaging 75°F/24°C are ideal – and winter temperatures that fall below 40°F/4.5°C (roughly USDA Zones 2 to 8). For quickest results, start with root divisions, also called sets (for a family of four you'll need about five plants). For each set, dig a site that's 1½'-2'/.45-.6 m square, and work in plenty of compost and well-rotted manure. Space sets 4'/1.2 m apart and plant them with the buds 1"- 2"/2.5-5 cm below the soil surface. Once they sprout, mulch heavily with grass clippings or chopped leaves and water regularly – they need 1"/2.5 cm of water per week. In fall cut back the tops. Top-dress rhubarb plantings annually in spring and fall with compost.

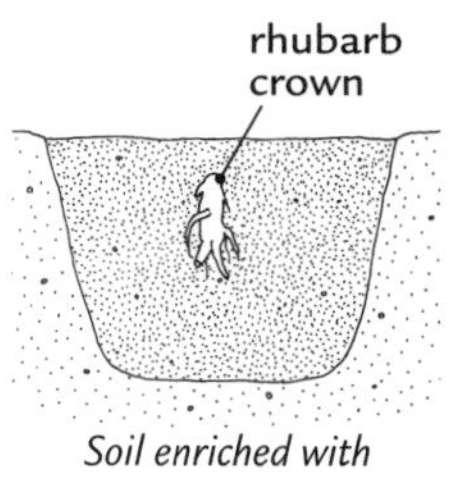

Soil enriched with organic matter

Q How do I harvest rhubarb?

A Don't harvest any stalks the first year, and harvest only a few stalks the second year. After that, harvest as many as you want for 2 months, beginning in spring when they are about as wide as a finger. To keep the plants producing new leaves, remove flower stalks as they appear. To harvest leaf stalks, either cut or twist and pull them off. Plunge stalks into ice water to cool them, then store in plastic bags in the refrigerator. Be sure to cut off the leaves and compost them. Only the stalks are edible; the leaves are poisonous.

Beans

LEGUME FAMILY, FABACEAE (LEGUMINOSEAE)

TIPS FOR SUCCESS

- Install a trellis, teepee, or other support for pole beans before sowing seeds.
- Wait to sow until the soil has warmed to at least 55°F/12.7°C.
- Cover seeded areas with floating row covers to protect seedlings from cold and insect pests.

Q Which kind of beans should I grow, pole beans or bush beans?

A Many gardeners grow some of each type. Bush beans are easy to grow and produce a crop quickly. They're self-supporting plants that do not need trellising. Pole beans, which take longer to bear, are climbing, twining plants that must be staked or trellised. Over the long run, they produce heavier yields and bear over a longer season than bush beans. Pole beans also take up less space in the garden; another advantage is that you don't need to stoop over to pick them.

Q Help! The bean descriptions on seed packets and in catalogs are confusing. What do I need to know?

A Beans *are* a confusing lot, because catalogs refer to the many different shapes and sizes, along with harvest times. If you experiment a bit, though, you'll find an interesting array of crops. All require basically the same care in the garden, and unless otherwise noted, all are available as either bush or pole beans.

- **SNAP BEANS.** Also called green or string beans, these are picked when the pods are still young and tender. Some cultivars have yellow pods (these are also called wax beans); others are purple podded.
- **FILET, OR FRENCH, BEANS.** Also called *haricots verts,* these are snap beans bred to be picked while still very slender.
- **ROMANO BEANS.** These are broad, flat snap beans that have a rich, beany flavor.
- **SHELL BEANS.** Also called horticultural beans or *flageolets,* these are beans that are harvested when the seeds have swollen but are still fleshy and the pods are tough and fairly dry, much like lima beans. Shell beans also can be left in the garden and harvested as dry beans.

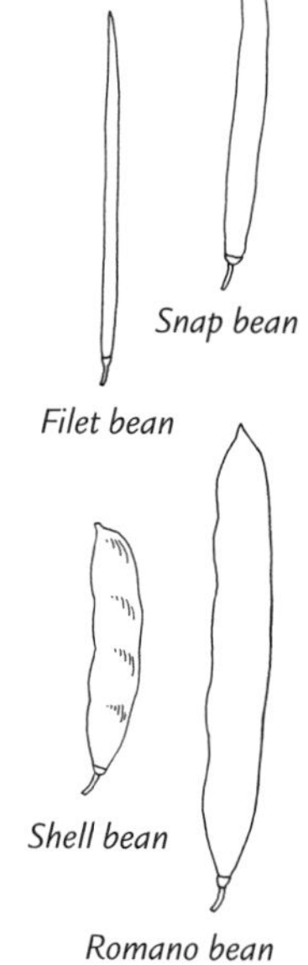

- **DRY BEANS.** Also called field beans, these are bush-type beans that are left in the garden until the seeds are hard and the pods are dry. They come in different colors and forms, including black beans, pinto beans, and kidney beans.

Dry beans

What about lima beans? How do I grow them? I live near Peoria, Illinois.

A Lima beans (*Phaseolus lunatus*) are a heat-loving crop, and most experts recommend limas for gardens in Zone 5 and warmer. You'll find both bush- and pole-type plants offered in catalogs. Bush-type plants begin bearing in 80 days, pole limas in 90. Since Peoria is in Zone 5, stick to growing bush limas; bush types are best in areas with less than 130 days of warm, summer weather. Planting short-season cultivars, warming the soil before planting, and protecting seedlings from cold in spring all help speed production. Both small- and large-seeded lima cultivars are available. Small-seeded limas are commonly called baby limas or butterbeans, while large-seeded ones are sometimes called potato limas.

Q **I like to experiment a bit in my garden. Are there other kinds of beans I can try that are easy to grow?**

A There's a wealth of crops closely related to beans that are great choices for home gardens. Unless otherwise noted below, all are grown much like snap or pole beans. In addition to the ones listed here, consider trying adzuki beans (*Vicia faba*), lentils (*Lens culinaris*), mung beans (*Vigna radiata*), or winged beans (*Psophocarpus tetragonolobus*), also called asparagus peas.

- **ASPARAGUS BEANS** (*Vigna unguiculata* var. *sesquipedalis*). Also called yard-long beans, these are heat-loving, subtropical pole-type beans with 1'–1½'/.3–.45 m-long pods with black seeds. Harvest when pods are young and tender, like a snap bean. Look for day-neutral cultivars, like 'Liana', which bear best in areas with long summers.
- **CHICKPEAS** (*Cicer arietinum*). These are also called garbanzo beans and Egyptian peas. They can be harvested when tender and used like a snap bean. To harvest dry garbanzos, pull the entire plant and lay them on a sheet or tarp in a dry, sunny spot until the pods have split to release their seeds.
- **COWPEAS** (*Vigna unguiculata* ssp. *unguiculata*). Also called Southern peas and field peas, these plants thrive in hot weather. They're also more drought tolerant than

other beans and bean relatives: Don't water them after the plants flower and pods have begun to form. Harvest when young and tender as snap beans, before the pods turn yellow as shell beans, or as dry beans. Blackeyed peas are one type of cowpea, but there are many other colors available. Most are bush-type plants, but pole cowpeas also are available.

- **FAVA BEANS** (*Vicia faba*). Also called broad or horse beans, these need cool, moist conditions and are grown like peas. Harvest them young, like a snap bean, or at the shell- or dry-bean stage. In hot-summer areas, try sowing in fall for overwintering or harvest in spring or fall.
- **SOYBEANS** (*Glycine max*). Also called edamame beans, soybeans are easy to grow. Treat them as you would any bush beans, harvesting when the seeds are plump and nearly touching in the pods but before the pods begin to turn yellow.

Q How early can I plant beans?

A Beans are a warm-weather crop, and the seeds simply sit and rot if they're planted in cold, wet soil in spring. Wait to plant until a week or two after the last frost date for your area. The soil temperature should be at least 55°F/12.7°C, but 60°F/15.5°C is better, and seeds germinate even faster in soil that has warmed to 75–80°F/24–26.7°C. (Fava beans are an exception to this rule: They prefer cool weather and are grown like peas.)

Q **What's the best spacing for beans? Are bush and pole beans grown the same distance apart?**

A Bush and pole beans are grown at slightly different spacings. Bush beans are normally grown in rows, with seeds spaced 2"–4"/5–10 cm apart. Thin seedlings to 4"–6"/10–15.2 cm apart. Space individual rows 1½'–3'/.45–.9 m apart or, for a higher-density planting, arrange bush beans in wide rows with several plants abreast so each row is about 2'–2½'/.6–.75 m wide (set individual plants at the regular spacing within the row). Leave 2'–3'/.75–.9 m between the wide rows, so you'll have room for tending the plants. Plant pole bean seeds 4"–6" apart and thin seedlings to 6"–9"/15.2–22.9 cm. Leave 3'–4'/.9–1.2 m between rows. Be sure to install poles or erect trellises before sowing to avoid trampling the soil to do it later.

Q **I want to grow my pole beans on trellises scattered around the garden. What's the easiest way to do that?**

A Plant your pole beans on hills with teepee-type supports. In this case, the number of plants will depend on how many supports are used to build the teepees. Build a hill large enough to accommodate the entire teepee, and use five to ten supports to build it. Plant two seeds per teepee support, and thin to one plant per support once the seedlings are up and growing. Leave 3'-5'/.9–1.5 m between hills.

SEE ALSO: *For details on how to set up teepees and trellises, pages 46–47.*

How do I sow the seeds?

A Plant beans 1"/2.5 cm deep to 1½"/3.75 cm deep in light-textured soil that's rich in organic matter, since it is generally warmer than heavier soil. For a late-summer crop of beans, sow seed slightly deeper than usual, about 2"/5 cm, to ensure they receive adequate moisture for germination. Since beans can take nitrogen from the air and use it to fuel their growth, there's one other sowing step that you may want to take. If you haven't grown beans before, purchase bacterial inoculant with your seeds. Beans need certain soil-dwelling bacteria in order for their roots to fix nitrogen, and applying bacterial inoculant ensures that the plants have plenty of bacteria available to form this mutually beneficial partnership. To apply it, moisten the seeds before planting and dust them with inoculant. After the first year, you'll probably have enough bacteria in your soil to inoculate future crops without dusting the seeds.

SEE ALSO: *For more information on inoculants, page 410.*

Q How can I keep my garden from producing bushels of beans one week and none the next?

A Anyone who has grown beans before knows that they produce a bumper crop all at once. To spread out the bean harvest – and your picking time – one option is to plant small crops of bush beans every 10 or 12 days. Continue planting up to 8 or 12 weeks before the first fall frost date for your area. As one batch of plants stops producing, begin picking from the next. Or grow both bush and pole types. Bush beans produce a week or two before pole types start bearing, and pole beans continue producing long after the bush-type plants are finished.

Care and Harvesting Tips

Q What care do beans need to stay healthy?

A Beans don't tolerate drought very well, so keep the soil evenly moist, especially while they're germinating, flowering, and growing pods. Don't overwater, though, because wet soil causes root rot and can cause flowers to drop off without producing pods. Once the plants are about to bloom, mulch them with 4"–6"/10.2–15.2 cm of light mulch. Plants don't need extra fertilizer during the season.

Q How can I encourage my pole beans to climb their trellis?

A Bean seedlings sometimes need a little help to begin climbing a trellis; otherwise they'll twine around each other or flop on the ground. When plants are still quite small, gently guide the vines around the trellis. Once they're in contact, they'll climb on their own. If your trellis starts several inches above the plants, try placing a thin garden stake next to each seedling that bridges the gap from ground to trellis. Then train the seedlings onto the stake to give them a leg up.

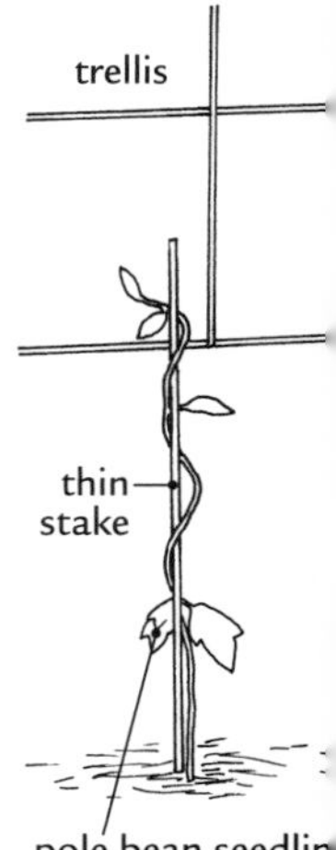

BIGGEST BEAN HARVESTS

For the biggest overall harvest, pick beans daily or every few days. If you wait longer between harvests, some pods will mature, which causes the plants to stop producing new ones. Pinch or cut off the pods — pulling at them can uproot the plants.

Q When are beans ready to pick?

A For tender green beans, pick them when they are about as thick as a pencil and the seeds inside the pods are just visible as small bumps. Pick shell beans once the seeds are full size but still tender. With both green and shell beans, the more you pick, the more the plants produce. Leave dry beans on the plants until the seeds are hard and rattle in the pods, or cut the plants once the pods are yellow and hang them in a warm, dry place. Store dry beans in jars with a tablespoon of powdered milk folded in a paper towel to absorb moisture.

What do I do once my bush beans stop producing?

A As the plants stop producing new pods, either pull them up and add them to the compost pile or dig them under to enrich the soil where they've grown. If you're digging the plants under, be sure to shred or chop up the foliage and stems first. Otherwise, they'll take quite a while to break down. Replant the bed with another crop or mulch heavily for planting later in the season.

Problem Patrol

I've heard that beans are susceptible to many diseases. What can I do about them?

The best line of defense is to plant resistant cultivars. Other steps that will reduce problems include:

- If possible, don't plant beans in a spot where other beans have grown in the past 3 years.
- Wait to sow seeds until the soil has warmed up.
- Soak seeds in compost tea for 20 minutes before planting.
- To avoid spreading disease spores, don't touch or work among wet plants.

- Water moderately; wet soil yields weak, stunted plants and may cause flowers or pods to fall off.
- Leave plenty of room between plants to encourage good air circulation.
- Use soaker hoses for watering so leaves stay dry, because wet leaves make it easier for diseases to spread.
- If disease strikes, pull up and discard plants; do not compost them. Also, rake up and discard any leaves or mulch around the plants to reduce the possibility of problems in future years.

SEE ALSO: *For information on specific plant diseases, chapter 4.*

Q What pests should I watch out for?

A The list of pests that love beans is long and includes aphids, various beetles — especially Mexican bean beetles — and leafhoppers. Installing floating row covers over bush beans when they're still small keeps out all of these pests; in addition, they provide protection from cool temperatures early in the season.

SEE ALSO: *For other options for dealing with common bean pests, page 153.*

Help! My bean plants were doing well, but then they stopped producing. What happened?

Diseases are one reason beans stop producing, but there are a few other causes for stalled pod production. Check the following:

- **UNPICKED MATURE PODS.** Check carefully for missed pods and pick them. Plants stop producing if seeds mature.
- **HEAT AND DROUGHT.** Flowers drop if the soil gets too dry or if the weather is too hot. Heat and drought may finish bush-bean production, but pole beans may resume production if you give them time and wait until conditions improve. To give pole beans a jump start, try removing pods and flowers, and cutting plants back to about 6'/1.8 m, then resume watering.
- **RAIN-DAMAGED FLOWERS.** Hard, pounding rain can damage flowers, which will cause plants to stop producing. Once they recover from the deluge, the plants will begin flowering and bearing again.

Beets, Radishes, and Other Root Crops

VARIOUS CROP FAMILIES

TIPS FOR SUCCESS

- Provide a spot in full sun for root crops if possible; if not, they'll tolerate partial shade.
- Sow seeds in a bed with deeply dug soil free of rocks and roots.
- Thin plants to encourage large roots to develop, but don't bother to thin if you are growing plants for greens alone.

Q I know I can grow radishes in spring. Can I plant any other root crops then?

A Beets, radishes, parsnips, rutabagas, and turnips share a love for cool weather, and growing them when temperatures are cool is the secret to sweet, crisp roots. Start sowing spring radish seeds as soon as the soil can be worked, and plants will be ready for harvest in as little as 3 weeks. Fast, even growth is the secret to a good crop. Sow new crops every week or 10 days until daytime

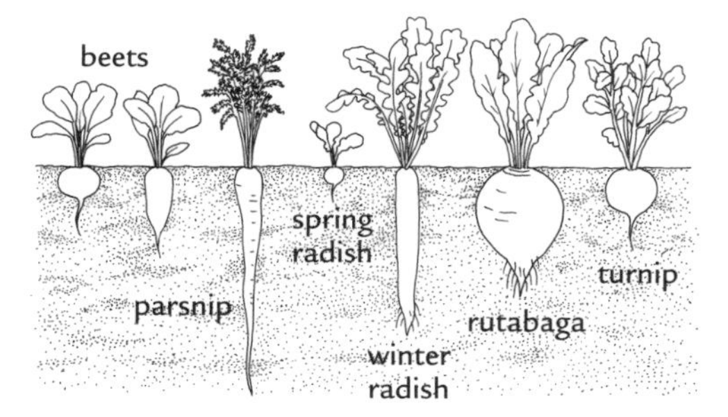

temperatures remain above about 65°F/18.3°C. After that, the roots will be bitter and tough, not spicy and crisp.

Beets and turnips also can be grown in spring, but they take slightly longer than radishes – from seed, beets take 1½ to 2 months, turnips 1 to 2 months. Beets germinate in 45°F/7.2°C soil, but you'll probably get better results if you wait a bit and sow both beets and turnips once the soil is at least 50°F/10°C. If you harvest turnips when they're still small, you can sow successive crops every 10 days until warm temperatures (daytime highs in the low 70s/21–23°C) arrive to spread out the harvest.

Some long-season or winter radishes also can be sown at the same time as beets and turnips in spring. Look for bolt-resistant cultivars that mature in 40 or 50 days, and sow as soon as the soil can be worked.

Parsnips are the slowpokes of this group. Sow them in early to mid-spring for fall harvest.

Q **My mom and dad always grew root crops, but I never paid much attention to how they took care of them. Are root crops hard to grow?**

A Root crops certainly aren't the rock stars of the vegetable garden, but gardeners who grow them love them. They all are easy to grow, need similar conditions, and, with the exception of radishes, are also quite nutritious. Here's a quick "who's who" of the root crops.

- **BEETS** (*Beta vulgaris*, Crassa group. Goosefoot family, Chenopodiaceae). Round or globe-shaped, red beets are best known, but home gardeners also can grow beets with thick, carrot-shaped roots, as well as ones with yellow, white, or red and white flesh. Primarily grown for their sweet-tasting, tender roots, all beets have edible leaves, too.

- **PARSNIPS** (*Pastinaca sativa*. Carrot family, Apiaceae). These produce long, white, carrotlike roots that are nutty and sweet tasting.

- **RADISHES** (*Raphanus sativus*. Mustard family, Brassicaceae). White-fleshed, red-skinned radishes are the best known, but home gardeners have many other choices. Spring radishes (Radicula group) are fast growing, while long-season or winter radishes (Daikon group) produce larger roots and take longer to mature. Flavor varies from spicy to mild, depending on the cultivar and growing conditions, and both types have edible leaves.

- **RUTABAGAS** (*Brassica napus*, Napobrassica group. Mustard family, Brassicaceae). A cross between turnip and cabbage, this little-grown crop is called by a variety of names, including yellow, Canadian, Russian, or Swedish turnip, or just plain swedes. Plants bear edible greens and round yellow- or white-fleshed roots that feature a sweet, mild taste.

- **TURNIPS** (*Brassica rapa*, Mustard family, Brassicaceae). This easy-care crop produces rounded roots that are sweet and mild tasting, plus nutritious, edible greens. Roots can be white, red, yellow, black, or bicolor (purple, red and white, or green and white).

SEE ALSO: *For information on carrots, another favorite root crop, pages 231–237.*

Q How do I figure out when to plant root crops for a fall harvest?

A All of the root crops will provide a good fall harvest if you time your planting right. To determine when to start any of these crops for fall harvest, start with the days to maturity, which you'll find listed on the seed packet or in catalog information. On a calendar, count back that number of days from the first fall frost date in your area to arrive at the date to sow your seeds.

For the best beets and spring radishes, harvest as quickly as they mature. For the best-quality turnips, rutabagas, winter radishes, and parsnips, the objective is to time crops so they are ready to harvest after a couple of light fall frosts, which improve both flavor and texture. That generally means mid- to late-summer sowing, but in warm climates, sow in fall for a winter crop. Keep in mind that while light frost improves texture and flavor, freezing destroys the roots. Dig them before a freeze or mulch heavily to protect the roots and lengthen the amount of time plants can be left in the garden.

SEE ALSO: *For information on mulching, pages 105–109.*

Q **What do I need to do to prepare the soil for root crops?**

A Root crops have similar soil preferences, and all will grow best in prepared vegetable garden soil that is well drained and rich in organic matter. However, a bit of extra soil preparation is necessary to ensure that the roots develop properly. To prepare the soil for any of these crops, dig deeply and incorporate compost or other organic matter throughout. While spring radishes grow fine in soil tilled to about 8"/20.3 cm, for other root crops dig soil and incorporate organic matter to a depth of 12–15"/30.5–38 cm or 18"–24"/45.7–61 cm for parsnips. Also, remove rocks, dirt clods, and roots, which cause forked or misshapen roots. Soil pH ranging from 5.5 to 6.8 is fine for radishes, while beets, parsnips, turnips, and rutabagas are happy in a pH of 6.5 to 7.5. Since heat and drought generally lead to small, woody roots, mulch is another essential for growing these root crops. Once plants are up and growing, cover the soil around them with organic matter — grass clippings, chopped leaves, or other light, loose mulch is fine — to keep conditions moist and as cool as possible.

I've tried parsnips before, but the seeds don't germinate. Any advice?

Parsnip seed is notoriously slow – it takes 3 to 4 weeks to germinate in 50°F/10°C soil. Try the following to get the seeds up and growing:

- Soak seeds in water overnight before sowing.
- Sow thickly in rows or wide beds when the soil is still cool. In warm climates, from Zone 8 south, sow in fall for an early spring crop.
- Sow parsnip seeds ½"/1.3 cm deep, then lightly sow some spring radishes ¼" deep in the same row or bed. The quick-germinating radishes help keep the soil from crusting and will be ready for harvest about the time the parsnip seedlings emerge. (Sow the radishes farther apart than you would normally, so you will be less likely to uproot any parsnip seedlings as you harvest the radishes.)
- Keep the soil evenly moist until seedlings appear.
- Cover the seeds with screened compost or packaged seed-germinating mix instead of garden soil. Or, cover the area with a very lightweight row cover.

BASIC BLOCKS

There's no rule that says your root crops have to be planted in arrow-straight rows, and sometimes other arrangements are easier, faster, and more space efficient. Wide rows are one alternative, but simple block planting is another great option. Simply mark out a square or rectangular space that's no more than about 3'/.9 m wide, so you can easily reach into the center of the bed to tend plants. Then scatter seed evenly across the entire block. Or mix tiny seeds with a bit of white sandbox sand so you can see where you've sown it. If you prefer, mark a grid on the soil surface with a trowel or other small hand tool — 3"x3" to 4"x4"/7.6x7.6 to 10.2x10.2 cm squares are fine — and then sow the same number of seeds in each square. Spread them out according to the proper spacing for the crop you are sowing.

SEE ALSO: *For advice about wide rows, page 22.*

Care and Harvesting Tips

Q Do I have to thin out root crop seedlings?

A That depends on whether you want roots, greens, or both. If you're growing for greens only, sow at the rates listed below, and don't worry about thinning.

If your goal is to harvest sweet, tender roots, be ruthless about thinning to the final recommended spacing. Thin when plants are still small – 2"–3"/5–7.6 cm tall – and cut the plants off rather than pulling them, to minimize damage to the remaining seedlings. All these crops grow well in rows spaced a foot/.3 m or so apart, or plant them in blocks and thin so plants are equally spaced on all sides. Mulch after thinning to suppress weeds and keep the soil cool.

Sow beets, radishes, and parsnips about ½"/1.3 cm deep; rutabagas and turnips ¼"–½"/.63–1.3 cm. Space and thin them as follows:

- **BEETS.** Sow 2"–4"/5–10.2 cm apart in rows, and thin to 4"–6"/10.2–15.2 cm apart while still small. In most cases each beet "seed" is actually a small fruit that contains a cluster of seeds, so no matter how carefully you space them out, you'll still need to thin. Cultivars described as single-seeded or monogerm bear one seed per "seed."
- **PARSNIPS.** Sow seeds thickly, and thin to 4"–6"/10.2–15.2 cm when they are still small.

- **RADISHES.** Sow seeds 1"/2.5 cm apart. Thin spring radish seedlings to 2"/5 cm; winter radishes 6"/15cm.
- **RUTABAGAS.** Sow seeds 1"/2.5 cm apart and thin to 8"/20.3 cm.
- **TURNIPS.** Sow seeds 1"/2.5 cm apart and thin to 4"/10cm.

Q What else helps root crops to grow quickly?

A Consistently even soil moisture is crucial, since uneven soil moisture yields tough or stringy roots and bitter taste. To encourage fast growth, mulch root crops with several inches of grass clippings, compost, or other organic mulch to keep the soil cool and preserve moisture. Make sure plants get 1"/2.5 cm of water per week.

PROTECT YOUR BABIES

To keep flea beetles and other insect pests at bay, cover beets, radishes, rutabagas, parsnips, and turnips with floating row covers (see page 134) as soon as the seedlings emerge.

Q Do root crops need feeding?

A Radishes, rutabagas, turnips, and parsnips don't need supplemental feeding, provided they're planted in well-prepared, compost-rich soil. Beets do benefit from supplemental feeding: Once their first true leaves are fully open, apply a low-nitrogen fertilizer every 3 weeks by sidedressing or foliar feeding. Or water weekly with a dilute solution of fish emulsion and kelp extract.

Q When do I harvest greens from these crops?

A You can harvest greens from all of the root crops except parsnips. Pick leaves when they are still young and tender. If you are growing for greens only, pull entire plants or pick as many leaves as you need. If you want roots, too, take only a few leaves from each plant, so there are enough left to fuel root growth. And don't forget that as you thin your seedlings, you can save and wash the seedlings you clip to add to salads.

Q How can I tell when the roots are ready?

A Pick spring radishes just before or as soon as they reach full size, since they decline quickly. (To check on the size of any of these root crops, gently brush soil away from around the plant to reveal the top of the root.) Bigger isn't better for any of the other crops either. Harvest when they are still small and tender: beets, 1"–2½"/2.5–6.3 cm wide; rutabagas, beginning when they are about 3"/7.6 cm across; turnips 1"–2"/2.5–5 cm wide. Harvest size for winter radishes varies depending on the cultivar, but small is best here, too. Dig parsnips anytime they're large enough to use, but along with turnips, winter radishes, and rutabagas, they're best if harvested after a few light frosts, so wait to harvest if you can.

Q What's the best way to harvest?

A For most root crops, pulling them up gently works fine, provided the soil is loose. You'll need to dig parsnips, which have fairly deep taproots. Dig any of these crops if you feel resistance when you try to pull them or the roots will simply break off in the ground. When digging, start outside the row to avoid bruising the roots. To store beets, parsnips, winter radishes, rutabagas, and turnips in the refrigerator, twist off the greens an inch or two above the root, and store in plastic bags. For longer storage (up to 6 months), pack the roots, dusted off but unwashed, in damp sand, peat, or sawdust at 32°–40°F/0°–4.4°C. (Check regularly, since low humidity causes shriveling.) All of these crops also can be mulched deeply and left in the garden for harvesting, as needed, at least until the ground freezes. You can leave parsnip roots in the ground over winter and harvest before new foliage emerges.

Problem Patrol

What's wrong with my beets? They're tough and woody.

A Tough, woody beets, turnips, and other root crops – along with bitter radishes – are all caused by poor growing conditions. Use these tips to ensure a tasty, tender harvest:

- Keep the soil evenly moist, never too dry or too wet.
- Harvest root crops when they're still small and tender.
- Incorporate plenty of compost into the soil at planting time.
- Time root crops so they either grow entirely or reach harvestable size when temperatures are cool.

Q **Something chewed slimy, winding tunnels in my turnips and radishes! How can I prevent this for the next crop?**

A Cabbage maggots probably caused this damage: Look for tiny grubs in the roots. Infested plants often have yellowed leaves and frequently wilt during the heat of the day because the tunneling damages the plant's root system. Pull and destroy any infested plants growing in your garden. To reduce populations apply beneficial nematodes before planting (follow package directions carefully). Also, at the end of the season make sure you remove all the roots in the garden. Otherwise, any larvae they contain can overwinter there.

Cabbage maggot tunnels in a turnip

Q **My root-crop plants have little tiny roots, not big fat ones. What happened?**

A Overcrowding is the most common cause when beets and other root crops don't develop. It's essential that you thin cut enough seedlings so that remaining roots don't touch one another. Soil that's too dry also prevents fleshy roots from developing. Be sure that plants receive 1"/2.5 cm of water per week.

Broccoli, Cauliflower, Cabbage, and Friends (*Brassica oleracea*)

MUSTARD FAMILY, BRASSICACEAE

TIPS FOR SUCCESS

- Grow these crops in spring, fall, or whenever temperatures in your area are cool for at least 8 weeks.
- Provide partial shade if temperatures are likely to be above 80°F/26.6°C during the growing season.
- Cover transplants with floating row covers to protect them from insect pests.

Q What do all these vegetables have in common?

A For one thing, broccoli, Brussels sprouts, cabbage, cauliflower, collards, kale, and kohlrabi all belong to one species, *Brassica oleracea.* They're collectively referred to as brassicas or cole crops, and while the timing is slightly different from crop to crop, all need similar cultural conditions. Some brassicas are easier to grow than others, but all are vegetables that thrive in cool weather and are primarily grown as spring or fall crops throughout much of North America. They all thrive in soil with a pH of 6.0 to 6.8. Brussels sprouts, collards, kale, and kohlrabi tolerate soil that is as acid as pH 5.5, while cauliflower takes soil that ranges up to pH 7.4.

Q **Can I grow broccoli, cabbage, and other brassicas in the same spot year after year?**

A The downside of the close family tie of these crops is that they also share a variety of pests and diseases. For best results, rotate the location of brassicas every year. Ideally, you want to maintain a 3-year rotation, so you grow a brassica in a particular spot only once every 3 years. Even then, common diseases may be a problem, because they persist in the soil for many years. Brassicas tend to be heavy feeders, so plant them after a legume crop, such as peas or beans, or after a legume cover crop, such as clover.

Q **I always grow a spring crop of cabbage. Can I add broccoli and cauliflower to my spring planting?**

A Yes, provided you time crops so they'll be ready to harvest before hot weather arrives. For spring crops it's also a good idea to select short-season or early cultivars for spring plantings. Although you can direct sow, for best results start seeds indoors. Be sure to harden off all seedlings before transplanting them to the garden.

- **BROCCOLI.** Start seeds 6 to 8 weeks before the last spring frost date; transplant 2 weeks before the last frost.
- **CABBAGE.** Start seeds 6 to 9 weeks before the last spring frost; transplant 1 to 3 weeks before the last frost once the soil is at least 40°F/4.4°C.

- **CAULIFLOWER.** Start seeds no more than 8 to 10 weeks before the last spring frost; transplant 1 to 2 weeks before the last frost, once the soil is at least 55°F/12.7°C. Younger seedlings transplant best, and transplanting at 4 to 5 weeks is ideal.

What spacing do brassicas need?

Unless otherwise noted below, space rows 2'–3'/.6–.9 m apart.

- **BROCCOLI.** In spring, space transplants 15"–18"/38–45.7 cm apart. Plants are a bit larger in fall, so space plants 18"–24"/45.7–61 cm apart.
- **BRUSSELS SPROUTS.** Space transplants 18"–24"/45.7–61 cm apart.
- **CABBAGE.** Space transplants anywhere from 12"–24"/30.5–61 cm apart, depending on the mature size of the head of the cultivar you are growing, in rows 1'–2'/.3–.6 m apart.
- **CAULIFLOWER.** In spring, space plants 15"–18"/38–45.7 cm apart. Space fall crops 18"–24"/45.7–61 cm apart.

Q **Do spring transplants need any special care? I know they like cool weather, but it's still really cold outside!**

A While brassicas thrive in cool temperatures, they do need protection from really cold weather. Harden off transplants, and cover them with row covers in the garden, which protect them from cold wind and also keep pests at bay. Use a double layer of row covers at first for a bit of extra cold protection, then switch to a single layer for pest control only. Set broccoli, cabbage, and cauliflower transplants slightly deeper than they were growing in their pots to protect their stems.

Q **How do I plan for a fall brassica crop? That means starting seeds in summer, right?**

A Exact sowing schedules vary, depending on what cultivar you're growing and where you live. To determine fall planting dates for crops that are to be harvested after the first fall frost, note the number of days to maturity on the seed packet or in the catalog. Also note whether that number is from transplanting or from seed sowing. Count backward that number of days from the first fall frost date in your area. Add 6 to 8 weeks if you are starting from seed and the days-to-maturity given is from transplanting. In general for brassicas, plan on sowing seeds for broccoli, cabbage, and cauliflower about 2½ to 3 months before the first fall frost date. Sow Brussels sprouts seeds indoors 3 to 4 months before the first fall frost. Move transplants to the garden about 6 to 8 weeks later.

Q **My broccoli transplants always get so stressed by the heat, and so do the other brassicas. What can I do to ease the transition?**

A While hardening off is important for all seedlings, brassicas that are transplanted into the garden in summer need extra TLC to weather the heat. Transplant on a cloudy day or during a spell of rainy weather. Try to look for a spot where the seedlings will be shaded by crops that are nearly ready for harvest so these other crops will be picked and cut down before frost. If you can't find a naturally shaded spot, it's a good idea to provide shade by propping bushel baskets over plants, covering them with burlap supported on wire hoops, or putting up temporary shelters of your own devising. Leave these temporary shelters in place for 2 or 3 days to give transplants time to adjust to the harsher conditions outdoors. Since these crops don't tolerate heat and drought well, and even temporary drought stress can damage the crop, be sure the soil is evenly moist at all times. Test it by sticking a finger into the soil, and water if the top couple of inches feels dry — daily if necessary.

Q **I live along the Gulf Coast, and our summers are much too hot for any of these crops. Is there a way that I can still grow them?**

A Yes. All the brassicas, from cabbage and broccoli to kohlrabi, are great candidates for growing from winter to early spring in the Deep South. You can try sowing seeds of early or short-season cultivars in late winter, but for best results, start crops in late summer or fall for harvest from winter to very early spring. Since the soil is hot in late summer, it's best to start seeds indoors and grow transplants. To spread out the harvest, plan on starting several small plantings in succession.

SEE ALSO: *For more about succession planting, pages 59–61.*

Q **My garden is in Maine, and it freezes early here. Can I grow some of these crops in summer?**

A Broccoli, cabbage, and other brassicas make fine summer crops in areas where average temperatures stay between 60–75°F/5.5–24°C. Broccoli and cauliflower are especially sensitive to warm temperatures, and probably won't produce a good crop if exposed to a long bout of temperatures in the 80s/26.5–31.6°C. If your area receives spells of 80°F/26.5°C weather, it's best to plan on a fall crop and use plastic row covers to protect plants from early freezes.

Care and Harvesting Tips

Q I've figured out my planting schedule for brassicas. Do I give all of them the same care after planting?

A Yes, for the most part they all need similar care. The soil should be kept evenly moist. To give your brassica transplants an extra boost, you may want to water them with compost tea once a week. All benefit from floating row covers, which prevent insect pest problems. Read on for special care and harvest tips about each crop.

CABBAGE

What do I need to know about selecting cabbage?

A Cabbages come in green (white at the center of the head) and red. In addition to smooth-textured types, there also are Savoy cabbages, which have a handsome corrugated texture and great flavor. There are early, midseason, and late cultivars as well. Keep the following distinctions in mind:

- **EARLY.** Also called spring cabbages, these take 50 to 60 days to mature from transplanting. They're mild tasting, great for fresh use, tend to produce smaller heads, and are perfect for growing a quick crop of cabbage in spring.

- **MIDSEASON.** These cultivars take 70 to 85 days from transplanting to mature. They are the most popular main-season cabbages.
- **LATE.** These take at least 85 days to mature from transplanting. They have stronger flavor and are better for storage than early and midseason cultivars.

Q What's the secret to growing good cabbage?

A It's important to time crops so that the heads develop when the weather is cool. Throughout much of North America, cabbage is grown in spring or fall. In the South and Southwest, it's a winter crop. Since cabbages are largely water, regular watering is important; the soil should be evenly moist at all times. Watch transplants especially closely in summer (for fall crops) to make sure they aren't stressed in hot weather. Mulch deeply. Stressed plants grow more slowly and may not form heads. Feed plants with a weak solution of fish emulsion for the first 3 weeks after transplanting or sidedress plants with well-rotted manure 3 weeks after transplanting.

Sidedressing cabbage

Q Is Chinese cabbage the same as regular cabbage?

A Although it's grown much like regular cabbage, Chinese cabbage is actually more closely related to turnips. (Both belong to *Brassica rapa*; turnips are Rapifera group, Chinese cabbage is Pekinensis group.) Chinese cabbage is typically planted in fall, although newer hybrids that resist bolting can be sown in spring. Plant seeds outdoors on the last frost date in spring. For an autumn crop, sow 3 months before the first fall frost date. Sow seeds 3"–4"/7.6–10.2 cm apart and thin plants to 1'–1½'/.3–.45 m apart. Thin seedlings when they are still small to minimize stress, and keep in mind that any kind of stress leads to bitter flavor. Plants need plenty of water to thrive (they're good candidates for soaker hoses or drip irrigation), as well as topdressing with compost manure or a high-nitrogen fertilizer and mulching so the soil will stay moist and cool. Smaller heads generally taste best, so don't wait too long to harvest. Pick the leaves individually or cut entire heads. Harvest your spring crop before hot weather arrives and your fall crop before the first freeze.

Smooth-leafed cabbage

Chinese cabbage

Savoy cabbage

Q **When do I harvest my cabbages?**

A Begin to pick them as soon as they are hard and firm, even if the heads are only 5"–6"/12.7–15.2 cm across. Use a knife, and cut just below the firm part of the head. Leave the uncut leaves and stem intact, and your plants may form a second crop of small heads.

Q **I don't have room in my refrigerator for more than a couple of cabbage heads. How can I harvest cabbage at the right time and still have room to store it?**

A There are two easy ways to spread out the cabbage harvest: Start small successive crops (as few as two or three plants) every 10 days to 2 weeks. To spread out the fall harvest, grow early, midseason, and late cultivars – the time they take to reach maturity will spread out the harvest for you. You can also plant small succession plantings of all three every 10 days. Close spacing also helps control size: For smaller heads, space cabbage transplants 12"/30.5 cm apart.

BROCCOLI AND CAULIFLOWER

Q **If I decide to plant broccoli and cauliflower in both spring and fall, do I plant the same cultivars or different ones?**

A Cauliflower needs temperatures in the 60s/15.5–20.5 °C in order for the heads to mature properly, and cool weather can be hard to come by in many parts of North America by late spring. If you get an early start by prewarming the soil and growing plants under a tunnel of plastic when the weather is still too cold, you may be able to harvest a crop before hot summer weather arrives. It's far easier to grow cauliflower as a fall crop.

Read catalog descriptions carefully and note their recommendations. You'll find cultivars recommended for quick or early spring crops that can tolerate a bit of summer heat. Heat-tolerant cultivars aren't necessarily the best for fall crops, though, where the ability to withstand frost is paramount. There are also cultivars with disease resistance, and these can eliminate major headaches if diseases are prevalent where you garden. If you haven't grown broccoli before, planting a mix of cultivars may be the best approach, since they perform differently. Nursery catalogs have recognized that this is a good approach, and you'll find seed of hybrid mixes offered.

Q How do I get cauliflower ready for harvest?

A To produce mild-tasting, snowy white cauliflower, you need to blanch the heads or restrict light. Starting when the heads are about 2"/5 cm across (the size of a chicken egg), gather up the leaves that surround the central head and tie them together with twine. Gather gently, and tie just tightly enough to cover the heads without crushing the leaves completely. Use a bow or a slip knot, because you'll need to check regularly for maturity. Once heads are 3"–4"/7.6–10.2 cm across, check daily and cut the heads while they are still tight and hard.

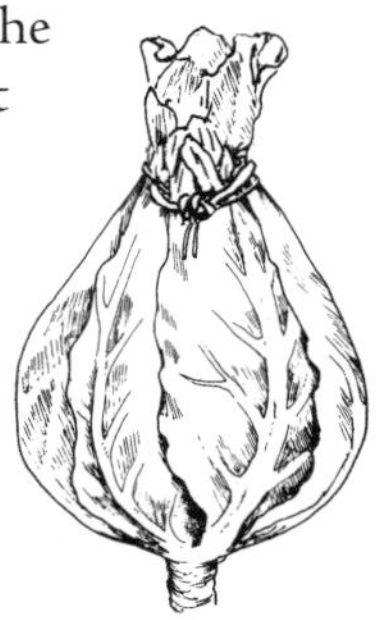

Blanching cauliflower

Q When is broccoli ready to pick?

A The heads, which are actually clusters of flower buds, are ready for harvest as soon as they are large enough to use. (Early on, when the head is small and first emerging, it may look yellow or yellowish green. Wait until it turns deep green as it enlarges.) After it has enlarged and turned green, be sure to cut the head before any part of it begins to turn yellow, which indicates the flowers are getting ready to open.

When I'm harvesting broccoli, is there a way I can encourage side shoots to form?

Cutting a broccoli side shoot

Use a sharp knife to cut about 2"/5 cm below the main head. After that, check plants frequently, and harvest smaller side shoots as soon as they are large enough to use. Frequent harvesting encourages new side shoots to continue to form.

COLLARDS, KALE, AND KOHLRABI

My grandmother used to grow collards and kale in her garden. Are they easy to grow?

Both crops are easy and quite forgiving, since they tolerate both heat and cold. Both are best grown in fall. For a spring crop, sow collards outdoors 3 weeks before the last spring frost date; kale, as soon as the soil can be worked. Indoors, start transplants 6 to 8 weeks before the last frost date, and transplant 2 weeks before the last frost. For fall harvest, sow collards or kale outdoors about 3 months before the first fall frost. Thin to 1½'–2'/.45–.6 m apart, and start harvesting as soon as the leaves are large enough to use. Or pull entire plants at any stage, and succession plant new crops every few weeks to keep the supply coming.

Q **Kohlrabi is the weirdest looking vegetable I've ever seen! Is it hard to grow?**

A While it looks something like the vegetable world's answer to a sea urchin, kohlrabi is actually a cross between a cabbage and a turnip. It's an easy, fast-growing crop with edible leaves and a crisp, swollen base that's tender and mild tasting. The bulbous stems are ready to harvest from 38 to 60 days from sowing, and it's easy to start them right in the garden. In spring, sow seeds outdoors 4 to 6 weeks before the last frost date. They're ideal fall crops: Begin sowing seed 8 to 10 weeks before the first fall frost. Space seeds 3"/7.6 cm apart, then thin to 6"/15.2 cm when the plants have a couple of true leaves. To spread out the harvest, plant small batches of seed every week or so in spring as long as the weather remains cool, then begin again in fall. In Zones 9 and 10, plant kohlrabi through the winter months.

Harvesting kohlrabi

BRUSSELS SPROUTS

Q **Can I grow Brussels sprouts in spring?**

A A touch of frost improves the taste and quality of the sprouts, so Brussels sprouts are best timed to mature after frost. Since they need a long season – they take about 3 months from transplanting – in areas with short seasons, you'll still need to start plants in spring and transplant to the garden roughly just after tomatoes go into the ground to have them ready in time.

Q **I remember Brussels sprouts from my mother's garden, and they didn't have leaves along the stems. Mine have lots of leaves. Do I need to pull them off?**

A Sprouts form all along the main stem of a Brussels sprouts plant, one sprout just above where each leaf stem is attached. Remove the leaves below the sprouts as sprouts form. Also remove any leaves that turn yellow. It's best to clip off the leaves with garden shears rather than pull them.

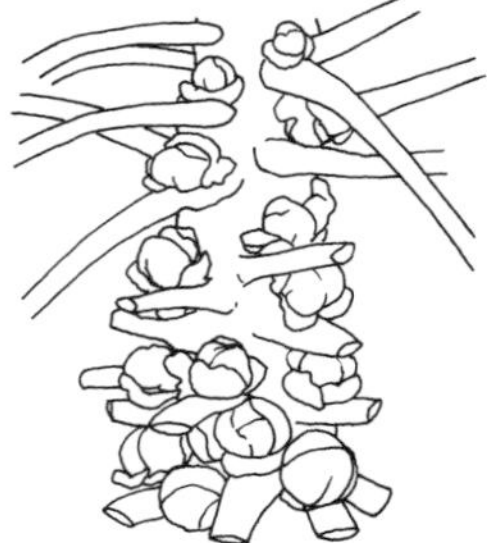

Cut off Brussels sprouts leaves as sprouts form.

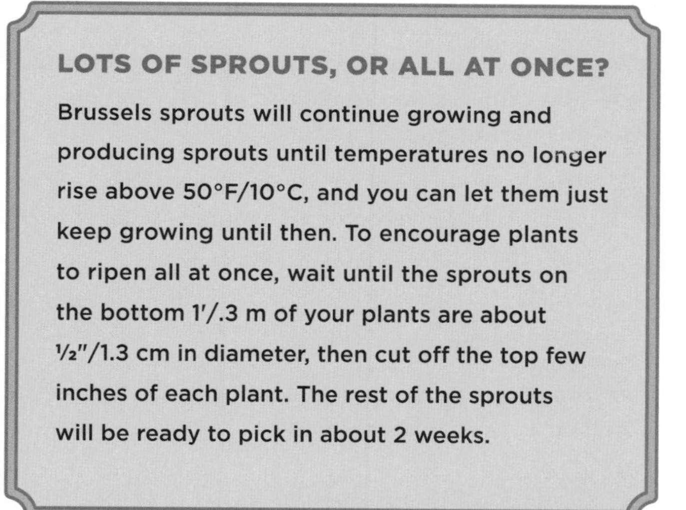

LOTS OF SPROUTS, OR ALL AT ONCE?

Brussels sprouts will continue growing and producing sprouts until temperatures no longer rise above 50°F/10°C, and you can let them just keep growing until then. To encourage plants to ripen all at once, wait until the sprouts on the bottom 1'/.3 m of your plants are about ½"/1.3 cm in diameter, then cut off the top few inches of each plant. The rest of the sprouts will be ready to pick in about 2 weeks.

Q Do I pick all the sprouts at once? How do I tell when they're ready?

A Sprouts are ready to use when they're about ¾"/1.9 cm wide, and you can pick them over the course of several weeks. Be sure to harvest sprouts while they are under 1½"/3.8 cm and still hard. Smaller sprouts are likely to be the most tender. You can also cut the entire stalk and store it in a cool spot.

Problem Patrol

I know I've seen insects eating my cabbage and broccoli leaves. What kinds of pests and diseases do I need to watch out for?

Brassicas do have their share of pests, but they are relatively easy to control if you use the tips below.

- Use row covers to keep pests off transplants. Tuck the row covers in along the edges with soil to make sure pests can't crawl underneath.
- If your plants aren't covered, handpick cabbage loopers and other caterpillars regularly.
- Clean up the garden thoroughly after each crop to prevent pests and disease organisms from surviving from one crop to the next or over the winter months.
- Include annuals and perennials with small flowers in your garden or in beds alongside it; these flowers attract beneficial insects that prey on aphids and other pests.
- To prevent diseases, look for brassica crops with built-in resistance or tolerance.
- Don't compost plants that show evidence of disease: Discard them in the trash.

SEE ALSO: *For more on pests and diseases, pages 146–162.*

Q My broccoli plants produced heads, but they were tiny and runty looking. What caused this?

A This condition is called buttoning, and it also can be a problem with cauliflower. Buttoning is caused by seedlings that are exposed to cold temperatures at the wrong time, and fortunately, it's preventable. Although really small seedlings can usually withstand cold temperatures, once they get larger (when stems are about as thick as a pencil) cold temperatures have a different effect, causing the transplants to produce small flower heads that never grow very large. Since exposure to a few days of temperatures in the 50s/10–15°C can cause buttoning, don't rush to transplant broccoli or cauliflower if spring weather is especially unsettled. Protect plants that are already out in the garden when cold weather is predicted.

"Button" head on broccoli

Q My cabbage bloomed instead of forming a head. What happened?

A Like cauliflower and broccoli, cabbage seedlings can be accidentally tricked into flowering too soon. Avoid exposing cabbage plants to temperatures that are too cold – below 50°F/10°C. Protect plants already in the garden with hot caps, cloches, or other protection.

Q **My cauliflower plants never did anything last summer. The transplants seemed really healthy, but they just didn't grow. Any idea what happened?**

A With all brassicas, it's important to avoid stressing the plants, because stress slows down growth or causes plants to stop growing altogether. When hardening off transplants, don't withhold water or nutrients. Instead, gradually expose them to increasing amounts of sunlight. Transplant on a cloudy day, and make sure the soil is evenly moist to minimize transplant shock. If you are aiming for an early start for your crop, plan on shielding transplants with cloches, hot caps, row covers, or other protection.

My cabbages were looking perfect, but then the heads cracked open! What happened?

A Too much water can cause heads to crack once they are near maturity. If there's a spell of rainy weather near harvest time, use a spade to slice about 6"/15.2 cm into the soil halfway around each plant. This cuts the roots and reduces the amount of water the plant takes up. It also slows growth and allows you to postpone harvesting. This trick is also a good one to use on one-third to one-half of your crop if all the heads are maturing at once.

Q **Sometimes a head of cauliflower separates into several sections as it develops instead of staying solid. What causes this?**

A A period of drought followed by a period of wet conditions can cause cauliflower heads to separate. Keep the soil evenly moist, especially after heads begin to form. Mulch also helps even out soil moisture. (Heat and drought can also lead to bitter-tasting heads.) Or you may have simply waited too long to harvest. Either way, it's worth it to cut the head and taste it. It is still probably usable. Leaves emerging from the center of the head can be caused by overmaturity, hot dry weather, or soil that contains too much nitrogen.

Q **My latest batch of kale was bitter and tough. What's the secret to the sweet, tender leaves I remember from my grandmother's garden?**

A Fast, even growth is the secret to the best-tasting collards and kale, so water regularly to maintain even soil moisture. Mulch also helps conserve soil moisture and hold weeds in check. One reason fall crops are better than spring ones is that taste improves after the plants are exposed to fall frost, so don't hurry to harvest if cold weather threatens. In fact, both crops can be harvested in the snow. In areas with severe winters, protect the plants with a deep layer of straw mulch or with heavyweight row-cover fabric. In warm weather cool the leaves quickly after picking them by plunging them into ice water.

My kohlrabi has tough, hard stems that are bitter tasting. What did I do wrong?

A Tough kohlrabi stems can be a signal that your soil either is too dry or doesn't drain well. But if the rest of your crops are thriving, perhaps the problem is hot weather, rather than your soil. Kohlrabi is happiest in cool weather, though it tolerates heat as long as it gets enough water. To make sure your crop isn't suffering from moisture stress, work in 1"- 2"/2.5–5 cm of extra compost at planting time. Mulching helps preserve moisture, which is critical to a good-quality crop. It's also important not to wait too long to harvest plants. Watch them carefully, and begin harvesting before the swollen stems become too large. In spring, cut them when stems are about 2"/5 cm in diameter; in fall they can reach 4"-5"/10.2–12.7 cm without being woody.

Carrots (*Daucus carota*)

SATIVUS GROUP, CARROT FAMILY, APIACEAE

TIPS FOR SUCCESS

- Prepare the soil deeply, removing rocks, soil clods, and other debris.
- Sprinkle vermiculite, potting soil, or sifted compost over seeds instead of using garden soil when sowing.
- Keep the seedbed evenly moist, watering twice a day if necessary. Floating row covers also help conserve moisture.

Q **I've tried to grow long, pointed carrots like you see in the grocery store, but in my soil, they never do well! Any suggestions?**

A While Bugs Bunny and many others like to snack on the long, narrow, tapered carrots called Imperators, they are not the best type for most home gardeners to grow. That's because Imperator cultivars were developed for mechanical harvesting, meaning they not only need deep, perfectly loose soil, but also are tougher or less crisp than other types, so that they don't break during harvest. Shorter-rooted types are a better choice for most home gardens. Try one or more of these:

- **NANTES.** Nantes carrot cultivars are the most popular for backyard gardens. They are 5"–7"/12.7–17.8 cm long and grow in a somewhat wider range of soils. Nantes carrots are both sweeter and crisper than Imperators.

- **BALL-TYPE.** For heavy soil, consider Paris Market types ('Thumbelina' is one), which are also called ball-type carrots. These are sweet, beet-shaped carrots with round 1"–1½"/2.5–3.8 cm roots.
- **CHANTENAY.** Chantenays are chunky, blunt-tipped carrots, 4"–6"/10.2–15.2 cm long, that are an especially good choice for growing in heavy soil. They're crisp and sweet-tasting.
- **DANVERS.** Developed in Danvers, Massachusetts, these carrots grow well in a wide range of soils but aren't quite as sweet as Nantes types.

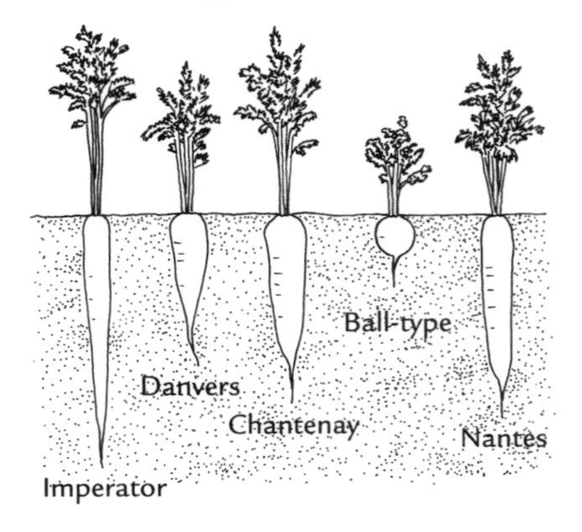

Q Are "baby" carrots just young carrots, or is there a difference? Are they easy to grow?

A Until recently, the ball-shaped Paris Market carrots, such as 'Thumbelina', were the only options for small carrots, but newer baby carrots are fun to grow, too, and a great crop for children's gardens. When growing baby carrots, select a cultivar developed specifically for its dainty roots, since full-size carrots won't necessarily have good flavor if they're harvested when they are still small. (Carrot flavor continues to develop as they grow and is at its peak after they've reached full size.) 'Bambina', 'Baby Spike', 'Little Finger', 'Minicor', and 'Short 'n Sweet' are all fingerling, or baby, carrot cultivars to look for.

Q How can I spread out my carrot harvest?

A Instead of sowing long rows of carrots all at the same time, to spread out the harvest, plan on sowing small crops of early- or short-season carrots every 2 or 3 weeks in spring. Carrots grow best at temperatures between 60–75°F/15.5–23.8°C, so stop sowing once temperatures routinely reach about 80°F/26.6°C. Wait until cooler weather returns in fall, then resume sowing.

Q What's the key to growing great carrots?

A Loose, deeply dug soil is crucial. For best results, it's worth it to double-dig a bed, so you end up with 12"-16"/30.5-40.6 cm of loose, prepared soil. Begin by removing grass and weeds from the site, then spread over the site at least a 3"-4"/7.6-10.2 cm-thick layer of compost or other organic matter, which will be worked into the soil.

1. Dig a trench about 8"/20.3 cm deep and 1'/.3 m wide along one edge of the planting area. Pile the removed soil on a tarp or in a wheelbarrow.

2. Spread at least an 1"/2.5 cm-thick layer of compost or other organic matter over the bottom of the trench, then work it into the soil with a garden fork.

3. Dig another trench next to the first, turning the soil into the previous trench. Then add more organic matter to the bottom of the new trench, and fork it in.

4. Continue this process until you reach the other end of the planting area. Fill the last trench with the soil removed from the first one. As you work, be sure to remove rocks, roots, and hard clumps of soil: Carrots that encounter even small sticks in the soil may fork or branch.

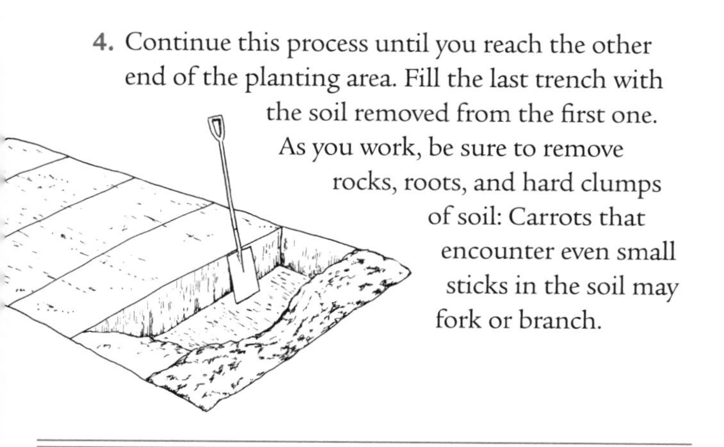

Q **I have clay soil. Does that mean I can't grow carrots?**

A Don't try to grow them in unamended clay, but if you work enough compost into clay soil – and then refrain from walking on it after that – you can grow great carrots. Short-rooted carrots like ball and fingerling types are good choices, but in deeply dug soil, so are Nantes, Chantenay, and Danvers cultivars. For even better results, grow carrots in raised beds filled with a mix of soil and compost, perhaps with as much as one-third vermiculite if your soil is really clayey. Another option is to use potting soil to fill raised beds. If you use bagged soil, avoid potting soil that contains chemical fertilizer. Organic bagged potting soil is okay, but make sure it does not contain too much nitrogen, which causes carrots to produce hairy, misshapen roots.

I have access to free cow manure. Is there any disadvantage to adding a lot of that?

Carrots do need plenty of organic matter, because it helps the soil stay moist and light, and moist soil yields sweet, crisp roots. But manure, along with too much of other sources of organic matter such as grass clippings or kitchen scraps, can cause problems. That's because carrots that have access to too much nitrogen – either from manure or from ordinary fertilizer – produce misshapen roots that have so many fine feeder roots they look hairy. Also avoid rough organic matter such as crop debris, because large particles in the soil, even if they're organic, can cause misshapen carrots.

How do I plant carrot seeds? I've had trouble getting them to come up in past years.

Carrots aren't the fastest plants out of the starting gate, that's for sure. Start sowing 3 weeks before the last spring frost date (in warm climates, plant carrots in fall for winter harvest). Set the seeds ¼"–½"/.6–1.3 cm deep. Use the shallower depth in early spring, when the soil is still cool; plant slightly deeper once it has warmed up. Try to sow about six seeds per 1"/2.5 cm, and sow in a wide band or in a block to make it easier to keep track of where you've sown seeds. Carrot seedlings are tiny, and crusted soil prevents them from coming up, so instead of covering the seeds with soil, try covering them with a mix of loose soil combined with screened compost to prevent a crust from forming. Also, mist plantings; don't water them heavily. Not only can water wash away the seeds, but pounding droplets cause crusting.

Double-cropping is another option that may work. Mix the seeds with spring radishes. The radishes germinate quickly, break up the soil crust, and will be ready for harvest about the time carrots are ready for thinning. Another option for encouraging seedlings is to prepare the soil and rake it smooth, water it, and sow seeds by spacing them out in blocks or wide rows. Cover the planting with a board or piece of plywood. Check daily for seedlings and remove the board the minute you see evidence of tiny white seedlings. Water very gently for the first few weeks, or you'll wash away the tiny seedlings.

Double-cropping radishes and carrots

Care and Harvesting Tips

I just hate thinning seedlings! Is there any way to avoid this chore?

A You can use a dibble and make tiny holes, then sow individual seeds. It's tedious, but it does eliminate the need to thin. Another option is to mix carrot seed with sand before sowing it. Or consider starting with pelleted carrot seed if you hate pulling up or cutting off those tiny, defenseless carrot seedlings. Pelleted seed is large enough to easily sow at the proper final spacing. Whatever you do, thin plants to 1"/2.5 cm spacing when they are 2"/5 cm tall, then thin again 2 weeks later so plants are 3"–4"/7.6–10.2 cm apart. For best results, thin by cutting off excess plants at the soil line using scissors, because pulling out seedlings may damage those that remain. If you don't thin your seedlings, your carrot roots will be misshapen.

Q **Once carrots are established and growing, is there anything else they need?**

A "Steady as she goes" is probably the best way to think about carrot culture. Mulch seedlings once they're large enough; the soil should be evenly moist but not wet. Spraying with compost tea helps plants grow quickly and can prevent disease problems. If the soil does dry out, rewet it gradually over the course of a few days; a sudden shift from dry to wet can cause your carrots to crack. Hand pull weeds or cut them off just below the soil surface to prevent damage to the roots. Floating row covers keep most insect pests at bay.

Q **My carrots always are green at the tops. Why?**

A Carrots push up out of the soil as they grow, and the part of the root that's exposed to the sun turns green and gets bitter. To prevent this, hoe soil up around the crowns throughout the season or cover them well with mulch.

Q **My carrots always seem to break off in the ground. How can I harvest them to prevent this?**

A Baby and fingerling carrots are usually easy to get out of the ground: Just stick your fingers into the soil to pull them up. Longer cultivars need a more focused approach to get them up and out of the ground intact. First, loosen the soil along the row, several inches away from the plants, with a digging fork. Then pull the carrots by hand; a fork will bruise them. Use a trowel to loosen carrots that are reluctant to leave the soil.

Q How often do I need to harvest?

A Pull carrots every couple of days during the summertime, or they'll go past their prime. In cool weather, they can remain in the soil for several weeks. To get them ready for storage, spread them out in the sun for a few hours to dry the soil that's still clinging to the roots. Then, brush off as much soil as you can (don't wash carrots before storing them), cut off the tops, and dry them in the sun for a few hours. Store them in plastic bags in the refrigerator. For longer storage, pack them in moist sawdust and keep them between 32°–40°F/0°–4.4°C.

I live in Georgia. What do I do for fall and winter harvests?

A In the South, you can plant carrots in fall for harvest in spring. Like gardeners in most parts of the country, you can also store carrots right in the ground. (Where the ground freezes, cover them with up to 2'/.6 m of mulch, to keep the soil and the roots from freezing. Roots that freeze and then thaw crack and appear waterlogged.) Continue harvesting into the winter months. If you miss harvesting any plants, they'll bring another benefit to your garden. Their lacy, white, flat-topped flowers attract a wide range of beneficial insects to the garden.

Problem Patrol

Q Ugh! Something has been tunneling in my carrots. Do I just throw them away?

A Both wireworms and carrot rust fly larvae tunnel through carrot roots. In either case, go ahead and harvest, then use a knife or a carrot peeler to remove the damaged sections. Use the damaged carrots promptly, though, since they won't last in storage. To prevent these pests, you'll need to identify the culprit.

- **CARROT RUST FLIES.** The larvae of these pests are maggots that eat root hairs and tunnel across or through the surface of carrots. Control them by covering beds of carrots with floating row covers to prevent the adults from laying eggs near the plants. To kill maggots in the soil, apply parasitic nematodes.
- **WIREWORMS.** These are the larvae of click beetles; they tunnel through carrot roots, leaving small, black entry holes. One way to control their numbers is to work the soil surface weekly in spring to expose them to birds and other predators. Use traps to control them before planting or even after your carrots are planted: Cut carrots or potatoes into 1"/2.5 cm cubes and stick them on a wooden barbeque skewer. Bury the pieces a few inches/cm apart and 2"–4"/5–10.2 cm deep, with the skewers still sticking out of the soil. Pull them up to check them

twice a week, and either pull out and destroy pests that have tunneled in or replace the pieces with fresh pieces of carrot or potato. Another way to control wireworms is to interplant carrots (or potatoes) with thick rows or bands of wheat, oats, or lettuce. Pull up and destroy these crops about 4 weeks after you planted them.

PESTS TO FOSTER

You may actually want to plant a separate patch of carrots to feed parsleyworms, which are green caterpillars marked with black and yellow. Then, whenever you find a parsleyworm in your garden, move it to the "caterpillar patch." Why protect parsleyworms? They're the larvae of beautiful black swallowtail butterflies!

Parsleyworm

Black swallowtail butterfly

Q My carrot seedlings don't look right. The leaves are yellow and misshapen, and overall, the plants are small and bushier than they should be. What's wrong?

A Aster yellows cause these symptoms – older plants may have purplish leaves, and the leaves are brittle and break off easily. The roots are usually bitter and woody. Aster yellows is spread by leafhoppers, and securing floating row covers over plants prevents them from feeding on carrots and transmitting the disease. Unfortunately, once plants are infected there is no cure. Pull up infected plants and compost them.

Q I love Bugs Bunny, but the bunnies that are eating my carrots are driving me crazy! Is there anything I can do to keep them out?

A The best solution for all animal pests is to erect a fence. For rabbits, it needs to be only 2'/.6 m tall, and poultry wire works fine. Be sure to use landscape pins along the base of the fence to make sure the rabbits can't wriggle under it. Short of a fence, try hanging shiny items like aluminum pie plates or old CDs from stakes so they flutter in the breeze. Some gardeners report success with repellents, such as blood meal, human hair, rotten-egg sprays, or predator urine. Repellents are best reapplied every 2 weeks.

Celery (*Apium graveolens*)

DULCE GROUP, CARROT FAMILY, APIACEAE

TIPS FOR SUCCESS

- Time your planting to allow for a long, cool growing season, ideally about 4 months, with daytime temperatures in the 60s/15.5–20.5°C.
- Amend the soil with extra organic matter, and water regularly, because celery plants are water hogs.
- Protect young plants if temperatures are going to drop below 50°F/10°C by covering them with floating row covers or cloches. Exposure to cold weather can cause them to flower prematurely.

I've never seen celery growing in anybody's home garden. Is it hard to grow?

A If you can give celery cool temperatures and rich, evenly moist soil, it isn't hard to grow. Plants require daytime temperatures between 65–75°F/18.3–23.8°C to grow well. Celery was originally a marsh plant, so amend the soil before planting with a generous amount of compost and/or well-rotted manure to duplicate the rich, mucky soil the plants thrive in. Also, start with short-season cultivars, which mature in 80 days.

Q **I'm in Indiana, where it's hot in the summer. When do I plant celery?**

A Grow celery as a spring or fall crop in areas like Indiana and Ohio, where it's hot in the summer. In the far north and in the Pacific Northwest, it grows well as a summer crop. In the South, plant it in fall for a winter crop.

Q **How do I start seedlings?**

A Sow indoors 8 to 10 weeks before you plan to transplant to the garden. Soak seeds overnight before sowing, and fill individual containers with sterile seed-starting medium. Press several seeds into the surface of the medium of each pot, then barely cover with a thin layer of sand, since the seeds need some light to germinate. Give them good drainage but plenty of water, and make sure the soil mix temperature stays above 55°F/12.8°C but below 70°F/21.1°C . Thin to one plant per pot. Harden off seedlings, and move them to the garden when they're about 6"/15.2 cm tall. Don't transplant until temperatures remain above about 50°F/10°C, because cool weather can cause plants to bolt. Space plants 6"–8"/15.2–20.3 cm apart, and water immediately when you transplant.

Care and Harvesting Tips

What do celery plants need once they're in the garden?

A Mulch plants, and make sure the soil stays evenly moist throughout the growing season. (Dry soil causes stringy, bitter stalks.) If you're transplanting in summer for a fall crop, try to grow them in a spot that's slightly shaded. They're heavy feeders, so fertilize plants every 2 weeks to prevent problems like cracking and spindly stalks. To prevent bolting, cover them with floating row covers if nighttime temperatures dip below 55°F/12.7°C for more than a couple of days.

I've heard you have to blanch celery. How do you do it, and why?

A Actually, green-stalked celery is most common and has slightly more nutrition than blanched celery does. If you'd like to try blanching, one option is to gradually hoe mounds of soil up around the plants as they grow, but don't cover up the leaves. You can also use paper milk cartons to blanch celery. Remove the tops and bottoms and open up the cartons along one side. Then place the

Blanching celery

carton around the plant and tie it in place with string. Or, box in plants with boards to keep out the sun. To harvest, cut the plants off just below the soil line with a sharp knife. In mild-winter areas, cut individual stalks as needed and leave the plants in the garden.

I want to grow celery as a fall crop. What are its storage requirements?

A Celery stores for several months in a cool place. Fill boxes with sand or moist soil, pull up the plants, and heel them in, covering their roots with sand or soil.

Corn (*Zea mays*)

GRASS FAMILY, POACEAE

TIPS FOR SUCCESS

- Wait for warm weather to sow corn, at about the time of the last average spring frost: The soil temperature should be at least 60°F/15.5°C.
- Ensure good pollination (and thus ears packed with plump kernels) by sowing corn in blocks of short rows rather than a single long row.
- Sow new crops every couple of weeks for an extended harvest.

What's the difference between various kinds of sweet corn? Are some sweeter than others?

You'll see three kinds of sweet corn listed in catalogs. Average production is about two ears per plant. Here's a rundown of their characteristics:

- **NORMAL SUGARY.** Cultivars of traditional sweet corn, called "Normal Sugary" or "su" cultivars, have varying amounts of sugar (from 5 to 10 percent) in the seeds. The sugars convert to starch when the ears are harvested, so they need to be eaten as soon after harvest as possible.

- **SUPER SWEET.** These cultivars have 20 to 30 percent sugar. They're also called "Shrunken" or sh_2 cultivars because the kernels are shriveled when they are dry. Sugar in Super Sweet corn cultivars converts more slowly to starch than it does in other types of corn, and ears last for several days in the refrigerator. Super Sweet cultivars are less vigorous, less tolerant of cold temperatures (don't sow seed that hasn't been treated with a fungicide until the soil is 75°F/23.9°C), and are far more sensitive to dry soil than other types of corn.

- **SUGARY ENHANCED.** Also listed as se or se+, these cultivars have very tender kernels and convert sugar to starch more slowly than Normal Sugary types but faster than Super Sweets. They're also more tolerant of cold and more vigorous than Super Sweets but less vigorous than Normal Sugary types. They also won't cross with nearby corn plants, as Super Sweets do, and thus can be grown next to other corn crops.

Q **I live in Minnesota. What kind of sweet corn is best up here? Our summers are pretty short!**

A Since the number of frost-free days in the average growing season in Minnesota ranges from 138 to 98 or fewer, early maturing cultivars, which ripen in 55 to 70 days, are best. Midseason cultivars take 71 to 85 days to ripen, while late cultivars take 86 days or more. For an extra-early start in cool climates, prewarm the soil by covering it with black or clear plastic for 2 weeks before planting. Also, try pregerminating corn or starting seedlings indoors in individual peat or newspaper pots, since seedlings don't transplant well.

Q **I live in southern Alabama, and my sweet corn just fries in the summer. Is there anything I can do?**

A In areas with superhot summers, plan on two seasons of sweet corn. Sow successive crops every 2 weeks in spring for early summer harvest, but stop sowing about 2½ months before searing summer heat is upon you. Start sowing again in late summer.

I got spotty germination from my corn last year. What can I do to get better results?

Corn is a warm-weather crop, and seeds need warm soil to germinate. Use these tips to get your corn up and growing:

- **SOW SEED AFTER ALL DANGER OF FROST** has passed, beginning about 2 weeks after the last spring frost date.
- **DON'T SOW UNTIL THE SOIL HAS WARMED** to at least 60°F/15.5°C. (Use a soil thermometer to be sure.) Seeds are more likely to be attacked by fungus diseases and insects when they're sown in cool soil.
- **SOAK SEEDS IN COMPOST TEA** for 20 minutes before planting.
- **FOR EARLY PLANTINGS,** prewarm the soil by covering it with black or clear plastic for 2 weeks.
- **SOME LAWN-GRASS PESTS** also attack corn plants, so try to avoid planting corn where grass was grown the previous year. An application of parasitic nematodes to the planting area also helps eliminate some pests.
- **SET SEEDS 1"–2"/2.5–5 CM DEEP** and about 7"/17.8 cm apart. Since germination averages about 75 percent, by the time seedlings are up they will be spaced at about 12"/30.5 cm apart, which is the correct spacing. If you

have better-than average germination, thin plants to 12"/30 cm apart when they are 3"–4"/7.6–10.2 cm tall.

- **COVER NEW PLANTINGS OF CORN** with floating row covers. Birds love to pull up and eat the seeds and baby seedlings, and row covers keeps them, along with various insect pests, at bay. Be sure to cover plants loosely, since they grow quickly.

Q **I've tried to grow Super Sweet corn before, but the ears tasted awful! What happened?**

A Super Sweet cultivars must be isolated from other types of corn or they will cross-pollinate, and the kernels will be stringy and starchy. Grow Super Sweets on a different schedule or plant them at least 250'/76 m away from other corn.

SEE ALSO: *For more about Super Sweet corn, page 248.*

Q **When my corn ripened last year, there was too much, and I couldn't eat it all before it turned starchy. How can I spread out the harvest?**

A Since corn ripens and then matures past its prime quickly, make a plan to spread out the harvest by staggering planting dates – sow a new batch of corn every week or two.

You can also grow cultivars that mature at different times. For example, plant 'Earlivee', which matures in 60 days, at the same time you plant cultivars like 'Seneca Horizon' (70 to 80 days) or 'Supersweet Jubilee' (85 days) and 'Silver Queen' (88 days) or 'Bodacious' (80 to 90 days). If your planting season is long enough, plant a second crop of 'Earlivee' one month after the first planting to spread out the harvest even farther.

Q I planted a big row of corn and the plants grew beautifully, but the ears had only a few kernels! What happened?

A Corn is wind-pollinated, and unless you're planting a field full of it, you need to think about how the pollen is going to get from the tassels (the male flowers on the tops of the plants) to the silks (the tips of the female flowers, which produce the kernels and emerge from the cobs). Plant a single row of corn, and the pollen simply blows away. If you are growing a small number of plants – from 15 or 20 plants up to a few rows in each succession planting – arrange them in a block that's at least 4'/1.2 m on a side, to ensure that wind can carry pollen from plant to plant.

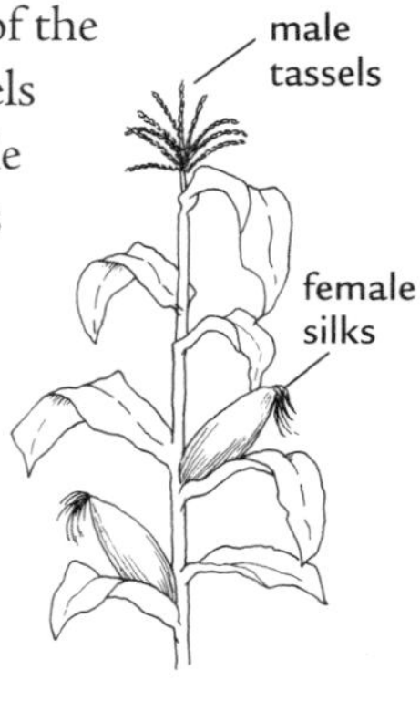

Care and Harvesting Tips

Q The farmers in our area don't water their corn. Do I need to water mine?

A Sweet corn needs evenly moist soil for best growth, so make sure plants get about 1"/2.5 cm of water a week from rain or watering – more if the weather is hot. It's especially important to water plants from the time they begin to produce tassels right through to when the ears are ready to harvest. Use soaker hoses or flood the rows, because spraying the plants with a hose or sprinkler can wash away the pollen. Also, to hold in moisture and reduce competition from weeds, mulch plants with grass clippings or other organic material once the soil has warmed up.

Q I've worked plenty of compost into my soil. Is that enough for sweet corn?

A Sweet-corn plants are heavy feeders, and they appreciate a bit of a boost about a month after planting and again when the tassels form. Sidedress them with compost or a balanced fertilizer. Some gardeners add a third feeding in between, roughly a month after the first, when plants are about 1½'/.45 m tall.

Q **My corn plants have roots around the bottom of the stalks that are up out of the ground. Should I cut them off?**

A No, leave them be. Corn plants continue to produce new roots, called nodal roots, *above* the first roots that emerge, and these help stabilize the plants as they grow taller. When spreading fertilizer or hoeing around corn, be careful not to damage the plants' shallow roots, which can extend 1'/.3 m from the base of the stalk. If plants begin to lean over, it helps to hoe soil up around the base, covering these roots, to give them more support.

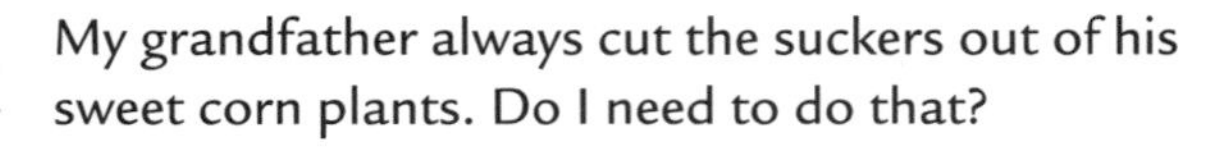

Q **My grandfather always cut the suckers out of his sweet corn plants. Do I need to do that?**

A Old-time gardeners typically removed the side shoots, or suckers, but recent studies have revealed that it's best to leave them on the plant.

Q How can I tell if the corn is ready to pick?

A Look closely at the silks. If they've turned brown but are still damp when you touch them, the ears are probably ready for harvest. Ripe ears also should have full-size kernels at the top, where the silks emerge. To make sure, try the thumbnail test by pressing your thumbnail into a kernel. If milky liquid spurts out, the ear is ready for picking. Clear liquid indicates the ear isn't quite ripe, while no liquid indicates it's past its prime.

Q What's the best way to pick corn?

A Pull ears off the plant with a downward twisting motion. Old-time gardeners will tell you to have the water boiling before you pick, since the sugars in corn kernels quickly turn to starch. Or, if you can't cook immediately, cool the ears quickly by plunging them into cold water and then refrigerate them. While sugars do convert more slowly in sugar-enhanced and supersweet corn, which can be kept in the refrigerator for a couple of days after harvest, corn is still at its best when eaten right out of the garden.

Problem Patrol

Q Half the ears of corn I've picked this year have caterpillars chewing into the kernels on the tips of the ears. Is there any way to keep them out?

A Corn earworms are the culprit; these pests also chew tomato fruits from the blossom end, eat into bean pods, and nibble lettuce. The best way to fight earworms is to take a multifaceted approach:

- **ATTRACT BENEFICIAL INSECTS** to your yard by planting annuals and perennials near your vegetable gardens. Annuals such as alyssum (*Lobularia maritima*) and cosmos (*Cosmos* spp.), as well as perennials such as yarrow (*Achillea* spp.) and those in the aster family such as coneflowers (*Echinacea* spp. and *Rudbeckia* spp.) all attract beneficials.
- **PLANT RESISTANT CORN.** Cultivars that have tightly wrapped husks are more difficult for earworms to enter.
- **AFTER THE SILKS EMERGE,** use a rubber band to hold the husks tightly together and prevent the earworms from entering.
- **ONCE THE SILKS HAVE BEGUN TO TURN BROWN,** place 5 drops of vegetable oil (corn oil works fine) at the base of the silks, next to the husks. The oil smothers the earworms as they climb inside the husks. Wait until

the silks are fully extended and begin to turn brown; otherwise, the oil affects pollination of the ears.

- **USE SPRAYS — BT OR SPINOSAD — AS A LAST RESORT.** You may have to spray several times, and worms that have already crawled into the ears won't be affected.

Cucumbers (*Cucumis sativus*)

SQUASH FAMILY, CUCURBITACEAE

TIPS FOR SUCCESS

- Cover cucumber seedbeds with floating row covers to protect plants from insect pests such as cucumber beetles.
- The soil should be evenly moist but not wet (a soaker hose along the row is ideal); otherwise, the fruit can taste bitter.
- Plant cucumber cultivars that feature built-in disease resistance, then follow spacing guidelines to reduce disease problems.

Q What's the difference between slicing cucumbers and pickling types?

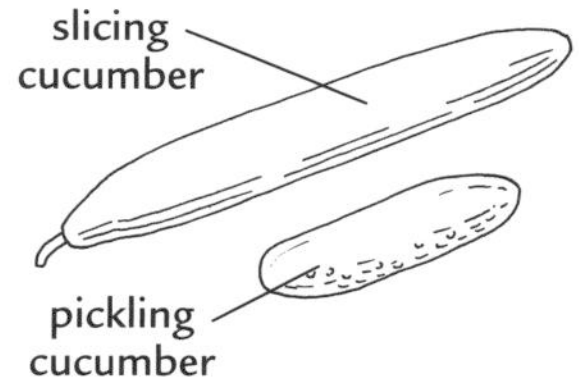

A Pickling cucumbers generally are fast-growing, short-season cucumbers that produce all or most of their fruit within a week or so, which is most convenient for pickling and canning. Picklers have thin, paler green skin than slicing cucumbers. Slicers, which produce dark green-skinned fruit, begin bearing about a week after pickling cucumbers and continue to produce for 4 to 6 weeks.

Q Can I still get a big cucumber yield even from a small-space garden?

A You probably can, especially if you trellis your cucumbers and choose the right type to grow. Typically, cucumbers bear separate male and female flowers and require bees or other pollinators to carry pollen from one to the other to set fruit. In recent years, though, plant breeders have introduced new types of cucumbers that bear especially heavily because they don't produce fruit by old-fashioned cross-pollination. Here are the types of cucumbers you'll encounter.

- **MONOECIOUS CUCUMBERS.** These cucumbers bear both male and female flowers on the same vine. You can grow a single plant of a monoecious cultivar and still get fruit. Like most squash-family crops, plants bear male flowers first before producing females.
- **GYNOECIOUS CUCUMBERS.** These extra-heavy producers bear only female flowers. The flowers require pollination to produce fruit, so you need to grow at least one monoecious cultivar to provide the pollen. Seeds for

gynoecious cucumbers usually are packaged with a few seeds of a monoecious cultivar, which are either dyed a different color or packaged in a separate envelope. You need to plant at least one of these seeds in order for gynoecious cultivars to produce fruit.

- **PARTHENOCARPIC CUCUMBERS.** These set seedless fruit without pollination. You can plant a single parthenocarpic cucumber plant, and you'll still get fruit. Be aware, though, that not all parthenocarpic cucumbers are suitable for outdoor culture: Many cultivars were developed for growing in greenhouses, where there are no bees or other pollinators. Look for a parthenocarpic cultivar designated for outdoor as well as indoor use, since greenhouse-only types may produce deformed fruit if the flowers do get pollinated.

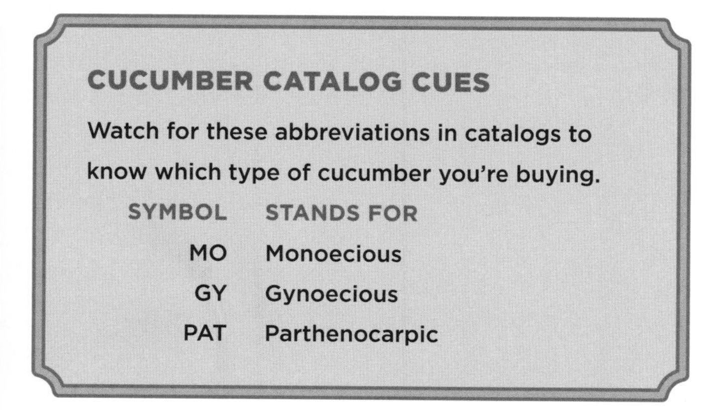

CUCUMBER CATALOG CUES

Watch for these abbreviations in catalogs to know which type of cucumber you're buying.

SYMBOL	STANDS FOR
MO	Monoecious
GY	Gynoecious
PAT	Parthenocarpic

Q **I usually prefer heritage cultivars. Why should I bother with newfangled gynoecious or parthenocarpic cucumbers?**

A A wide range of diseases attack cucumbers, and many of the newer hybrids feature resistance to many of them. By planting cultivars that resist anthracnose, bacterial wilt, cucumber mosaic virus, downy mildew, powdery mildew, and other diseases, you can increase yields and reduce problems by little more than selecting the right seed. For example, if cucumber beetles have ruined your crops in the past, you can plant a parthenocarpic cultivar. ('Diva' is both gynoecious and parthenocarpic.)

How do I tell the difference between male and female cucumber flowers?

The secret is to look at the base of the flower, behind the petals. Female flowers have a tiny cucumber that is already formed; male flowers do not. Keep in mind that the fruits on the female flowers don't automatically grow. In monoecious and gynoecious cucumbers, they need to be pollinated to enlarge.

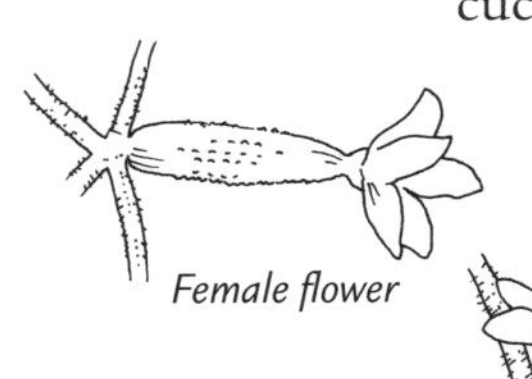

Q I have a small garden in downtown Louisville, Kentucky. Should I grow bush-type cucumbers?

A Bush cucumbers, which are actually compact vines, are a perfect choice for small gardens, since they take up less space than rambunctious vining types. They're also easier to care for, and it's easier to pick the fruit. If you have enough space for even a single section of trellis, though, a couple of plants of a vining cultivar may be in order. Vining types bear slightly later than bush types and produce much more heavily, although they do need considerably more space. Big garden or small, locate trellises for vining cucumbers on the north side of your garden or in rows that run east to west, so they don't shade the rest of your crops.

Q I can't wait for the first garden-grown cucumbers every year. How early can I plant them in spring?

A Cucumbers originated in the tropics, and it doesn't pay to rush them into the garden, because they simply can't take cold weather. Wait until *at least* 2 weeks after the last spring frost date to sow seeds or move transplants to the garden. Cucumbers do appreciate prewarmed soil, so mulch with clear or black plastic for 2 weeks before planting. Or, plant in hills of soil or raised beds; both tend to be warmer than ground-level planting sites.

Can I start seeds indoors?

Yes, but since the seedlings don't transplant well, take steps to ease their transition into the garden. Sow seed no more than 3 weeks before your projected transplant date, so the seedlings don't get too large to transplant well. Sowing in individual peat pots or newspaper pots is best. Be sure to harden off seedlings before moving them to the garden. Because of transplant stress, cucumbers that were transplanted take as many as 10 days longer than direct-sown ones to produce their first fruit.

What's the best approach for sowing cucumber seeds right into the garden?

Cucumbers grow just fine in ordinary, well-prepared garden soil. Plant cucumber seeds ½"/1.3 cm deep and 2"/5 cm apart. Cover newly planted beds with floating row covers to protect seedlings from pests like cucumber beetles, which transmit bacterial wilt, a disease that kills plants. Thin seedlings of vining cucumbers to 8"–10"/20.3–25.4 cm apart once they have about three leaves. Thin bush types to 6"–10"/15.2–25.4 cm. Space rows 4'–5'/1.2–1.5 m apart, since good air circulation helps prevent diseases.

HEAT THINGS UP, COOL THEM OFF

When direct-seeding cucumbers, if the soil is still a bit on the cool side — below 60°F/15.5°C — cover the newly sown bed with clear plastic for up to 5 days to help warm up the soil. Remove the plastic as soon as seedlings appear.

In midsummer, however, when you sow a second crop, the soil may be too hot for good cucumber seed germination. To get seeds off to a good start, soak them in water for 24 hours before sowing. Water once the seeds are in place, then shade the site with boards propped up on bricks or with burlap to keep the soil cool and moist until seedlings appear.

Q Can I grow more than one batch of cucumbers a summer?

A Cucumbers mature relatively quickly – they're ready for harvest in 50 to 65 days, depending on the cultivar – and in most parts of the country, there's enough time for a couple of crops of cucumbers. For the biggest harvest, plan on growing successive crops throughout the summer. Sow seed every 2 or 3 weeks, up to 3 months before the last frost date. Although they may not do well in searing summer weather, in the South and Southwest, it's warm enough to grow cucumbers as a fall crop. In south Florida and southern California, it's warm enough to grow them as a winter crop as well.

I'm growing two rows of gynoecious cucumbers. Do I need only one monoecious plant to get fruit?

A That depends on how many plants you have. To ensure adequate pollination and plenty of fruit, plant one monoecious cultivar for every seven or eight gynoecious plants. Be sure to mark the locations of the monoecious seeds, so you don't thin them out by mistake.

SEE ALSO: *For more about monoecious and gynoecious cucumbers, pages 258–259.*

Do I have to grow my cucumbers in a straight line along a trellis? What are the different ways to arrange them?

A Arranging cucumbers in rows along a trellis is one popular way to grow them. Another option is to grow cucumbers in 2'–3'/.6–.9 m-wide hills, with three plants per hill (start with seven or eight seeds and thin to the healthiest seedlings). Install a teepee or stakes for the plants to climb, or if you'd like something more ornamental, consider an obelisk or arbor. Yet another option is to fasten together two pieces of lattice to make an A-frame tent, then train cucumbers on both sides. In summer use the space under the tent to grow baby greens, which will appreciate the shady spot that's created. In hot climates, a low tent or arching length of wire fencing is a good choice, since it keeps the vines close to the ground and protected from drying winds and hot sun.

A-frame trellis for cucumbers

Care and Harvesting Tips

Q Do cucumbers need fertilizing?

A If you amend the soil with plenty of compost or well-rotted manure at planting time, cucumbers need fertilizing only once: Sidedress with a balanced organic fertilizer or another dose of compost when they are about a month old. Mulch the plants to preserve soil moisture.

Q **I live in Texas, and I could water all day, but the soil still wouldn't be cool and evenly moist the way cucumbers like it. Any other options?**

A In areas with searingly hot summers, you may want to grow cucumbers from spring to early summer, take a break during midsummer, and begin planting them again in late summer for fall harvest. Also, consider a trellising structure that keeps plants closer to the ground, because it helps them cope with the hot, dry weather. A low, wire, arch support is a good choice, because it helps protect plants from drying winds and also shades and cools the soil a bit.

Q **How do I know when it's time to pick?**

A One clue to watch for is when the flower drops off the end of the fruit. You can harvest cucumbers any time after that. Smaller is better when it comes to harvesting, since younger fruit is higher in quality. Even though they can grow quite a bit larger, slicing cucumbers are at peak quality when they are 6"–8"/15.2–20.3 cm long, European types when they are about 10"/25.4 cm, and pickling types when they are 2"–4"/5–10.2 cm. If you are growing a cultivar that has spines on the fruit, wait until the dimples around the spines fill out and disappear.

Q **I live in upstate New York, and we have a short growing season. Is there any way to make sure all my cucumbers ripen before frost?**

A About 4 weeks before the fall frost date, start picking off all the female flowers. This stops the plants from forming new fruit and directs the plant's energy to ripening the fruits that have already formed.

Problem Patrol

Q **My plants have all male flowers, but no female ones! What do I do?**

A Be patient! Like all squashes, pumpkins, and melons, cucumbers produce male flowers first (at least, the monoecious types do), then begin bearing females. You should see female flowers in a few days.

SEE ALSO: *For an illustration of male and female flowers, page 260.*

My cucumbers are really odd looking! They aren't fat all the way down. What causes that?

A Two things can lead to misshapen cucumbers. The first is moisture stress. The soil should be evenly moist but not wet. For best results water deeply when the top few inches of soil are dry. Consider delivering water via drip irrigation or soaker hoses, because keeping the soil dry helps prevent disease. Uneven pollination can also cause misshapen fruit. Try hand-pollinating – taking a male flower and manually transferring pollen to female flowers – to help new fruits to fill out completely.

SEE ALSO: *For an illustration of male and female flowers, page 260.*

Q **Help! My plants are producing new cucumber fruits, but they shrivel up instead of growing. Otherwise the plants look healthy and perfect.**

A If a plant has one big fruit on it that's producing seeds, the rest of the cucumbers won't form. Search the plant carefully for a full-size cucumber that you may have missed. If you don't find a full-size cucumber, pollination may be the problem. Check to see if you planted a gynoecious cultivar, which produces all female flowers but no male ones, and thus no pollen and no fruit. Try hand-pollinating by picking a male flower and carrying the pollen to a female flower yourself.

Q **My cucumbers are producing, but the fruit is so bitter I can't eat it. Did I plant the wrong kind?**

A Cucumbers need warm weather and even moisture to produce the best fruit, and adverse conditions can easily lead to bitter-tasting fruit. Beginning when fruit starts to form, make sure the soil stays evenly moist but never sopping wet; plants don't appreciate wet feet. Instead of watering every day, water deeply a couple of times a week to encourage deep roots. Overripe fruit is bitter; discard fruits that have a touch of orange or yellow next to the flower. Cool temperatures also can cause fruits to be bitter. Make a note of the name of the plant that produced bitter cucumbers, then try a different cultivar for the next crop.

Eggplants (*Solanum melongena*)

NIGHTSHADE FAMILY, SOLANACEAE

TIPS FOR SUCCESS

- Don't rush to transplant eggplants into the garden. Wait until soil and air temperatures are consistently in the 70s/21–26°C.
- Provide stress-free conditions: Make sure the soil is evenly moist, and control insect infestations and diseases promptly.
- Harvest eggplants when they are large enough to use but before the skin loses its glossy texture.

I love eggplant, but I've never had any luck with it in the garden. What do they need to grow well?

A Eggplants love summertime heat and humidity, and if you try to get them out into the garden too early in the season, they'll just sit and suffer. Exposure to cool temperatures can also permanently stunt eggplants. To get your eggplants excited about growing, give them the following:

- **GOOD SOIL.** They like soil that's rich in organic matter, well drained, and warm. Prewarm the soil by covering it with black or clear plastic a couple of weeks before transplanting.
- **A HEAD START.** Start seedlings indoors or purchase transplants at the garden center.
- **LATE TRANSPLANTING.** Work compost into the soil before planting, and don't transplant seedlings to the garden until the soil and air temperatures both reach 70°F/21°C.
- **EXTRA COVER.** Protect plants with floating row covers to shield them from cool temperatures and to keep pests such as flea beetles at bay.
- **PAMPERING.** Eggplants are the drama queens of the vegetable garden. They go into shock if the weather is a little too cool, if they don't get enough water, or if they are exposed to any other factors that cause stress.

How early should I start eggplants indoors?

Sow seeds 8 to 10 weeks before the last spring frost date. To get them up and growing quickly, set the pots on a heat mat or other source of bottom heat that will maintain the soil at 85°F/29.5°C. Once the seedlings are up, keep them in a spot that is 70–80°F/21–26.6°C during the day and only slightly cooler at night. Begin to harden off seedlings a week before transplanting, and don't plan on moving eggplants to the garden until 2 to 3 weeks after that last spring frost date (check the soil temperature before moving them).

What spacing do they need?

Set eggplant transplants 1½'–2'/.45–.6 m apart in rows spaced 2'/.6 m apart. Use hot caps or row covers to keep the seedlings toasty warm if conditions are still cool.

Q I live in Vermont. Can I grow eggplants?

A The best areas for growing eggplants are from USDA Zone 5 south, since most cultivars take 100 to 150 days to produce fruit and require warm weather to do so. They're best in areas with long, hot summers and mild falls. In USDA Zones 3 and 4, they need an extra-long head start in spring along with extra protection from cool temperatures, such as a plastic-covered tunnel or other shelter, such as that shown on page 285. (The plants stop growing altogether if exposed to temperatures below 50°F/10°C for any length of time.) Gardeners in areas with short growing seasons should look for cultivars that mature in 60 to 70 days from transplanting.

Care and Harvesting Tips

Q Do eggplants need much fertilizer?

A Eggplants are like most other vegetables: They appreciate soil that contains a good dose of organic matter, but they don't need anything more than the standard soil preparation. Since they also need warm, well-drained soil, a spot in a raised bed is perfect for eggplants. Feed plants monthly for best production.

Q **Do I have to worry about bees not being able to find my eggplant flowers for pollination?**

A The flowers pollinate themselves and don't need the help of bees or other insects. That means you can cover them with row covers from planting until harvest if you like. If you garden in the North, keep in mind that eggplants need warm nights for pollination to succeed. If overnight temperatures dip below about 60°F/15.5°C, flowers may just drop off without being pollinated. To prevent this, keep an eye on predicted overnight lows, and cover your plants overnight with a blanket or plastic row cover when cool nights are in the forecast. Be sure to uncover them so that the hot summer sun won't cook them during the day.

 **Do I need to stake my plants?**

A Eggplants can be grown without staking, but they may benefit from a stake or even a lightweight tomato cage. Staking is especially important when plants are laden with fruit.

Staking eggplant

Q How do I tell when the fruit is ready to pick?

A Eggplants are at their best when they're still small – at about half their potential full size. The skin should turn from glossy to slightly dull. Press the skin with a fingernail to make an indentation. If it doesn't spring back, the fruit is ready to cut off (use a knife or garden shears) and enjoy. Set eggplants in a cool spot (do not refrigerate them) as soon after harvest as possible.

Q Help! I've got nearly ripe eggplants in the garden, but it's going to get chilly overnight! I don't want the fruits to be ruined. What should I do?

A Cover the plants with several layers of floating row covers, sheets, or lightweight blankets. Install stakes, cages, or other supports first to support the extra covering and prevent it from smashing the plants.

Lettuce, Spinach, and Other Leafy Crops

VARIOUS CROP FAMILIES

TIPS FOR SUCCESS

- Rake the seedbed well before planting to remove surface stones and debris and break up clods. Sow seeds shallowly because some types need light to stimulate germination.
- Plant in full sun in cool weather but in light to partial shade during warm weather.
- Water deeply once a week in cool weather; water daily during warm and hot weather to prevent wilting and bitter-tasting leaves.

Q How do I figure out what kind of lettuce to grow? There are so many different kinds!

A These days, lettuce can be one of the most beautiful crops in your garden, and it's much easier and more intriguing to grow than in the days when iceberg lettuce was the salad-bowl staple. Here's a guide to the full range of lettuce choices.

- **LEAF.** These fast-growing, easy lettuces take only 45 to 60 days from seed to full-size plants and are also called cutting and looseleaf lettuce. Many cultivars are available, and leaf edges can be wavy to curly, very frilly, or lobed (like oak leaves).

Leaf lettuce

- **ROMAINE OR COS.** These form loose heads of long, broad leaves that mature in 50 to 70 days from seed.

Romaine lettuce

- **BUTTERHEAD.** Also called Boston or bibb lettuce, these form a loose head and have exceptionally tender, succulent leaves. Plants take from 50 to 75 days to mature from seed.

Butterhead lettuce

- **SUMMER CRISP.** Also listed as French crisp lettuce, summer crisp lettuces are intermediate between Butterhead and Crisphead lettuce. They have crisp leaves that eventually form a firm head and generally take 50 to 75 days to mature from seed. Pick the leaves individually, or wait to harvest the entire head.

- **CRISPHEAD.** Also called iceberg lettuces, these produce firm, solid heads of crisp, juicy leaves. Older cultivars need 75 days of cool weather to form heads, but newer ones released for home gardeners make this crop easier to grow. Still, crispheads ideally need about 2 months of days in the 60s/15.6–20.5°C to form a head. Batavian or summer crisp-type cultivars usually form heads (and will not bolt) as long as temperatures don't exceed about 75°F/23.8°C during the day and stay above 50°F/10°C at night.

Crisphead lettuce

Q **How about Popeye's favorite treat? What are the best options for spinach?**

A Smooth-leaved spinaches are probably the best choice if fresh eating for salads is your goal. The leaves are easier to clean and more tender than savoyed spinaches, which have crinkled and puckered leaves. Savoyed spinach leaves are harder to wash but tend to hold up better for cooking. Savoyed spinach cultivars also tend to tolerate more heat and have more resistance to diseases like downy mildew.

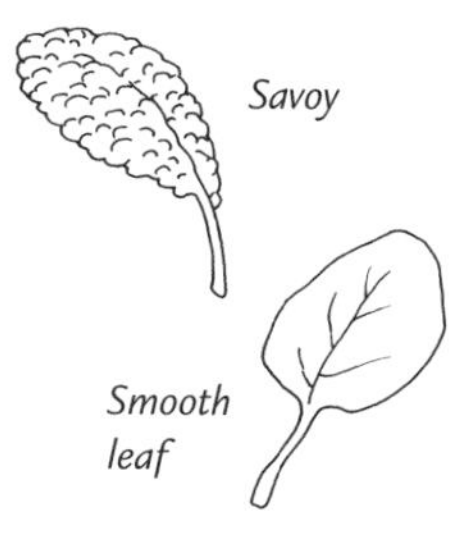

Q **My garden is in Cookeville, Tennessee, and I always have trouble with my spring spinach crop. The plants flower too soon, and that makes the leaves inedible. Is there a way to prevent flowering?**

A Two factors cause spinach to bolt quickly in spring: increasing day length and bouts of warm weather (temperatures above 70°F/21.1°C encourage bolting). For a spring crop, try to get as early a start as possible, and look for cultivars that are bolt resistant. Plant spinach in a raised bed to ensure perfect drainage, and sow 8 weeks before the last spring frost date. To protect plants from hot weather that ends the harvest, use shade cloth to protect plants and harvest as soon as possible. The good news in areas with warm climates is that fall is perfect for growing spinach, since days are shorter and cool weather rules. In Zones 9 and warmer, winter is a great time for growing spinach, lettuce, and other cool-weather leafy crops like mesclun.

Pretty Mixes

I've heard of mesclun. What is it?

A Mesclun, French for *mixture*, is actually a mix of leafy crops. Ideally, mesclun mixes include plants with a variety of leaf colors and shapes that make a pretty, flavorful salad. You'll find that seed catalogs offer preblended mesclun mixes, as well as individual packets of a variety of crops that are typically included in mesclun.

In addition to lettuces and spinach, mesclun mixes contain other leafy crops, including the following: arugula (*Eruca sativa*), beets (*Beta vulgaris*, Crassa group), bok choy (*Brassica rapa*, Chinensis group), chervil (*Anthriscus cerefolium*), corn salad or mâche (*Valerianella locusta, V. eriocarpa*), endive (*Chicorium endivia*), garden cress (*Lepidium sativum*), miner's lettuce (*Claytonia perfoliata*), mustard (*Brassica* spp.), orach (*Atriplex hortensis*), radishes (*Raphanus sativus*, Radicula group), sorrel (*Rumex acetosa, R. scutatus*), and swiss chard (*Beta vulgaris*, Cicla group).

Q **Are mesclun mixes the best way to go, or should I blend my own?**

A Seed companies that specialize in vegetables generally offer several mixes, and these may be the best way to go if you haven't tried growing mesclun before. You'll find mixes that are blended for taste, from mild to tangy. Other types are customized for growing at different times of year — cold-tolerant mixes for spring or fall and heat-tolerant crops for summertime harvests. Mixes are easiest to sow, and they tend to be less expensive, since you don't have to buy seed packets of all the different crops in the mix. Try several to see which mixes perform and taste best for you.

You may also want to experiment with buying and growing the individual ingredients separately, and mixing them together after you harvest. This prevents the problem that sometimes occurs with premixed blends when one type of plant outcompetes the others, leaving you with more mustard than you'd like, for example. By buying seeds of the individual crops and planting small blocks of each, you can grow and harvest salads that feature the exact tastes and colors you prefer.

Q How do I plant a mesclun mix?

A It is as easy to grow as lettuce. Ideally, all the crops in a mesclun mix need the same growing conditions: rich, well-prepared soil and full sun or afternoon shade in warm weather. Typically, mesclun mixes are sown in rows, wide rows, or blocks and then harvested all together when the plants are only a few inches tall. Sow thickly – as close as 1"/2.5 cm between plants – and don't worry about thinning, because you'll be harvesting them before the plants grow large.

Q What kind of soil do I need for salad crops?

A It's easiest to prepare soil for all your leafy crops at once. In general, lettuce, spinach, and other leafy crops prefer rich soil that's evenly moist. If possible, work organic matter into the soil the season before you plan to plant – in fall for a spring crop and in spring for a fall crop. While lettuce is fairly adaptable and grows in a range of soils (pH 6.0 to 6.8 pH is ideal), spinach prefers soil that's close to neutral (6.5 to 7.5) so testing and adjusting pH the season before is a good idea. Test soil the season before you plant so that amendments you add to adjust pH have time to work their effect. Yellow or brown

Salad Crops that Bite Back

MUSTARDS (*BRASSICA* SPP.) ARE SPICY-TASTING leafy crops perfect for adding a bit of zing to salads. Most are more able to tolerate heat than lettuce and are well worth growing at any season for the tasty bite they add to salads. They can also be included in mesclun mixes. Pungent mustards include broad-leaved types that have large 12"–20"/30.5–50.8 cm-tall leaves that are crinkled or savoyed and tolerate both heat and cold, but there are many others. The mildest of the mustards is mizuna, which produces 1'/.3 m-wide rosettes of deeply cut leaves. Give mustards full sun in spring and fall but partial shade during the summer to help them withstand heat. Ordinary well-prepared vegetable garden soil is fine, and even moisture is essential. Plants grown in soil that is too dry will become very hot tasting.

If you develop a yen for spicy salads, you can turn up the heat by adding some of these crops, too:

- Arugula (*Eruca sativa*)
- Chives (*Allium schoenoprasum*)
- Garlic greens (*A. sativum*)
- Green onions (*A. cepa*)
- Nasturtium leaves and blossoms (*Tropaeolum majus*)
- Sorrel (*Rumex acetosa*)

leaf edges signal that plants are growing in soil that is too acid. To sweeten acid soil, follow directions from your soil-test results or dust with lime or wood ashes in fall before spring planting.

Q What's the best way to plant lettuce?

A You can start lettuce right in the garden or sow plants indoors. Outdoors, sow seeds in a prepared seedbed about 4 weeks before the last spring frost date. Be sure to rake the soil carefully and remove surface clods and rocks, since lettuce seeds are very small. Thin plants once they have two or three leaves. Leaf lettuces generally need to be spaced 8"-10"/20.3–25.4 cm apart, other types 12"-16"/30.5–40.6 cm. Use the thinnings in salads.

Indoors, sow seeds in small flats or pots 3 weeks before the last spring frost date. Transplant seedlings to individual pots about 2 weeks later. Either way, cover the seed very lightly; ¼"/.64 cm is the recommended planting depth, because light aids germination.

Lettuce, spinach, and other leafy crops are perfect candidates for planting in blocks or wide rows, because the plants are fairly small, and it's easy to reach over the row to tend the plants. You can broadcast seeds in a band and thin them or set seedlings out at their proper spacing.

Q What's the best way to get my spinach crop growing?

A Spinach is also quite cold tolerant, and you can begin sowing seeds outdoors 4 to 6 weeks before the last spring frost date. Plant in a raised bed if your soil tends to be wet in spring. Since seedlings resent transplanting, it's usually best to direct-sow outdoors. Soak the seeds in water for several hours before sowing to speed germination, then set them ½"/1.3 cm deep and 1"–2"/2.5–5 cm apart. Once seedlings are about 4"/10.2 cm tall, thin them to 6"/15.2 cm. Use the thinnings in salads. Sow new crops every week to 10 days until 1½ months before temperatures are in the mid-70s/23.3–24.4°C.

Q How do I plant mustards?

A Despite the fact that they're heat tolerant, mustards are easiest to grow in spring or fall in all but the coolest portions of North America. Or grow them as a winter crop in the South and Southwest. For a spring crop, sow seeds directly in the garden 2 to 3 weeks before the last spring frost date. For fall, sow them in mid- to late summer. Set seeds ¼"/.64 cm deep and 1"/2.5 cm apart, then thin when seedlings are several inches tall; the distance depends on the mature size of the cultivar(s) you are

COLOR SALADS WITH FLOWERS

To make salads even more colorful and appealing, plan on using a sprinkling of the many edible flowers commonly grown in gardens. Add them fresh to salads, either whole or as petals. Edible flowers include basil (*Ocimum basilicum*), borage (*Borago officinalis*), cornflowers (*Centaurea* spp.), dill (*Anethum graveolens*), fennel (*Foeniculum vulgare*), glads (*Gladiolus* spp.), honeysuckle (*Lonicera* spp.), lavender (*Lavandula* spp.), nasturtiums (*Tropaeolum majus*), pinks (*Dianthus* spp.), oregano (*Origanum vulgare*), marigolds (*Tagetes* spp.), pansies and violets (*Viola* spp.), peas (*Pisum sativum* ssp. *sativum*), pot marigolds (*Calendula officinalis*), roses (*Rosa* spp.), squash and pumpkins (*Cucurbita* spp.), and thyme (*Thymus* spp.). Be sure to harvest flowers only from beds where no chemical sprays have been used.

Garnish salads with edible flowers

growing. Add thinned seedlings to salads. You can start harvesting individual leaves as early as 4 weeks after sowing, or pull up entire plants when they reach maturity.

Q Our garden is in northern Pennsylvania, and the growing season ends far too soon! What can we do to extend the lettuce- and spinach-growing season?

A As weather cools off in fall, lettuce, spinach, and other leafy crops mature more and more slowly, so you won't have to rush to harvest the way you do when warm summer weather is on the horizon. The cool fall weather offers gardeners a big advantage, since the plants basically stop growing and you can plant a large crop all at once and then harvest over time. Instead of "going by" in a matter of days, as they do in spring and early summer, the plants last for 4 to 6 weeks in the garden, and you can harvest plants as you need them. Once temperatures drop into the low 30s/–1.1–.5°C, plan on protecting plants by covering them with row covers or erecting a plastic tunnel over the rows. Be sure to remove covers on warm days and replace covers at night.

A plastic tunnel extends the growing season

What salad crops tolerate summer heat? We still like to eat salad in summer!

A One way to extend the salad season beyond spring is by growing heat-tolerant cultivars of salad greens. (Catalog descriptions are a good guide to appropriate cultivars.) To give them as cool a spot as possible, plant on the north or east side of your house or in the shade of a trellis. Keep them mulched and watered, too. Here are some ideas for summer salad greens:

- **SWISS CHARD.** Perhaps the best candidate for summer culture is Swiss chard (*Beta vulgaris,* Cicla group). Plants produce clumps of tall leaves on fleshy stems that can reach 2'/.6 m, but the leaves are ready to harvest beginning when they're only 5"/12.7 cm tall. Either way, the leaves are nutritious and mild tasting. Swiss chard actually prefers cool weather, so sow plants outdoors 1 to 2 weeks before the last spring frost date. Water generously, especially once the weather is warm. Look for cultivars like 'Rhubarb' or 'Bright Lights' for a colorful addition to salads.
- **SUMMER SPINACH SUBSTITUTES.** Other summer-salad crops include malabar spinach (*Basella rubra*), a tropical vine that can reach 6'/15.2 m and requires a trellis. Harvest new, very young leaves, which have a mild taste. Older leaves become mucilaginous. New Zealand spinach (*Tetragonia tetragonioides*) also tolerates heat but

needs plenty of moisture to produce tasty leaves that are high in vitamin C. Pick young leaves and stem tips, since older leaves become tough and bitter. Finally, try vegetable amaranth (*Amaranthus tricolor*), which is also called *calaloo* and resembles coleus. Its nutritious, oval- to pear-shaped leaves taste like spinach. Pick young leaves and pinch plants to encourage branching.

Q My wife and I can't wait for our first homegrown salads in the spring. What can we do to have our plants ready to harvest as early as possible?

A Plan on starting some seed indoors and some out. Hardened-off seedlings can go into the garden at the same time you can sow seeds, which gives you a head start on your first crop. Seven or 8 weeks before that last spring frost, sow your first batch of seeds indoors. Sow additional batches indoors each week after that. Transplant your first batch of seedlings — and sow seeds — outdoors about 4 weeks before the last fall frost date. (Lettuce seedlings are fine outdoors provided temperatures remain above 30°F/–1.1°C.)

Lettuce matures fairly uniformly, so all the seeds you sow will be ready to harvest at about the same time. Keep that in mind, and sow small amounts at a time — perhaps a 1'–2'/.3–.6 m row, or a dozen transplants. Continue seeding and sowing until about a month before temperatures are routinely in the 70s/21.1–26.1 °C. Plant spinach, mesclun, and other leafy crops the same way. You can use the same system to spread out the fall harvest.

Care and Harvesting Tips

What's the right way to water lettuce and spinach?

A If possible, when the weather is cool, water these crops deeply once a week. Lettuce plants have shallow roots, though, and in warmer weather they probably will need watering every other day — daily in dry climates. The soil should be constantly moist but not wet or soggy. To avoid wetting the leaves, use soaker hoses if you can. Also, try to water in the morning — by midday at the latest — so there is plenty of time for the leaves to dry out before nightfall.

Do salad greens ever need fertilizer?

A In well-prepared soil, they probably will do just fine, but to speed growth even further, water with fish emulsion a couple of times during the season.

Q I live in Richmond, Virginia. We have nice spring weather, but the temperature can pop up into the upper 70s/25–26°C without much warning. What can I do to save my lettuce crop during hot spells?

A Hot weather usually brings an end to spring lettuce and spinach harvests, but you can buy your plants a little time nonetheless. Plan to shade plants, especially in the hot afternoons. Erect a framework over the rows with wire or PVC pipe and drape it with shade cloth, which comes in degrees of screening that block 25 to 50 percent of the light and heat. For Zone 7 areas, such as Richmond, try 50 percent shade cloth when temperatures get close to 80°F/26.7°C. Or prop up sheets of lattice or picket fencing on the west side of plantings. For lettuce and spinach that will mature about the time that hot weather arrives, plant on the north or west side of a trellis.

Even if you plan to use shade cloth, also sow bolt-resistant, heat-tolerant cultivars all through the spring season. That way, if a freak hot spell occurs and all your other lettuce bolts, you'll still have some lettuce to eat. Also, be sure to mulch and water regularly (daily if necessary) to keep the roots moist and cool.

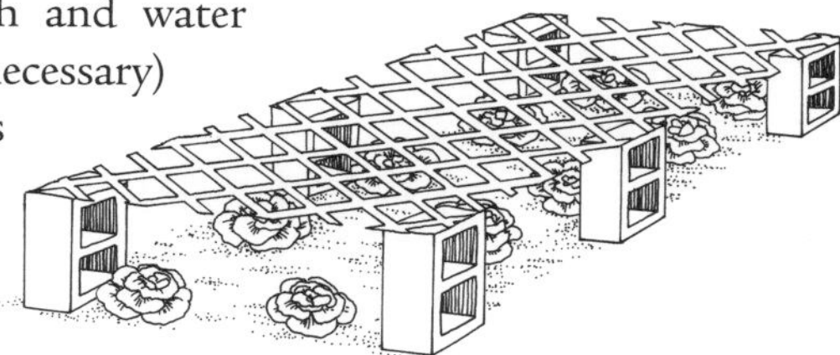

Lattice shading summer lettuce

Q How do I tell when my leaf lettuce and spinach are ready to harvest?

A You can begin harvesting leaf lettuce, spinach, and most other leafy crops as soon as the leaves are large enough to be picked. When picking leaves, pinch them off gently or cut them with scissors. Since the spring season is short, and hot weather causes plants to go from mature to bitter very quickly, pulling or cutting off whole plants is the best course of action in most areas. In fall, picking individual leaves is best, since the plants produce for several weeks. Once temperatures are routinely in the 30s/–1.1–3.9°C, harvest entire plants, since they won't grow much more. To get lettuce at its best, harvest in the morning, when the leaves are most turgid.

When are crisphead lettuces ready for harvest?

A To determine when crisphead, romaine, and summer crisp lettuce is ready to pick, feel the heads. They should be firm and fully formed but probably won't be as hard as grocery-store lettuce. If hot weather is in the forecast and you need to catch them before they bolt, you may want to go ahead and harvest even if the plants haven't formed a head yet. Use a sharp knife to cut the heads off just above the soil surface.

Q How do I harvest mesclun?

A Begin harvesting about 6 weeks after sowing, when the plants are perhaps 6"/15.2 cm tall. Use scissors to cut bunches of leaves 1"/2.5 cm above the ground. After that, water the patch gently with compost tea. The plants will resprout for at least a second, and perhaps a third, harvest.

Problem Patrol

Q My spinach and lettuce always go to seed before I have a chance to pick them. What can I do to get to them in time?

A Both lettuce and spinach form flowers and go to seed in response to warm temperatures and increasing day length in spring. This is called *bolting*. Once temperatures exceed 80°F/26.6°C, the plants' main stems begin to elongate, and flowers form very quickly. Once that happens, pull up your plants and compost them, because bolting causes the leaves to turn bitter. To avoid losing your crop, watch the weather forecast for your area. If hot weather threatens, act quickly to harvest all of your spinach and lettuce (or as much of it as you'll be able to eat and store).

Q **A friend gave me a flat of lettuce seedlings that were large and gorgeous, but they never grew much once I transplanted them to my garden. Is there something wrong with my soil?**

A Probably not. The best lettuce seedlings are small – only 3 or 4 weeks old, in fact. Although they look tiny, young seedlings outperform large transplants almost every time.

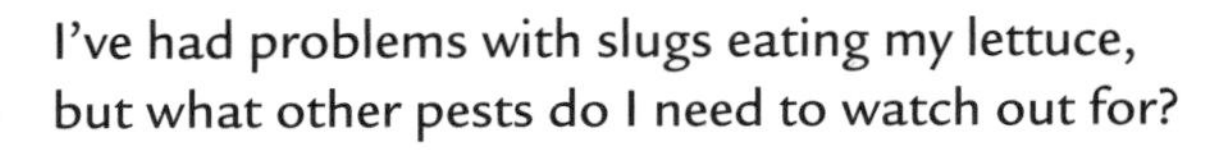

Q **I've had problems with slugs eating my lettuce, but what other pests do I need to watch out for?**

A Slugs do love lettuce, and the slimy trails and ragged holes they leave in lettuce are none too appetizing. Two other pests to watch for are aphids and thrips. Aphids are small, rounded insects that feed by sucking sap from leaves. Their feeding causes curled leaves and stunted plants. Thrips rasp the leaves, leaving silvery streaks. They are very tiny insects and are hard to see. To check for thrips, hold a piece of white paper under a leaf and tap or shake the leaf. Thrips will show up as tiny black specks on the paper.

SEE ALSO: *For tips on slug control, page 151; for thrip control, page 149; for aphid control, page 147.*

Q My lettuce plants have been developing dark rusty-looking patches on the bottom leaves; then all the bottom leaves turn slimy and brown. What's causing this?

A Look carefully at the rusty patches: If they are sunken and oozing, a disease called bottom rot is the culprit. Remove infected plants or pull off outside leaves that show signs of rot, and compost them. To prevent future outbreaks, add extra compost to your soil the next time you plant and/or plant lettuce in raised beds. Bottom rot is caused by a fungus that thrives in poorly drained conditions, and both compost and raised beds improve soil drainage. It also helps to reduce watering, allowing the soil surface to be slightly dry, as well as to water in the morning so plants have dried off by nightfall. Also, water remaining plants with compost tea to encourage beneficial microorganisms.

Melons and Watermelons
(*Cucumis melo, Citrullus lanatus*)
GOURD FAMILY, CUCURBITACEAE

TIPS FOR SUCCESS

- Let the soil and air warm up before planting; both should be at least 70°F/21.1°C, and nighttime temperatures should dip no lower than 60°F/15.6°C.
- Give plants enough, but not too much, water for best flavor: Water if the plants wilt before midday or if the top 4"/10.2 cm of soil dries out.
- Pinch off shoot tips and extra fruit starting in midsummer to direct the energy of the plants to ripening existing fruit, especially in short-season areas. Melon plants bear about six fruits per vine, maximum; large watermelons, two or three.

What's the best kind of melon for a beginning gardener to try growing?

A The most popular melons to grow in backyard gardens are muskmelons — *C. melo,* Reticulatus group, for readers who want the proper name for these sweet treats. These range from 2–3 pounds/.9–1.4 kg and have tan, netted rinds and usually pale orange flesh. Ideally, start out with a cultivar bred for its resistance to or tolerance of diseases such as fusarium and powdery mildew. (Although muskmelons are also called cantaloupes, true cantaloupes have hard, warty-textured rinds and orange flesh.) Muskmelons mature in 70 to 80 days from transplanting. If you'd like to try some of the other types of melons, look for fast-maturing cultivars that mature in about the same number of days.

Q **What about plant size? Are the bush-type plants as good as the full-size ones?**

A In general, full-size or long-vined melons and watermelons produce better-quality fruit than compact or bush types. That's because they generally have more leaves and thus more energy to produce fruit. If you have only enough room for compact or bush-type plants, don't despair, though. Thin the fruit so that each plant bears only two melons. That ups the ratio of leaves to fruit and also helps plants yield sweeter fruit.

Compact or bush-type cultivars should be spaced about 2'/.6 m apart. Trellising is another option that works well for small-space gardens. For trellising, stick to small-fruited melons and icebox-type watermelons that produce smaller fruit – up to about 10 pounds/4.5 kg. Use strips of soft cloth to tie the vines to a sturdy trellis or fence. If you train melons on a fence, keep in mind that you'll need to train the vines on the south-facing side of a fence that runs east and west to ensure that they'll receive enough sunlight.

Q I live in Sacramento, California. With such a long growing season, I'd like to have some fun and experiment. What other kinds of melons can I grow?

A Gardeners in Zones 8 through 10 are the lucky ones when it comes to cultivating melons, because they have a long, warm growing season (temperatures in the 90s/32.2–37.2°C are ideal for melons and watermelons). Most commonly grown melons mature in 70 to about 80 days from transplanting; winter melons (*C. melo,* Inodorus group) such as casabas and crenshaws require much longer but are still easy to schedule whether you live in Sacramento or anywhere else in Zones 8 to 10. Here's a rundown of the types of melons you may want to consider. All bear succulent, sweet-tasting fruit:

- **ANANAS MELONS.** These oval, 2–4-pound/.9–1.8 kg melons have white flesh and a yellow-orange rind. Maturity is around 80 days from transplanting.
- **BUTTERSCOTCH MELONS.** These are smooth-skinned melons with pale yellow-green or whitish green rinds and two-toned green and pale orange flesh. Maturity is 75 to 80 days from transplanting.
- **CASABA MELONS.** These winter melons generally weigh 5 pounds/2.3 kg and have yellow rinds that are ribbed and rough with greenish flesh. Maturity is around 110 days from transplanting.

- **CHARENTAIS-TYPE MELONS.** Usually weighing in at about 2 pounds/.9 kg, these have a smooth-textured gray-green rind and especially fragrant, extrasweet orange flesh. Maturity is around 80 days from transplanting.

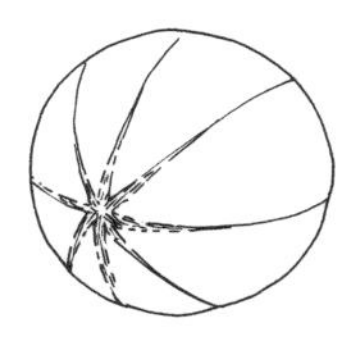

Charentais

- **CRENSHAW MELONS.** A winter melon, crenshaws weigh about 6 pounds/2.7 kg and have smooth-textured, yellow-green skin and pale green or pale orange flesh. Maturity is 90 to 110 days from transplanting.

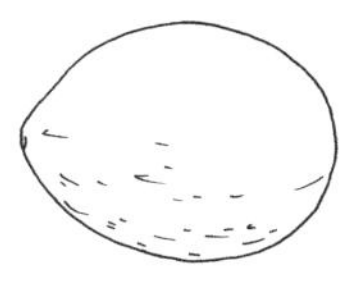

Crenshaw

- **HONEYDEW MELONS.** A winter melon that averages about 3 pounds/1.4 kg, honeydews have smooth, pale green to white rinds and pale green flesh. Maturity is 80 days or more from transplanting.

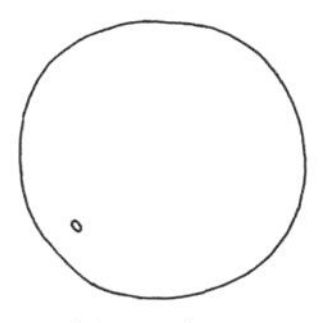

Honeydew

- **OTHER TYPES.** Once you've grown some of the most popular types, you'll probably want to experiment even further. Look through catalogs or on the Internet a bit, and you'll find all sorts of melons to try, including white-fleshed Asian-type melons, tennis-ball-size single-serving melons with striped or mottled rinds, and melons that look just like lemons.

Q I live near Minneapolis, Minnesota, where we have a pretty short growing season. Can I still grow melons or watermelons?

A Provided you start with a short-season or early maturing cultivar – look for a days-to-maturity rating of 70 to 75 days from transplanting – you should be able to grow a crop of either melons or watermelons. Both melons and watermelons can be grown in gardens from Zone 4 south, but to get a jump on the season, gardeners in cooler regions should plan on starting seedlings indoors and prewarming the soil with clear or black plastic for a couple of weeks before moving seedlings outdoors. Cover plants with row covers in spring to keep them warm, and leave them covered as long as possible. If it's still chilly when the first female flowers form, remove the covers, hand-pollinate by picking a male flower and carrying the pollen to the female flower yourself, and then put the covers back in place.

I just moved to northern Louisiana. Can I grow watermelons here?

Any gardeners living in Zones 8 through 10 – and that certainly includes everyone in Louisiana – have the long, hot summers that watermelons require, and it's in the South where the walloping big ones are produced.

Watermelons typically take a minimum of 70 to 85 days from transplanting, which means at least 110 days overall from seeding to ripe fruit. Gardeners farther north can still grow them, but early maturing or short-season cultivars are easier to grow.

Q **I could eat melons or watermelon every day of the year! How can I spread out the harvest?**

A First, it's important to know that all of the melons on a single vine ripen at about the same time, so you need to succession plant to spread out the harvest. Plant your first crop in spring — and start early by prewarming the soil and keeping plants under row covers. Then plant another batch of melons 3 to 5 weeks later. In the South, you have time for more crops. Look at the days-to-maturity listed on the cultivar you'd like to grow, and count backward from the first fall frost date to determine planting time. (It's best to add a couple of extra weeks to your estimate so you have plenty of time to let the fruit ripen before cold temperatures arrive.)

Wherever you garden, if you have melons ripening in late summer or fall, be sure to cover the plants on cool nights, since temperatures below 50°F/10°C will stress plants. Use a couple of sheets, old blankets, or a tarp.

Q **Do I plant seeds out in the garden or start melons and watermelons indoors?**

A Anywhere the growing season is long and warm – from about Zone 8 south – sow seeds outdoors directly in the garden. Elsewhere, start them indoors 3 to 4 weeks before it's time to transplant. Either way, soak seed in compost tea for 20 or 30 minutes before sowing, and plant seeds ½"/1.3 cm deep.

Keep in mind that neither melons nor watermelons transplant well. Since smaller seedlings transplant much more reliably than larger ones, don't start too early. Ideal transplants have only two or three true leaves, and transplants that have four or more leaves or produce any tendrils have difficulty putting down roots once they're moved to the garden. To ensure transplants that are the right size, you may want to wait and sow them indoors about 1 week before the last spring frost date. Follow these guidelines to help them make the move with flying colors:

- **USE INDIVIDUAL POTS** to minimize transplant stress.
- **SOW SEVERAL SEEDS IN EACH POT.** Three-inch/7.6 cm pots are best. Peat or newspaper pots also help minimize transplant trauma.
- **SET SOWN POTS ON A HEAT MAT** to maintain soil temperatures at 75°F/23.8°C.

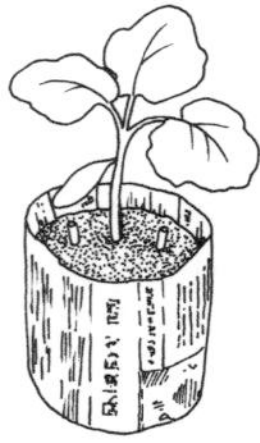

Newspaper pots minimize transplanting stress.

- **WHEN SEEDLINGS ARE 2"/5 CM TALL,** use scissors to clip off all but the strongest one in each pot.
- **BEGIN TO HARDEN OFF SEEDLINGS** a week after the last frost date and transplant to the garden 2 to 3 weeks after the last spring frost date has passed. They'll tolerate 60°F/15.6°C soil but really appreciate soil that is lots warmer – 85–90°F/29.4–32.2°C.
- **COVER SEEDLINGS WITH FLOATING ROW COVERS** to keep pests at bay and give them a little protection from cool temperatures. Be sure to remove row covers when flowers appear or hand-pollinate to ensure fruit set.

Q What kind of soil prep is best?

A Melons and watermelons prefer well-drained soil that holds moisture well and is rich in organic matter. Since their roots normally reach a depth of 8"–10"/20.3–25.4 cm, dig the soil to at least 1'/.3 m – somewhat deeper than a shallow-rooted crop such as lettuce would require. Gardeners in dry areas should dig even deeper; this encourages roots to delve deeply and makes plants less susceptible to heat and drought. If you're growing some of the longer-season melons, keep in mind that their roots can tunnel down several feet, so double-digging the soil may be worth the effort. Melons and watermelons do appreciate an extra dose of organic matter – in addition to the amount you apply annually as part of your overall soil improvement plan. Since they don't go into the garden until late, there's plenty of time to work 2"–3"/ 5–7.6 cm of well-rotted manure or compost deeply into the soil in spring before it's time to plant. In dry regions, try to incorporate 4"–6"/10.2–15.2 cm of organic matter.

SEE ALSO: *For information about double digging, pages 234–235.*

I want to trellis my melons. What type of structure would work best?

A Try making an A-frame trellis. Use wood, bamboo stakes, PVC pipe, or galvanized pipe to create the frame, and wire-mesh fencing or sturdy wooden crosspieces for the surface. Make individual slings to support the fruit. Slings made from old pantyhose are ideal for this purpose, since they expand as the fruit grows. Slings made of mesh bags, bird netting, or old cotton T-shirts also are suitable. Try growing lettuce or other greens underneath it during the summer months, because the shade will help them cope with heat.

A-frame melon trellis

MORE OF A GOOD THING

To create an extra-special planting site for melons or watermelons, dig a hole that's 1'/.3 m deep and 1'/.3 m wide at each spot where you are planning a hill for planting. Fill the hole with compost or well-rotted manure, then use the soil you removed to build a hill on top of the site that's 1'/.3 m tall and 2'–3'/.6–.9 m wide. Once their roots are long enough to reach down into this special cache, your plants will appreciate the extra dose of organic matter.

Q I remember that my grandfather always planted melons in hills in his garden. Is that the best way to plant them?

A While they will grow in rows, melons and watermelons are especially happy growing in mounds of rich, loose soil amended with compost and/or well-rotted manure. Sow about six seeds per hill, then thin to the three strongest plants when they are about 2"/5 cm tall. Space hills for melons about 4'–6'/1.2–1.8 m apart. Watermelons need more room – from 6'–12'/1.8–3.7 m. Bush-type melons don't need quite as much space: Plant them about 2'/.6 m apart. Both crops also perform well in raised beds.

If you live in a dry climate, though, digging down is the best option, since raised mounds of soil dry out more quickly. Whether you grow your melons in hills, raised beds, or sunken beds, cover the plants with floating row covers to prevent pests from attacking the plants. If you prefer to grow in rows, space seedlings 3'–4'/.9–1.2 m apart in rows that are 5'–6'/1.5–1.8 m apart.

SEE ALSO: *For planting in sunken beds, page 86.*

Care and Harvesting Tips

How much water do melons and watermelons need?

A Water crops whenever the top 3"–4"/7.6–10.2 cm of soil are dry — just stick a finger down into the soil to test for moisture. Both crops routinely wilt on hot summer afternoons, but if the plants wilt before noon, they need to be watered. While they need a steady supply of water to grow and set fruit, stop watering about 2 weeks before the fruits are ready to harvest. Holding back water at this point makes the fruits sweeter tasting.

Q **My melons don't seem to be growing as fast as my neighbors' are. Is there anything I can do to speed them up?**

A Melons appreciate amended soil, but they also benefit from feeding during the growing season. From the time transplants or seedlings begin growing vigorously until the first female flowers appear, water plants weekly with a dilute solution of fish emulsion fertilizer (1 tablespoon/14.8 ml per 1 gallon/3.8 L of water).

Q **I never know when to pick my muskmelons! What's the secret?**

A Harvesting muskmelons can be tricky. Since they don't become any sweeter after harvest (they just get softer), it's important to pick them at the peak of ripeness, not too early or too late. Muskmelons "slip" from the vine when they're ripe, meaning that the vine naturally detaches from the fruit. Most gardeners pick just before this – at the half-slip stage, about 2 days before full slip – to ensure that the fruit won't be overripe. To harvest at half slip, pick when gentle pressure at the point where the vine attaches to the melon detaches it. Another clue to ripeness is the color of the melon beneath the netting on the rind. When it turns from green to paler green or yellow, the melon is probably ready.

What about watermelons? I've tried thumping, but I'm not sure what to listen for!

A Harvesting watermelons is part art and part science. They don't become any sweeter after they've been picked, so it's crucial to get them out of the garden at just the right time. If you want to try the scientific approach, mark your calendar on the day the female flowers open fully. Then count off 35 days; that's when the fruit will be ready. Here are some other cues to ripening:

- The tendril on the stem nearest the fruit dries up and turns brown.
- The spot on the bottom of the fruit turns from white to yellow or creamy yellow in color. Try pressing a fingernail into the spot on the bottom of the fruit. It's probably ripe if it doesn't dent easily, the skin peels back easily with a little bit of scraping, and the flesh under the skin is greenish white.
- The top of the watermelon turns dull in color and the contrast between the stripes diminishes. Thump your watermelon, and you should hear a deep, hollow sound.

Pay attention, and even make notes in your garden journal, and you'll gradually become more expert at telling exactly when your watermelons reach the peak of ripeness. Cut the fruit from the plant, and leave a short stem. Pulling or yanking fruit damages the remaining vines.

STORAGE STRATEGIES FOR THE HEIGHT OF HARVEST SEASON

Your fridge and countertops fill up quickly during harvest time, especially once tomatoes, squash, corn, and other vegetables begin to ripen. A healthy melon and watermelon crop makes the storage dilemma even more critical! Our ancestors stored all their homegrown bounty in the root cellar, which offered ideal cool (45–50°F/7.2–10°C), dark conditions, but suburban homes don't come equipped with root cellars these days. Instead, consider setting up in a garage or basement an old refrigerator that's used only during harvest time to keep produce. Or, if you have a cool basement, a set of metal shelving (the kind sold in home stores) makes a good temporary storage spot. A crawlspace may also provide the proper temperatures for storage: If so, add wood pallets or make a frame, and cover it with hardware cloth so you can store produce up off the floor.

How can I tell when honeydews, casabas, and true cantaloupes are ripe?

Unlike muskmelons, most other melons won't slip from the vine even when they're fully ripe. Here are some tips to catch these crops at the peak of sweetness:

- Watch the skin color. Rind color on honeydews and other melons changes when they are ripe, often to gold or white.
- These melons generally have small hairs on the fruit that fall off when it's ripe. Stroke the melon to feel for hairs. The skin should be slightly slippery and smooth.
- Smell the fruit on the end where the flower was originally located. You should be able to smell the sweet, fruity fragrance.

Q What can I do to prevent melon diseases?

A Look for cultivars bred for disease resistance or disease tolerance. Powdery mildew resistance is especially important in humid areas, because infected plants produce flavorless fruit. Use soaker hoses or drip irrigation if possible when watering melons so the foliage will stay dry, since this helps cut down on diseases. A thick layer of mulch helps too, and mulch also holds weeds in check and keeps the fruits clean.

Problem Patrol

Help! I've got flowers, but I don't see any female ones! Did I do something wrong?

A Both melons and watermelons bear male flowers first. Be patient, and you'll eventually see female flowers, which usually follow the males by about a week and have tiny melons formed just below the base of the flower.

Q My plants each formed a dozen or more melons, but most of them shriveled up and died. Why did this happen?

A Each plant generally ripens only three to four melons, and it's actually best to remove surplus fruit. This directs the plant's energy into ripening only the amount of fruit the plant can support. In midsummer, remove all immature fruit and flowers to direct the plant's energy into ripening fruit that is already growing before cool fall weather arrives.

Q Ugh. I tried to harvest my perfect-looking melons, but they're rotted on the bottom! What can I do to keep this from happening again?

A The easiest and best way to prevent rot is to get the fruit up off the soil surface so it will stay dry. Slip a board, a flat rock, or a piece of paver under each fruit when it is about half grown. This trick also speeds ripening, especially if you choose a prop that absorbs heat during the day and releases it at night.

Ripening melon propped on a board

Okra (*Abelmoschus esculentus*)

MALLOW FAMILY, MALVACEAE

TIPS FOR SUCCESS

- Select a warm, protected site for planting.
- Soak seeds overnight before sowing, or freeze them for 2 to 3 days to break the seed coat and speed germination.
- Pick okra daily or every other day, about 4 days after the flowers fall, when pods are still quite small and tender.

Q I've never grown or eaten okra. What part of the plant do you harvest, and how do you cook it?

A Okra is one of those love-it-or-hate-it crops. It's grown for the seedpods that follow the flowers, each of which opens for 1 day. The pods are picked in summer and are an essential ingredient in a traditional stew called *gumbo.* Okra pods also are served steamed or boiled, pickled, sliced, or breaded and fried. Their taste has been described as a cross between the flavors of green beans and oysters. Their texture is mucilaginous (meaning slimy).

Some gardeners also grow okra plants as an ornamental accent in a flower bed. The handsome plants bear yellow bell-shaped flowers with red centers, and the leaves are attractive, too. Plants range from 3'–6'/.9–1.8 m or more. Keep in mind that some people get a rash from working around okra's spiny leaves. Plant a spineless cultivar or wear gloves and long sleeves when working around the plants.

Okra blossom and pods

Q What are the secrets to success with okra?

A Okra plants appreciate richer soil than most vegetables, so work plenty of compost or well-rotted manure into the soil, digging it in to a depth of 8"–10"/20.3–25.4 cm. Soak seed overnight in water and sow it 1"/2.5 cm deep after the soil has warmed up to at least 65°F/18.3°C. The seeds simply sit and rot if the soil is too cold, so don't be in a rush to plant. Space seeds about 4"/10.2 cm apart in rows that are 18"/45.7 cm apart. Thin seedlings so they are 2'/.6 m apart when they're about 8"/20.3 cm tall. Cut off the excess seedlings with scissors to minimize root disturbance to the remaining plants. Feed with a balanced organic fertilizer after thinning and again when they begin to form pods.

Q I live in Michigan, on the Upper Peninsula. Can I grow okra?

A There's no doubt that okra is a heat-loving tropical crop, but as long as your garden is located in USDA Zone 4 or warmer, you can probably manage to fit in a crop. Look for an early- or short-season cultivar that begins to bear about 50 days from transplanting (most cultivars take 70 days to bear). A warm spot protected from winds is the best choice. It's also best to prewarm the soil by covering it with clear or black plastic for 2 weeks before planting. Your harvest will be smaller than the bumper crops this plant produces in the South, however.

Can I start okra seeds inside?

Yes, start them indoors if you live in the North or want an extra-early crop. Since okra resents transplanting, sow in individual pots 4 to 6 weeks before the last spring frost date. Harden off plants, and move them to the garden after all danger of frost has passed. Space plants 2'/.6 m apart.

How do I harvest the pods?

Use scissors or gardening shears to cut them off when they are 2"–4"/5–10.2 cm long. Leave a short stem on each pod. Don't wait until they get larger to harvest, because larger pods are tough. Use the pods as soon after you harvest as possible, since they decline quickly. And don't put them in the refrigerator because the cold temperatures cause them to turn black.

I had flowers on my okra plants, but no pods formed. What's up?

While okra plants love heat, temperatures above 90°F/32.2°C can cause poor pollination and thus flowers that don't yield pods. Wait for cooler weather to return. A few other cultural problems can cause poor pollination, including temperatures that dip below 50°F/10°C, dry soil, not enough light, and too much nitrogen.

Onions and Garlic (*Allium* spp.)

ONION FAMILY, ALLIACEAE

TIPS FOR SUCCESS

- Pay attention to regional schedules: In the South, plant short-day onions in fall; north of Zone 7, plant long-day cultivars in spring.
- Start weed control early, since weedy garden invaders can quickly overtake the delicate foliage of onions and their kin.
- Check your crop frequently to harvest at the right time — before the outer skins begin to break down. Dig up bulbs carefully to avoid damaging them.

I know that onions and garlic are related, but aren't they grown differently?

A Onions, garlic, leeks, and chives are all alliums. While they're not all grown exactly the same way, their cultural needs are similar. All are happiest in full sun, but they also tolerate partial shade and need similar soil conditions. The biggest difference is in the scheduling of each crop. Here are the basics on these savory crops:

- **CHIVES.** *Allium schoenoprasum.* Hardy in USDA Zones 3 to 9, chives produce clumps of thin edible leaves and edible flowers as well. This easy-to-grow perennial is most commonly grown in herb and flower gardens.

- **GARLIC.** *Allium sativum.* Grown primarily for its edible bulbs, garlic also produces tasty leaves that can be chopped and used like chives. The best crops of garlic are planted in fall and harvested in midsummer the following year. Plants are hardy from USDA Zones 2 to 10. Although garlic crops are typically harvested each year, they also can be left in the garden and grown as perennials as well.

- **LEEKS.** *Allium ampeloprasum,* Porrum group. Another hardy onion-family plant, leeks can be grown in USDA Zones 2 to 10, although there are both hardy and non-hardy cultivars available. They're planted in spring and harvested the same season. Leeks are biennials.

- **ONIONS.** *Allium cepa,* Cepa group. Biennials that are grown as annuals, onions can be a bit confusing, since there are many different colors and kinds to choose from. They can be grown throughout North America, but planting times and cultivars vary depending on day length. They're generally planted in spring, although in warm climates they're grown as a winter crop. Harvest time varies depending on the size and type you are growing.

What kind of soil do onions and garlic need?

All these crops produce bulbs and thrive in loose, deeply dug soil that drains well but also retains moisture. While they'll grow in average garden soil, for best results incorporate an extra 1"–2"/2.5–5 cm layer of finished compost. Make a 4"/10.2 cm-deep furrow between your rows and sprinkle about 1 cup/.23 L of a balanced organic fertilizer along 10'/3 m of row. Cover the furrow with soil, then plant; once your onions are large enough to reach the fertilizer, it will give them a boost.

SEE ALSO: *For more soil management advice, chapter 2.*

Anything else to keep in mind when preparing the soil?

Onions and their kin all have grassy leaves, and since they don't shade the soil very well, weeds can become a big problem relatively quickly. Remove weed roots and shoots when you prepare soil, and especially avoid tilling grass or other weeds into the soil, because the chopped-up roots will yield many more weeds. Once plants are in the ground, a 2"–4"/5–10.2 cm layer of mulch helps suppress weeds. To avoid causing the necks of the bulbs to rot, don't push the mulch up closely around the onion-plant stems.

Planting Onions

Q I've heard that some onions are short-day onions and others are long-day onions. What does that mean?

A Onion-bulb formation is triggered by day length. Short-day onions begin to produce bulbs as soon as they start receiving about 12 hours of daylight per day. Long-day onions need 13 to 16 hours of daylight to trigger bulb formation. Gardeners in the South should grow short-day onions. Long-day onions need to be planted for summertime production in the North – although we might assume differently, summer days are longer in the northern states and Canada than they are in the South. The 35th parallel of latitude is the approximate dividing line between long-day and short-day onion growing. This line runs just south of Raleigh, North Carolina, slightly north of Little Rock, Arkansas, through Albuquerque, New Mexico and near Santa Barbara, California.

There also are intermediate-day length cultivars that can be grown in the regions in between. Keep in mind that wherever onions are growing, it's important that plants produce plenty of foliage before they receive the trigger to start forming bulbs; otherwise, the bulbs will be puny.

Q **Deciding which onions to grow seems complicated! What do I need to know?**

A In addition to red, yellow, and white onions, there also are gradations of shape and flavor (from sweet to pungent). For gardeners, though, the place to start is probably based on usage – whether the onions will be put in salads, sliced for hamburgers, or stored for later use. Here are the types you'll encounter in catalogs:

Green onions

- **GREEN ONIONS.** Also called scallions and spring onions, green onions have fleshy stems that have little or no bulb or swelling at the bottom. (Most don't belong to *A. cepa,* as common kitchen onions do. They're *A. fistulosum* or crosses between *A. fistulosum* and *A. cepa.*)

Storage onion

- **STORAGE ONIONS.** Not surprisingly, these are hard onions developed especially for their ability to last in storage. They have a pungent taste but actually contain more sugar than milder onions. The pungency cooks away, leaving great taste. They also become milder in storage.

Slicing onion

- **SLICING ONIONS.** These are sweet and mild tasting but have softer flesh than storage types and do not last as long in storage. They're also called Bermuda or

Spanish onions. Slicing onions are usually lighter in color than storage types.

- **PEARL ONIONS.** These are small, mild-tasting onions usually used for pickling.

Pearl onions

Q What are onion sets?

A Sets are small bulbs grown the previous year, and they produce bulbs quickly after planting, so they're an easy option for growing a crop of onions. Garden centers and even many grocery stores sell onion sets in spring, but they usually offer only a couple of color choices. (If you live in the South, you'll have to store sets in the refrigerator for fall planting.) Keep in mind that larger isn't necessarily better. Sets should be no more than about ½"/1.3 cm in diameter. Larger ones are more likely to bolt, meaning they'll go to seed rather than produce bulbs.

Starting your own onions from seed allows you a wider selection of varieties. Another option is to order onion transplants from catalogs or through the Internet (especially from onion specialists). They generally come bundled in groups, and they look like skinny scallions.

Q How do I plant sets? What about transplants?

A Plant sets or transplants 2"/5 cm deep and from 3"–6"/7.6–15.2 cm apart, depending on the final bulb size of the cultivar you are growing. Sets go in the ground pointed end up. It's important to sort them before you plant: Discard any that are soft or have already begun to sprout, because these will likely bolt. Even if you are growing cultivars that produce large bulbs, plant them half the final recommended spacing distance, and then pull every other plant about 5 or 6 weeks later to use as green onions.

Q I live in Iowa. Should I plant onions in the spring?

A Plant onions in early spring north of USDA Zone 7. Start with sets or transplants of long-day cultivars, and set them out as soon as the soil can be worked, about 4 to 6 weeks before the last spring frost. The soil should be at least 40°F/4.4°C. Onions grow best when temperatures are between 55–75°F/12.7–23.8°C. Cool weather promotes healthy foliage growth. As the days grow longer, it signals the plants to start forming bulbs. At that point, the warmer the weather, the faster the bulbs grow.

Shallot Simplicity

SHALLOTS (*Allium cepa,* Aggregatum group) are an easy-to-grow gourmet treat. They're perennials that are grown as annuals, and producing them is a snap compared to growing a crop of regular onions. Start with sets or transplants 2 to 4 weeks before the last spring frost date — or in fall if you're located in the South. They need well-prepared moist soil, just like onions do. Space sets or transplants 6"–8"/ 15.2–20.3 cm apart. You can harvest the tops as you would green onions or garlic greens in 30 days by cutting a few leaves from each plant; don't cut the new leaves, just the mature ones on the outside of the cluster. Harvest green shallots in about 45 days and mature ones in 90 to 130 days. Cure shallots by spreading them on newspaper in a dry spot out of direct sun for several days. Be sure to set aside the largest and best-quality bulbs for replanting the following year.

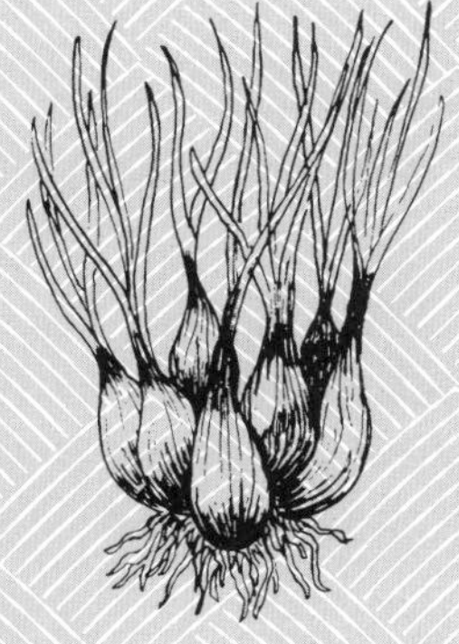

Shallots

SEE ALSO: *For advice on soil preparation, page 316.*

I live in South Carolina. When should I plant onions?

In the South and Southwest, plant sets or transplants of a short-day cultivar in fall for harvest in winter or early spring. When cool winter weather arrives, mulch the plants, then uncover them in late winter or spring. You can also plant intermediate-day onions in early spring.

How do I grow onions from seeds?

You can sow seeds outdoors in spring 3 to 4 weeks before the last spring frost date, but for best results start them indoors 10 to 12 weeks before the last spring frost date in pots. Sow thickly, and dust soil mix over the top of the seeds. Keep the soil moist and warm (above 65°F/18.3°C) until germination occurs. Thin or transplant to 1"/2.5 cm spacing, when the seedlings are still small. The ideal temperature for growth is 40–55°F/4.4–12.8°C, so if you can, move the pots to a cold frame. If the seedlings get too tall (about 5"/12.7 cm) use scissors to cut them back to about 3"/7.6 cm. Harden off the seedlings, and move them to the garden 2 to 3 weeks before the last spring frost date. If you want to plant onions in the fall, start seeds in late summer.

A Leek Lesson

LIKE ONIONS AND GARLIC, leeks are easy to grow. They need well-prepared soil that's deeply dug and rich in organic matter. As long as you're following a yearly soil-improvement plan, they'll probably do just fine. They do best in full sun but also grow in partial shade. If there's a secret to growing top-quality leeks, it's producing long white fleshy stems by blanching, or keeping them covered with soil. Blanching makes leeks tender and mild tasting.

Long or Short

There are two kinds of leek cultivars, hardy long-season ones and early or short-season types that aren't hardy. Short-season leeks are planted in spring for harvest in summer or fall. They have a milder taste than long-season types and also don't store as well. Long-season cultivars, which take 100 or more days to mature from transplanting, are planted in fall. They store well and also can be overwintered in the garden and harvested any time the soil isn't frozen.

Starting from Seed

For spring planting, sow short-season leeks 8 to 10 weeks before the last spring frost date. For fall planting, sow long-season leeks 8 to 10 weeks before the first fall frost. Follow the steps on the next page for a bumper crop:

(Leek Lesson continued)

1. **SOW THE SEEDS ½"/1.3 CM DEEP,** and sow thickly in pots or flats, then set them on a heat mat or another spot that keeps the soil at 70°F/21.1°C.

2. **TRANSPLANT SEEDLINGS TO INDIVIDUAL POTS** or thin to 1"/2.5 cm apart when they are 3"/7.6 cm tall. (Deep pots, up to 6"/15.2 cm are best.) Keep them cool (60–65°F/15.6–18.3°C) until it's time to transplant — around the last spring frost date.

3. **THE EASIEST WAY TO TRANSPLANT** is to use a broomstick or tool handle to poke holes in the soil — space holes 8"–10"/20.3–25.4 cm apart in rows 12"/30.5 cm apart — then stick individual leek seedlings into the holes. Set the seedlings up to the depth of their stem, just below where the leaves separate.

4. **DON'T REFILL THE HOLES.** Instead, water the plants gently, and let soil gradually fill in the hole around the seedlings. Hill up the soil a bit if too much stem seems to be exposed.

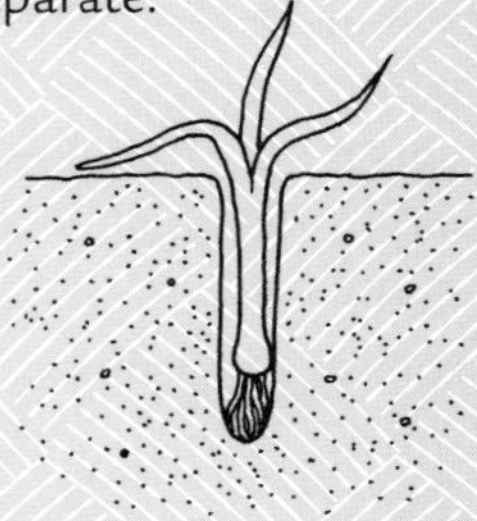

Planting a leek seedling

Enjoying the Harvest

For fresh use in salads, begin harvesting leeks any time. For full-grown plants, wait until the stems are about 1½"/3.8 cm thick. To dig them, loosen the soil along the row and then pull the plants; otherwise, they'll break off rather than come up. Cut off all except 2"/5 cm of leaves and store them in the refrigerator. For long-term storage, pack them in damp sand in a cold (32–40°F/0–4.4°C), dark spot.

Garden Storage

Unlike onions and garlic, leeks keep well right in the garden for long periods if conditions are right. From the warmer portions of Zone 8 and south, you don't even need to mulch the plants – simply harvest them as you need them. In colder areas, mulch leeks heavily when cold weather threatens in fall. To harvest, pull back the mulch and dig. From Zone 7 north, either dig the entire crop before the soil freezes or leave the plants mulched over the winter and harvest in late winter or early spring. Don't delay once spring arrives, though, because the plants will bolt soon after they "wake up" from their winter sleep.

Planting Garlic

I love cooking with garlic. Do I just buy a few cloves at the grocery store and plant them?

A In most cases, garlic sold in grocery stores is treated to prevent sprouting, so you're better off buying from a local garden center or by mail. If you are an aficionado, ordering by mail is best, since you'll find a wealth of different cultivars to try. Or ask a friend or neighbor who already grows it to give you a few cloves to start your own patch.

Q What about starting garlic from seeds?

A Most garlic is reproduced vegetatively – that is, by dividing the bulbs – and is not grown from seed. Even the curling flower heads that some garlic bulbs produce in summer rarely produce seeds. Instead, they produce clusters of tiny bulbils, which can be saved and planted much like seeds. Bulbils take 2 years to produce bulbs large enough to use.

Q How do I decide what kinds of garlic to buy?

A While there are hundreds of cultivars, all fall into two basic types: hardneck and softneck garlic. Bulbs of hardneck garlic have a stiff stem at the center that's surrounded by one or two rows of cloves. Each bulb produces a flowering stem in early summer that curls at the top. Softneck garlic has a soft stem in the center of the bulb. Softneck garlics store better than hardnecks, but hardneck garlics are hardier. Softneck garlic is the type to buy if you want to make garlic braids. Elephant garlic (*Allium ampeloprasum*) is a type of bulbing leek that is grown like garlic.

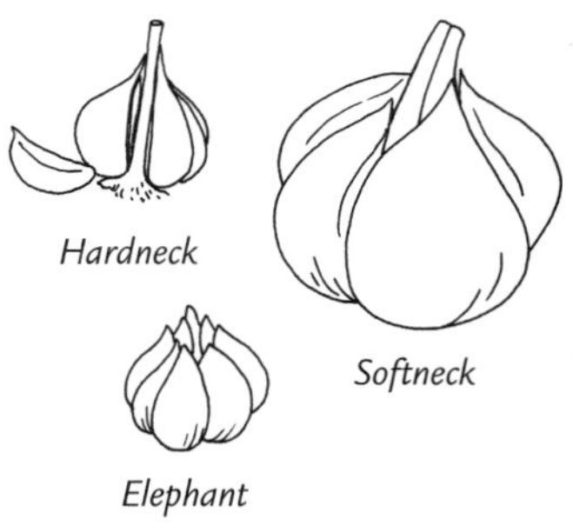

Q When's the best time to plant garlic?

A The best time to plant is in fall, about 6 weeks before the soil freezes for the winter. Depending on where you live, that could be as early as September or as late as November. The plants overwinter and are ready for harvest in midsummer the following year. Fall-planted bulbs produce a larger, better harvest than spring-planted.

Q How do I plant garlic?

A Each bulb is made up of individual cloves. Separate the cloves and plant them pointed end up. If you have more cloves than you need for planting, use the smallest ones for cooking, and plant only the biggest ones. Don't peel the papery covering off the individual cloves before planting. From Zone 7 south, plant cloves 1"–2"/2.5–5 cm deep; set them slightly deeper in the North – from 2"–4"/5–10.2 cm. Space cloves about 5"/12.7 cm apart. (Plant elephant garlic 3"/7.6 cm deep and 8"–10"/20.3–25.4 cm apart.)

Care and Harvesting Tips

Once I get my onions into the garden, what problems do I have to watch out for?

A Keep after weeds, which can quickly overtake onions. If onion maggots have been a problem in previous years, cover the plants with floating row covers until they're ready to harvest; install wire hoops to support the row covers so they won't flatten the foliage. If the bulbs push up out of the ground, cover the tops lightly with mulch to protect them from sunscald. Give plants 1"/2.5 cm of water a week.

Q My garlic has produced curving flowering stems. What do I do with them?

A Garlic doesn't produce pretty flowers like ornamental onions do, and many gardeners simply cut them off, because they take energy away from bulb formation. Don't just compost them, though. Cut them while they're still young and tender, chop them up, then mix them with olive oil. Use the mixture to flavor sauces and other foods.

Q How do I know when my onions are ready to dig?

A Begin harvesting green onions or scallions grown from sets when they're about 6"/15.2 cm tall. On full-size onions, wait until the leaves turn yellow or brown and fall over. (If some of your onions don't turn yellow and the leaves don't bend over, harvest them and use them fairly quickly, because this indicates they probably won't store well.) Once the tops are completely brown, dig or pull the onions. If you have to harvest your onion crop while some plants still have green leaves, go ahead and dig, but be aware that onions that are dug while the leaves are still green won't store well. Spread harvested onions out and let them dry in a bright spot out of direct sun. For maximum onion storage, cure the bulbs by spreading them out on screens in a well-ventilated spot until the outer skins are papery and the tops are completely brown. Then cut off the tops and store them in a cool (35–40°F/1.7–4.4°C), dry, dark spot.

A LEAFY HARVEST

Garlic produces flat leaves, unlike the round leaves borne by chives and onions. They're tasty, though — like mild garlic — and can be chopped and used like chives. Harvest only a couple of leaves from each plant, or your plants won't produce very large bulbs. Or plant a separate patch of garlic for leaf production only, and you can pick all the leaves you need. Dig up the clump in midsummer to divide and replant if it becomes too crowded. Picking foliage is an option if you missed planting your fall crop for some reason — just plant your cloves in spring and pick all the leaves you like, since the spring-planted bulbs won't enlarge much anyway without the cold treatment that overwintering in the garden supplies.

Q When should I dig garlic bulbs?

A Harvest fall-planted garlic in midsummer, when about three-quarters of the leaves have turned yellow. When digging, start at the outside of the row and dig carefully, since bulbs that are damaged by spades or digging forks won't store well. It's best to dig a plant or two and examine the bulbs. If the bulbs are still mostly solid and it's hard to separate the cloves, leave them in the ground and test another plant in a week or two. Ripe bulbs should have developed skins that separate the individual cloves, but the outer skin should still be quite firm and intact. Set aside the largest cloves from your harvest, and store them for planting the following year.

Q What's the best way to store garlic?

A All garlic needs to be cured before it can be stored. Spread freshly dug garlic plants on screens or tie them loosely in bunches and hang them. For either method, leave the roots and tops attached, and put the garlic in a warm, dark spot that has good air circulation. The bulbs should be dry in 2 or 3 weeks. After that, cut off the roots and tops, and store them in a cool (40–50°F/4.4–10°C), dry spot.

Problem Patrol

My onion bulbs split while they were still in the ground. What happened?

A Extremely dry soil can cause bulbs to split. For best growth, keep the soil evenly moist, but avoid sopping-wet soil. Ideally, the soil should be moist like a damp sponge that's been wrung out. Applying a thick layer of mulch – straw or grass clippings are fine – helps keep moisture in the soil and prevents weeds.

My plants had loads of leaves, but they have dinky little bulbs. What's going on?

A Onions appreciate doses of compost or a balanced organic fertilizer early on, but withhold extra fertilizer starting about 2 months before harvest. Otherwise, they'll keep making leaves and won't produce bulbs.

My onions went to seed, and they didn't produce bulbs. What did I do wrong?

A Onions that are exposed to cold temperatures tend to bolt (go to seed). In this case, cold means a few days below 50°F/10°C or even a couple of days below

30°F/–1.1°C. Don't be in a rush to plant if spring weather is unsettled. Onion sets that are too large also tend to bolt. When planting, sort your sets and plant the larger ones all together with the bulbs nearly touching, then harvest them as soon as they're ready to use as green onions.

Peas (*Pisum sativum*)

LEGUME FAMILY, FABACEAE

TIPS FOR SUCCESS

- Choose a site with full sun and good air circulation.
- Plant in early spring or late summer so plants can grow while the weather is cool.
- Install a trellis or other supports at planting time.

Q I want to grow peas, but I'm not sure how to get started. Are snow peas and edible pod peas the same thing as regular peas (the kind I usually buy canned or frozen)?

A Peas are great garden plants, whether you choose old-fashioned shelling types or snap peas, which you eat pod and all. Growing techniques are the same whatever type of pea you decide to grow, but the timing of harvest varies. Whatever you decide to grow, be sure to choose cultivars that offer disease resistance. Here's a rundown of types to try:

- **SHELLING PEAS.** Also called English and green peas, these have inedible pods. Harvest when the pods are full size and the peas are round and full. Pick before the pods begin to turn yellow, or the peas will be starchy and past their prime. Baby peas, or *petit pois,* are small-seeded green peas. There are cultivars developed specifically to be harvested as *petit pois*, but any pea that's picked early can be used this way.
- **SNOW PEAS.** Also called sugar or Chinese peas, these should be picked when the edible pods are large and flat, but before the peas inside them have begun to swell.
- **SNAP PEAS.** The newest crop in the pea lineup, these originated as a cross between shelling and snow peas. They bear crisp pods and sweet peas, both of which are edible. They are sweetest when the peas inside the pods are round and full.
- **DRY PEAS.** These are left in the field until the pods are brown, then are shelled, dried, and stored. They're also known as soup or field peas.

SEE ALSO: *To learn about other types of crops that are sometimes called peas, pages 187–188.*

Q **I know that peas should be planted early, but how early?**

A The standard recommendation – to plant as soon as the soil can be worked in spring – can be confusing. In general, sow seeds about 5 weeks before the last frost date for your area. They'll germinate, albeit slowly, in 40°F/4.4°C soil but may rot at lower temperatures. Seeds germinate quicker in 50–60°F/10–15.6°C soil. For extra-early planting, warm the soil by covering it with black-plastic mulch for 2 weeks before planting.

Q **What's the best way to plant peas?**

A Soak pea seeds in compost tea for 20 minutes before planting, and set seeds 1"- 2"/2.5–5 cm deep and 2"–3"/5–7.6 cm apart in a prepared garden bed or row. Space rows 3'/.9 m apart or plant two rows 6"–8"/15.2–20.3 cm apart with strings or light trellises running down the center. Don't worry about thinning, since peas don't mind crowding. Mulch plants when they are about 3"/7.6 cm tall to keep the soil cool.

Q Do peas need support?

A Peas have tendrils, which attach themselves to strings, small-gauge wire, netting, and each other. Climbing or vining peas definitely need a trellis or strings to climb on. They make efficient use of garden space and can climb to 8'/2.4 m. A narrow A-frame trellis made from 2×2s/38×38 mm and strung with twine or covered with netting works well.

Dwarf types actually benefit from some support to keep the pods up off the ground. Stick pea stakes – pieces of twiggy brush – along the row, or consider installing short trellises along the rows.

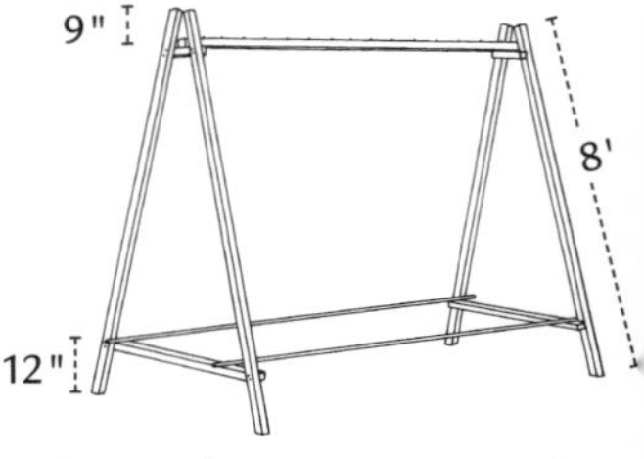

A-frame trellis to support pea netting

Q I'm growing bush-type peas and beans this year. Is there an easy way to stop the plants from flopping all over the place?

Pea brush

A One of the simplest methods is to use pea stakes, which are nothing more than short lengths of twiggy brush. Cut pieces that are perhaps 3'/.9 m long with a straight, unbranched section (about 1'/.3 m long) at the base and a branched top. Stick them in the ground along the row. The peas or beans will grow up among the branches of the brush, which keeps them upright.

Q **One spring crop of peas isn't enough! How can I keep them coming?**

A To spread out the harvest, plant new crops every 10 days as long as the plants will mature before summertime temperatures get too high. In warmer climates or for crops that mature in summer, plant heat-tolerant cultivars. Or grow both short- and long-season cultivars.

Peas are also a terrific fall crop. Plant 6 to 8 weeks before the first fall frost, although daytime temperatures may still be above 80°F/26.6°C. To help seedlings cope with the heat, plant them in some shade – ideally in the shade of a crop that will be removed around the last frost date, leaving your pea crop in full sun. Also, water regularly to cool the soil. In areas with mild winters, sow in fall for late winter to very early spring harvest. Keeping plants cool is crucial. Try planting them in the shade of pole beans, corn, or tomatoes, all cold-sensitive crops that will be finished before peas are ready to bear. Deep planting may help protect seeds from heat as well. Plant the seeds in 6"/15.2 cm-deep trenches, but cover them with only 2"/5 cm of soil. Gradually fill in the trench with more soil as the seedlings grow.

TASTY TREATS

The tendrils from vining peas are great for adding to stir-fry dishes or salads, as are the fresh young shoots. Pick tendrils from the top 8"/20.3 cm of the plant. Flowers from garden peas (*Pisum sativum*) are edible, too. Note, though, that flowers and seeds from sweet peas (*Lathyrus odoratus*) are poisonous and should never be eaten or used to garnish a dish.

Problem Patrol

Help! Something pulled up my pea plants!

A Birds will pull up pea plants to get at the seeds. Cover new plantings with bird netting to protect the seedlings.

Q My peas never germinated. What happened?

A Peas like cool temperatures and cool soil, but they don't like cold, wet soil. Make sure your soil has plenty of organic matter and is well drained. Check the soil temperature, then try again once it's a little warmer. If your soil tends to be wet, try planting peas in raised beds. Some gardeners also swear by starting seeds indoors on damp paper towels, then planting them outdoors 3 or 4 days after they've germinated.

SEE ALSO: *For more on pregermination, pages 28–29.*

Q My plants aren't producing. What's going on?

A Hot temperatures or too much rain can cause pea flowers and pods to drop. Wait until adverse weather conditions change, and plants will resume blooming. If hot summer has arrived, however, it's time to replace pea plants with crops that are more heat tolerant. If vines are dark green and healthy but aren't producing flowers or pods, it's a sign that the soil is too rich in nitrogen. Peas can fix their own, and high-nitrogen fertilizers encourage foliage, not flowers.

Peppers (*Capsicum annuum*)

NIGHTSHADE FAMILY, SOLANACEAE

TIPS FOR SUCCESS

- Wait until the soil is at least 65°F/18.3°C before transplanting peppers into the garden.
- Keep the soil evenly moist for best pepper production. For best flavor cut back slightly on watering as fruits mature.
- For the biggest crop, pick peppers before they're ripe, just as they're turning their final color, and let them ripen indoors.

I've never had good luck with peppers. What do they need to produce a really great crop?

Like many vegetables, peppers need full sun as well as warmth and good soil to grow really well. Here are the basics for keeping them happy:

- **ADD ORGANIC MATTER.** Peppers don't need extremely rich soil, and if you follow an annual soil improvement plan for your entire garden, that should be enough. If your soil isn't as rich as you would like it to be, add a generous shovelful of compost to each planting hole. Ideal pH is near neutral, or 6.7 to 7.0.

- **GIVE 'EM GOOD DRAINAGE.** Adding organic matter to your soil gives peppers the drainage they prefer. If your soil is clayey or often wet in spring, it's best to plant peppers in raised beds filled with soil that has been amended with organic matter.

- **WARM THINGS UP.** A couple of weeks before pepper-planting time, cover the soil with black- or clear-plastic mulch to prewarm it to the proper temperature for transplants.
- **WAIT 'TILL IT'S TOASTY.** Don't move peppers to the garden until the soil is at least 65°F/18.3°C. While transplants may survive cooler conditions, they will sit and do nothing and may not recover. Exposure to cool temperatures can affect growth the entire season, and transplants you move later will beat ones exposed to cold every time.

Q How long does it take to grow a crop of peppers?

A That depends on what cultivars you plant and whether you want to harvest when the fruit is green or when it's fully ripe. Sweet bell peppers begin producing green fruit that's ready for harvest in 50 to 60 days from transplanting. They'll have ripe fruit, which can be red, orange, or yellow and even purple or chocolate brown, in about 80 days from transplanting. Most other peppers have a similar timetable, but some peppers, such as 'Habanero', need as much as 100 days to produce ripe, red fruit.

Hot, Hotter, Hottest

WANT A LITTLE BITE FROM YOUR PEPPERS, but not too much? In the past, fruit shape was a pretty good indicator of heat – if a pepper was tiny, or long and thin, chances are it would be a hot pepper. Now, though, there are mild cultivars of traditionally hot peppers like jalapeños and chiles, so the best way to choose is to read descriptions carefully in catalogs or on labels. Look for rating scales like mild, hot, and very hot.

Another way to judge a pepper is by looking at its Scoville rating. Most peppers contain a compound called *capsaicin,* which is what gives them their spiciness: the more capsaicin, the hotter the pepper. Inside hot peppers, the capsaicin is concentrated in the tissues around the seeds. (Sweet bell peppers contain no capsaicin.) Chemist Wilbur Scoville developed a rating scale based on Scoville Heat Units (SHU) that grades peppers on the amount of capsaicin they contain and thus how hot they really are.

- Sweet bell rates 0 on the SHU scale.
- Chili powder rates 500–1,000 SHUs.
- Mild jalapeños range from 2,500–5,000 SHUs.
- Commercial Tabasco sauce rates 5,000–15,000 SHUs.
- 'Cayenne Long' hot peppers rate 30,000–50,000 SHUs.
- 'Habanero' and 'Scotch Bonnet' peppers both rate an astounding 100,000–500,000 SHUs.

Q **I live in southern Georgia. Is summertime the only season I can grow peppers?**

A Yes. Peppers need summer heat in order to successfully produce a crop. Gardeners in warm climates like yours – Zones 8 to 10 – can plant a second crop of peppers from late June into July for harvest in the fall. Gardeners in most regions can plant pepper transplants out in the garden up to 3 months before the first fall frost.

Q **What's the best way to start the seeds?**

A For best results, start pepper seeds indoors 8 to 10 weeks before the last spring frost date. Sow three to four seeds per pot, and give them bottom heat from a heat mat or other source. Once seeds germinate, keep them in bright light in a warm spot (70°F/21.1°C, 65°F/18.3°C at night). Thin seedlings when they have about two sets of true leaves by cutting off all but the strongest seedling in each pot.

Q **Okay, I gave my peppers everything – good soil, warm temperatures – and they just didn't produce last year or even grow much. Any ideas?**

A Pepper plants are more subject to transplant shock than many other vegetables, and a little mishandling can compromise your entire season's harvest. Keep the following points in mind.

- **CONSIDER USING PEAT POTS** to minimize shocks to the root systems. Be sure to pull off the top portion of the pot when transplanting, because if it sticks out above the soil, it will wick away water.
- **WATER TRANSPLANTS** with lukewarm water.
- **BEGIN HARDENING OFF SEEDLINGS** a week before transplant time.
- **BE SURE TO PINCH OFF** any small fruits that form before transplanting.
- **TRANSPLANT TO THE GARDEN** 2 to 3 weeks after the last spring frost date once temperatures are consistently warm, spacing the plants 14"–16"/35.6–40.6 cm apart. If possible, transplant on a cloudy or rainy day.
- **PROTECT TRANSPLANTS** in sunny weather with an upturned bushel basket or other cover for the first four days outside.
- **WATER** them in with compost tea.

Care and Havesting Tips

We're going to have a cold snap tonight! How can I protect my pepper plant?

Peppers don't tolerate chilly temperatures, during the daytime or at night. Whenever cool weather threatens, protect plants with cloches, row covers, or hot caps. If you're using cages to stake your plants, you can wrap them in plastic or sections of row covers. Whatever type of protection you're using, leave it in place until the weather stabilizes and is consistently warm.

SEE ALSO: *For more on protective devices, including some you can make yourself, page 55.*

Do peppers need staking?

Pepper plants do benefit from staking, especially once they're weighted down with ripening fruit. While you can use conventional stakes (4'/1.2 m tall) next to each plant, small-size tomato cages offer an especially easy way to cage plants. Whether you use stakes or cages, install support systems when you move transplants to the garden to minimize disturbance to the roots after they've become established.

Staking peppers

How about food and water? Should I feed peppers?

For the biggest crops, sidedress peppers with a balanced organic fertilizer once when the plants begin to flower and again 3 weeks later. After that, they should be fine with the compost you added at planting time. Peppers require evenly moist soil to produce fruit, so water regularly throughout the summer to keep the soil from drying out.

How do I tell when peppers are ready to harvest?

Peppers can be harvested when they're green or left on the plant to ripen and turn color. Pick sweet bell peppers as soon as they're large enough to use, or wait until about two-thirds of the fruit has turned its final color. Hot peppers don't develop their fire until they have fully turned color, although you can harvest them for milder heat as soon as they're large enough to use.

With peppers, the more you pick, the more your plants will produce, so harvesting early and often is the best course of action.

Q What's the best way to pick them?

A Since pepper stems are brittle, it's easy to break off branches or otherwise damage the plants if you try to pull off the fruits at harvest time. Instead, use scissors or garden shears to cut cleanly through the stem near the top of the fruit.

Q Ouch! I didn't wear gloves! What can I do to stop the burning after I cut up hot peppers?

A If you've ever cut up hot peppers, you've no doubt discovered one important-to-remember fact about capsaicin: It isn't easy to wash off. Here are some home remedies to keep in mind if you forget and cut hot peppers without protection.

- **WASH THE AREA** with milk.
- **TRY WASHING** with automotive waterless hand cleaner, vegetable oil, or tomato juice.
- **DIP HANDS IN RUBBING ALCOHOL,** then coat them with an ointment like Bag Balm.
- **SOME GARDENERS RECOMMEND** using evaporated milk, full strength, for washing or drinking to cool internal burns.

- **COAT BURNING HANDS** with yogurt.
- **WASH HANDS THOROUGHLY** with dish soap, dry them, and then rinse with lemon juice.
- **SOAK HANDS** in ice water.

Q What precautions should I take when cutting hot peppers?

A To protect your hands, wear gloves when cutting up peppers – surgical gloves provide good protection, as do rubber gloves. Never touch your face, and especially your eyes, when cutting up hot peppers. Also, remember that the juice (and thus the capsaicin that causes irritation) will end up on the rubber gloves, the knife, and the cutting board. If you do get hot pepper juice in your eyes, call your doctor or local poison-control center. For mild exposure try running water into your eyes for several minutes, and then douse them with a moisturizing tears product.

Q **We're expecting an early cold snap. Is there anything I can do to protect my crop? I'm not ready to harvest them just yet.**

A If temperatures are going to dip below 55°F/12.8°C, protect your crop with a double layer of row covers. Ideally, drape one layer directly on the plants and suspend the other over hoops. If temperatures are going to drop much below 50°F/10°C, harvest the entire crop.

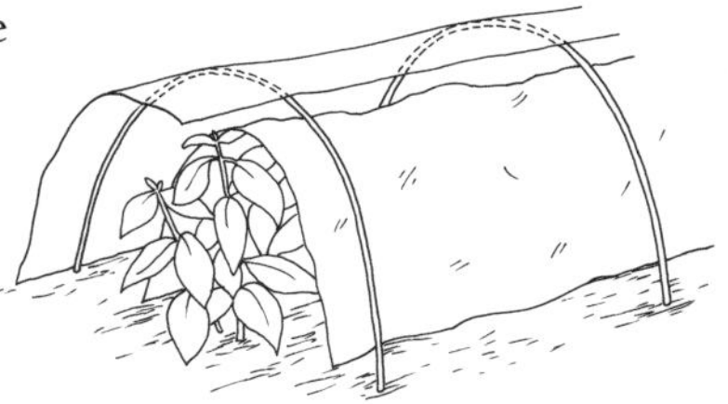

Double row cover protector

Problem Patrol

Q **It's summertime, and my garden is located outside Atlanta, Georgia. My peppers are blooming, but they don't seem to be producing any fruit. What's wrong? Do I need bees to get fruit?**

A Peppers are self-pollinating, so you don't need to worry about whether or not bees have been visiting your plants. They do stop bearing fruit during the summertime when daytime temperatures exceed 85–90°F/29.4–32.2°C. (Temperatures under 60°F/15.6°C can cause the same problem.) This is especially an issue with larger-fruited cultivars; some smaller-fruited peppers bear right through bouts of torrid weather. Keep your plants well watered, and wait a few weeks. You'll undoubtedly see fruit forming once slightly cooler weather arrives.

Q The fruits on my pepper plants have sunken patches on their upper shoulders that aren't as brightly colored as the rest of the fruit. I don't see any bugs, though. What could be the problem?

A Sunscald causes this kind of damage on peppers, and it's especially problematic during very hot summer weather. In warm-climate gardens, locate midsummer pepper crops where they'll be shaded somewhat by taller nearby crops. A spot that receives afternoon shade is ideal. Also, take steps to control leaf diseases and keep plants fed and watered, since a thick canopy of foliage protects fruit from sunscald.

Potatoes (*Solanum tuberosum*)

NIGHTSHADE FAMILY, SOLANACEAE

TIPS FOR SUCCESS

- Plant in full sun and well-drained soil.
- Mulch plants to control weeds and to keep the soil moist and relatively cool.
- Harvest new potatoes when flowers appear on the plants; dig the main crop about 2 weeks after the tops die back.

Q What do I need to know to choose the best kind of potatoes to grow in my garden?

A While grocery stores and garden centers may offer a few types of potatoes for planting in spring, you'll find a wider variety if you order by mail or over the Internet. Ordinary white potatoes, sometimes called Irish potatoes, are good all-purpose spuds for adding to soups or for making potato salad. They have a medium starch content, while russet potatoes have a higher starch content and are better for baking or mashing. Red potatoes generally have red skins and white flesh and also are good for all-around use. If you'd like to try growing something unusual, look for gold-fleshed cultivars such as 'Yukon Gold', as well as spuds with red flesh and purple flesh. Fingerling potatoes are small and relatively thin, and feature thin skin, a waxy texture, and great taste.

Cultivars are generally divided according to the length of the growing season, so you'll see the designations "early," "midseason," and "late" in descriptions. Early cultivars are ready for harvest about 65 days after planting. They're not good for storing and are at their best if eaten fairly quickly after harvest. Midseason cultivars are ready to dig from about 80 days onward, while late-season potatoes take 90 days or more. Both mid- and late-season potatoes tend to be better candidates for storage. Also look for disease resistance when picking out spuds for your garden, and always purchase certified disease-free seed potatoes.

Q Do I start my potato crop from seed?

A To grow potatoes, you'll start by planting small potato tubers or pieces of tuber referred to as "seed potatoes." Many mail-order suppliers cut seed potatoes into the proper size for planting. If you get larger tubers for planting, cut them into pieces the day before planting so the cut surfaces have time to dry before being put in contact with the soil. Each piece of tuber should have at least two buds, or eyes, and in general, the pieces should be about

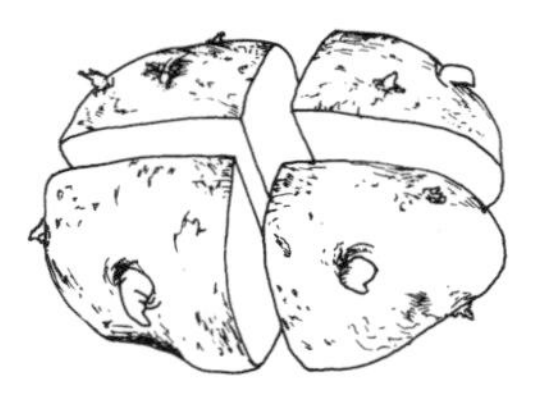

Cutting a seed potato

1½–2 ounces/44.4–59.2 ml, or about 1"–1¼"/2.5–3.2 cm in diameter. Plant very small seed potatoes (under 1½ ounces/42.5 gm) whole. Always start with certified disease-free seed potatoes, since a number of diseases are spread by infected tubers.

Q **Can't I just buy the regular potatoes that are sold in the grocery store and cut those up?**

A Most potatoes sold in grocery stores have been treated to prevent sprouting, making them worthless for cutting up and planting in the garden. In addition they may carry disease organisms in the tuber that could ruin your crop. In the spring, some stores carry seed potatoes especially for planting, however, and these are fine for using in your garden.

My seed-potato order arrived, but I can't plant them yet. What should I do?

A Healthy seed potatoes are fleshy, and it's important to store them properly. Keep them in the refrigerator or a cool (40–50°F/4.4–10°C) dark spot until you are ready to plant.

TUBER TUTORIAL

Although tubers form below the surface of the soil, they're actually modified plant stems, not roots. When seed potatoes sprout, they send conventional stems up toward the soil surface. Above ground, these stems produce green foliage. Roots branch off the stems and head downward into the soil. Long underground shoots, called *stolons*, also branch off from the stems and stretch out horizontally through the soil. The stolons may extend 1'/.3 m or more away from the stem. Tubers form on these stolons. Hilling or mulching potatoes expands the potential area through which stolons can spread and thus creates the potential for more and larger tubers to form.

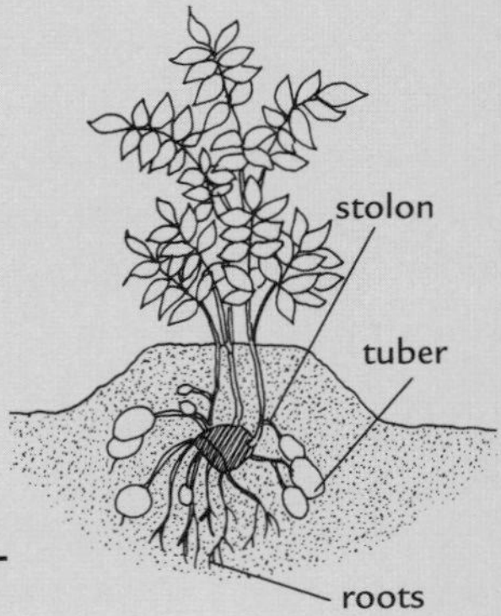

Q **How early can potatoes go into the ground?**

A Plant seed potatoes 2 to 4 weeks before the last spring frost date. Wait to plant if the soil is too wet to work or is cooler than 40°F/4.4°C. Otherwise, the potatoes tend to rot rather than grow. Don't worry too much if frost threatens after you plant: Even though aboveground shoots are killed by light frost, new sprouts will emerge in about 2 weeks. Continue planting new crops every few weeks until about 3 months before the first fall frost.

Q **I live in Alabama. Can I still grow potatoes? I understand they don't like hot weather, and we certainly have plenty of that!**

A Since potatoes don't appreciate hot weather (temperatures over 90°F/32.2°C), plan on spring and fall potato crops. In Zones 7 and 8 get them out early in spring – from February into March – so the plants can mature in cool spring weather. You also probably have time to grow an early-season cultivar if you plant outside in April. Plant another crop in fall toward the end of September, and plan on harvesting your potatoes in December or January. In Zone 9 along the Gulf Coast, plant in fall for harvest the following spring. In the Southwest, plant anytime from late fall to winter for harvest in early spring.

Q How about adding manure to make the soil really rich?

A Overfeeding potatoes can lead to cultural problems such as hollow heart, which causes tubers to have a hollow cavity in the center. Using manure in the soil isn't a good idea, since too much manure can lead to a disease called potato scab. Instead, depend on compost or a balanced organic fertilizer product, or grow and dig in a cover crop that adds nitrogen to the soil, such as alsike clover, Austrian winter peas, berseem clover, cowpeas, or clover.

Q On a seed potato, which end is up?

A Plant seed potatoes with the cut side down. The eyes should point up, since they produce the stems that grow toward the soil surface.

Q So, do I bury my seed potatoes? If so, how deep?

A After amending the soil and loosening it to a depth of 1'/.3 m, plant seed potatoes 2"–3"/5–7.6 cm deep. Space them about 1'/.3 m apart or grow them in wide rows with plants spaced 1½'/.45 m on all sides.

Leave 3'/.9 m between rows or beds. Cover the seed potatoes by pulling a couple of inches of loose soil over the top of them with a hoe. You'll see sprouts in 2 to 3 weeks; sooner in warmer weather. When the plants are 6"–8"/15.2–20.3 cm tall, cover them again with loose mulch or soil. You can use compost, compost and soil, straw, leaves, or any combination thereof. Don't cover the foliage at the top of each plant, so it has access to light and can make food. Continue hilling up more mulch or soil as the plants grow until the hills are at least a foot tall. The objective is to encourage the plants to produce long stems and thus more stolons and more potatoes. It's also important to keep the developing potatoes covered so they are not exposed to sunlight.

Care and Harvesting Tips

Q What about watering? Do I need to worry about it?

A Potatoes are mostly water, and if the soil is too dry, they won't develop properly. Keep the soil evenly moist from the time the foliage is fully developed until it begins to turn yellow. After that, the tubers have formed and may rot if the soil stays too wet.

Prepare for Potato Beetles

COLORADO POTATO BEETLES ARE A MAJOR PEST of potatoes, and unfortunately, they don't limit themselves to living in Colorado — these pesky beetles range throughout most of the United States and Canada. Cover plants with floating row covers to hold them — as well as other pests like aphids and leafhoppers — at bay. The covers should be loose, so the plants have room to grow, but be sure to pile soil or place boards all along the edges to prevent bothersome pests from crawling in under them. (Be sure to check under the row covers early on to make sure no beetles happened to emerge right where you planted your potatoes. Otherwise, they'll go to town!) Another way to keep damage to a minimum is to time plantings. The beetles are most active in summer, so growing a quick early spring crop and a second crop from late summer into fall helps avoid serious damage.

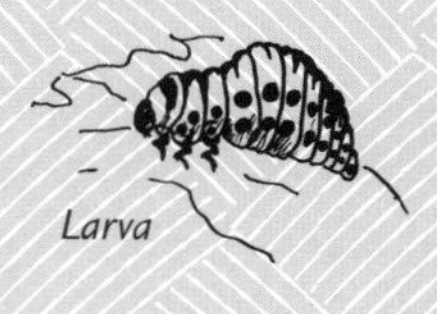

Larva

Colorado potato beetle

Q **I have potatoes growing right on top of the soil! They've developed a greenish color. Is that okay?**

A Potatoes that are exposed to sunlight form an excess of a compound called *solanine,* which is poisonous and makes the tubers taste bitter. Block sunlight by hilling the base of the plants well with mulch, straw, soil, or other organic matter. This not only prevents the formation of solanine, it also encourages the main stem of the plants to elongate and encourages more side shoots, and thus potatoes, to form.

Q **Are new potatoes a special kind of potato? When do I harvest them?**

A New potatoes are young tubers harvested early from any kind of spud you grow. Begin looking for new potatoes as soon as the plants begin to flower. Harvest by gently brushing away the hill of mulch and soil from around the plants and picking tubers that are large enough to use. Or you can dig an entire plant.

Q When do I harvest mature potatoes?

A Watch the plants: When the foliage begins to turn yellow, the tubers are full size, and you can dig them. Dig all the tubers if they mature when the weather is warm or rainy. Fall crops can be left in the ground until just before the first frost.

My potato plants aren't turning yellow, but I want to dig them soon. What should I do?

A If you need to dig your spuds to fit in another crop, or because the end of the season is near but they don't seem to know it, cut the tops off, then wait about 2 weeks before digging. The delay helps the tubers harden, which prolongs storage.

Q Is there a best way to dig potatoes?

A Use a spading fork, and lift the plants by digging along the edge of the row. Try to avoid damaging any of the tubers, but if you do nick some of them, use them right away, since they won't store well. To store undamaged tubers, brush off the loose soil but do not wash them, and spread them in a dark place at about 40°F/4.4°C. Potatoes can be stored for several weeks at that temperature, but if you don't have a spot that cool, they'll keep at room temperature for a couple of weeks. Don't store them in the refrigerator, because cooler temperatures cause starches in the tubers to turn to sugar, resulting in a sweeter taste.

Squash and Pumpkins (*Cucurbita* spp.)

SQUASH FAMILY, CUCURBITACEAE

TIPS FOR SUCCESS

- Use row covers to control insect pests, but remove the covers when plants begin to flower to ensure pollination.
- Don't rush to plant squash: Wait until the soil is at least 60°F/15.6°C. Use black plastic mulch to warm the soil and speed up plant growth.
- Harvest zucchini and summer squash, every 2 or 3 days, when the fruits are about 6"/15.2 cm long for best flavor and tenderness.

Q **What's the difference between the squash and zucchini you can pick in the summer and the kind of squash that isn't ready until fall?**

A Squash that are harvested during the summertime – including yellow squash, green-skinned zucchini, and patty-pan types, which look something like miniature flying saucers – are collectively referred to as summer squash. They're all grown the same way and are harvested when the fruit is small and still has a thin, tender skin. They're eaten raw or cooked and have a mild flavor. Winter squash come in a wide range of sizes, shapes, and colors, including small, 2-pound/.9- kg ribbed acorn squashes, large pear-shaped butternuts, and huge 12–15-pound/5.4–6.8-kg Hubbards with bumpy, gray-green skins. Pumpkins are winter squashes as well. Just as with summer squash, the winter types are all grown the same way but are always cooked before they're eaten. Flavor var-

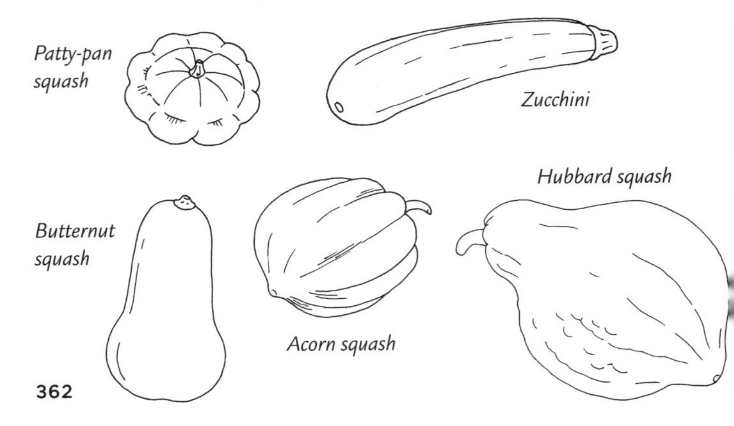

ies, and winter squashes are usually described as sweet or very sweet and nutty tasting, although some are simply used ornamentally for fall displays. They are harvested when the squash is mature and the skins hard, although some cultivars also can be picked when still immature and used as summer squash.

Q Are pumpkins a type of squash?

A Yes, pumpkins are a type of winter squash and are grown the same way. Some types of pumpkins are best suited for carving because they have thinner walls and a more uniform surface. Others have thick walls and sweet flesh for baking. Still others serve well for both purposes.

Squash and pumpkin plants are typically large vines that can cover a good deal of ground, but breeders have developed more compact cultivars for smaller modern-day gardens. Today, most gardeners grow bush-type cultivars for their summer squash crop, because the plants are extremely productive and a couple of plants produce all a family can eat. You'll still find that most winter squash is produced on full-size vines, but today there also are bush-type cultivars available as well. In addition, there are two other sizes that fall between vine- and bush-type plants: semibush and semivining. Select the size that matches your available garden space most effectively.

A Pumpkin Primer

I want to bake pumpkin pies. What kind of pumpkin should I plant?

A For best results, start with a cultivar developed for cooking, not carving. Most baking-type pumpkins belong to *C. moschata*. They have thick, sweet-tasting, finely grained flesh and weigh from 5–10 pounds/2.3–4.5 kg. Read catalog descriptions and look for cultivars that describe the taste, color, and thickness of the flesh. 'New England Pie' is a classic pie pumpkin, but there are many others, including heritage cultivars.

What about pumpkins for carving?

A Jack-o'-lantern, or carving-type, pumpkins have been developed primarily for their symmetrical shape and their thinner – and thus easier-to-carve – flesh. Carving pumpkins look like baking types but actually usually belong to a different species, *C. pepo.* Keep in mind that while they are completely edible, in most cases you'll bake better pies from cultivars developed specifically for the taste and texture of their flesh.

Q **I want to grow minipumpkins. How much space will they need?**

A Most minipumpkins are produced on full-size vines, so they need just as much space as any other kind of pumpkins. If you want something more compact, read cultivar descriptions, looking for the term "semi-bush" ('Wee-B-Little' is an example).

Q **My family loves pumpkin seeds. Can we eat seeds from any kind of squash?**

A Yes, squash and pumpkin seeds are edible. To prepare them, first clean the stringy flesh off the seeds (do this manually, and don't wash them, because it destroys the flavor). To roast them, preheat your oven to 300°F/149°C. Spread them out on a baking pan, drizzle them with olive oil, and sprinkle them with salt. Toast for about 30 minutes, stirring periodically. Take them out when they turn light brown. Or first boil the seeds for about 10 minutes in lightly salted water, then spread a couple of tablespoons of olive oil in a baking pan and toast them until they are lightly browned – about 20 minutes – at 300°F/149°C. You can eat the seeds whole, hull and all, or crack them to remove the inside. Better yet, try growing a hull-less, also called naked-seeded, pumpkin, which produces pumpkin seeds that have paperlike hulls.

Growing "The Great Pumpkin"

START BY CHOOSING A CULTIVAR known for producing giants. 'Atlantic Giant' and other really whopping-big pumpkins are actually neither jack-o'-lantern nor pie pumpkins; they belong to *Cucurbita maxima.* Once you've picked out which cultivar you're going to grow, here's what you need to do to grow a giant:

- **START SEEDS INDOORS.** Growing transplants gives your pumpkins an extra head start. Thin to one plant per pot.
- **PREPARE A RICH GARDEN SPOT.** Give each plant a 5'x10'/1.5x3 m bed (about 50 square feet/4.7 sq m) and work 5 bushels (40 gal/176 L) of organic matter into the soil; a mix of compost and well-rotted manure is ideal.
- **BABY TRANSPLANTS.** Transplant once the weather has settled, and use row covers to minimize stress.
- **HAND-POLLINATE FOR EARLIEST FRUIT SET.** Pick a male blossom and move its pollen to a female flower, which will have a tiny, preformed pumpkin at the base of the flower.
- **KEEP PLANTS FED AND WATERED.** Feed plants every 2 weeks with high-nitrogen fertilizer, and water regularly.
- **THIN TO ONE FRUIT PER PLANT.** Once fruit has set, remove all but one pumpkin so that all of the plant's energy is directed into producing a giant. Also, remove any other flowers that form.

Planting Tips

Q How should I prepare the soil for my squash patch?

A Both squash and pumpkins grow well in ordinary garden soil. Follow your annual care schedule for adding organic matter, and they'll be satisfied. If you are growing them in an area outside the vegetable garden because of their large size, incorporate plenty of organic matter 2 or 3 weeks before planting – well-rotted manure and/or compost are ideal. The roots travel fairly far in search of moisture and nutrients, so incorporate organic matter and loosen the soil over a wide area.

Q Can I just plant pumpkin and squash seeds outside, or do I need to start them indoors?

A Pumpkins and squash can be planted directly outside beginning about 2 weeks after the last spring frost date. If you want an extra-early start or live in an area with a fairly short growing season, sow seeds indoors a week before the last spring frost date. It's important not to start too soon, because the seedlings grow quickly, and smaller plants are best for transplanting. Sow seeds in individual 3"–4"/7.6–10.2 cm pots a week before the last spring frost date, and you'll have transplants ready to move to the garden 2 weeks after the last frost. Be sure to harden off seedlings beginning a week before they're scheduled to be planted outdoors. Ideally, you want to transplant no more than a few days after the first true leaf appears. If your seedlings get to this point, and you can't transplant because the weather is still too cool, move seedlings to larger pots so their growth won't be checked.

Are there any special planting techniques that ensure successful outdoor sowing?

Try these tricks for a top-notch crop of squash:

1. Prepare planting hills before you're ready to sow; you can build them several weeks before the last spring frost if you have the time.
2. Wait to plant seeds until the soil temperature is at least 60°F/15.6°C, because pumpkin and squash seeds won't germinate in cool soil.
3. Soak seeds in compost tea for about 15 minutes before you sow – studies have shown that this improves germination – and water the hills before sowing if the weather has been dry.
4. Plant the seeds 1"/2.5 cm deep, then mulch the soil with grass clippings or chopped leaves to keep it from crusting.

Q Is there any advantage to planting more than one crop of winter squash?

A Yes. Starting more than one crop of winter, as well as summer, squash buys you some insurance against pests and diseases. If you plant more than one crop, or transplant and direct-sow on the same day, one group of plants may miss the main flush of cucumber beetles or other pests for the year.

Q How much space do I need to grow pumpkin and squash vines?

A Spacing isn't an exact science with squash, especially since the vines can travel 15'/4.6 m and even bush-type squash plants can spread to 5'/1.5 m. Fortunately, the plants mix together quite happily in the garden provided they have rich soil to sink their roots into. For vining types especially, look for a spot where you can give them a bed of prepared soil for planting alongside plenty of room to let the vines wander widely.

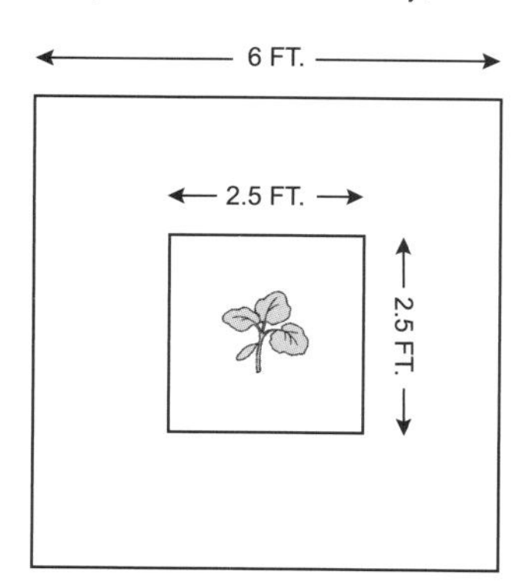

Does growing squash and pumpkin plants in hills change their spacing requirements?

A You'll need to adjust the spacing according to the size of the plants you're growing. Space the hills for vining types from 3'/.9 m to as much as 8'/2.4 m apart. Space hills for bushy cultivars 2'–4'/.6–1.2 m apart. (While they don't reach quite the size vining types do, they still are not small plants.) Space semivining squash slightly closer, from 3'–4'/.9–1.2 m apart. Don't be tempted to crowd your plants, because crowded squash and pumpkins are more subject to diseases, especially in areas with humid, rainy summers.

Q **I live on the edge of a suburban area near Columbus, Ohio, and I don't have room for pumpkins in my main vegetable garden. Can I grow them somewhere else?**

A Build planting hills on the edge of your property, then just let them ramble. Squash and pumpkins also are very happy growing on top of a finished compost pile. Plant a few seeds in the top, and they'll give it a decorative cover of rich green throughout the summer, plus a bumper crop!

Both pumpkins and squash can be trained to grow up a sturdy fence or trellis. Choose mini- or at least small-fruited pumpkins, as well as small winter squash, such as acorn types. Be sure you have a sturdy fence, with steel or well-set wooden posts. An A-frame trellis is another good option. Be sure to locate trellises so they will not shade the rest of your garden. You'll need to support each fruit with a sling made of old pantyhose, T-shirt fabric, or other stretchy material. Tie slings to the trellis to keep the fruit from weighing down the vines, and check the slings periodically to make sure they don't get too tight.

SEE ALSO: *For an illustration of supports for trellis-grown crops, page 302.*

Care and Harvesting Tips

Q **Do seedlings and transplants need special care?**

A Both squash and pumpkins are easy to establish. It's a good idea to water the soil before sowing or transplanting, but mainly they require row covers to keep cucumber beetles and squash bugs at bay. Have covers ready and waiting to cover seedlings as soon as they sprout or transplants as soon as you move them to the garden.

(Row covers also hold in some heat and provide a bit of protection for transplants from cool, breezy weather.) Tuck in the edges of the row covers all around with soil to be sure insects can't get through, but leave enough slack to allow for growth. You'll need to pull back covers to thin the seedlings if you have direct-sown your crop. In addition, since bees and other insects are required for pollination, you'll need to remove row covers once the plants begin flowering.

ROOT INSURANCE

As winter squash and pumpkins spread, cover the vines with moist soil at the leaf nodes — the point where a leaf stem joins the main stem of the vine. This encourages additional roots to form at the nodes, which help support the ripening fruit. It also helps plants survive even when they're invaded by squash-vine borers: The borers disrupt the flow of water and nutrients from the central root system, but the new roots can continue to supply the foliage and ripening fruit.

Q Do I really have to thin my squash plants? All of the seedlings look so healthy!

A Yes, thinning is necessary to raise a healthy crop, whether you have sown seeds indoors or out. Thin your pumpkin and squash plants to two plants per hill once they have at least one true leaf. Thin pot-grown plants to one plant per pot at the same time.

Q Do plants need feeding beyond the initial soil prep?

A With good soil prep, squash and pumpkin plants grow fine with minimal feeding. You can sidedress the plants with compost or well-rotted manure (for winter squash and pumpkins only) at the time that the first fruit sets. Or douse plants every other week with compost tea. Keep the soil evenly moist but not soggy or wet. Squash and pumpkins need from 1"–2"/2.5–5 cm of water a week, especially once they begin flowering and setting fruit.

Q My zucchini are as big as baseball bats! When should I pick them?

Early and often is the best motto for harvesting summer squash. While zucchini and yellow summer squash will grow to humongous proportions, they are best picked when small, about 6"/15.2 cm long. The outer skin should be glossy and tender; you should be able to cut into it easily with a fingernail. Harvest patty-pan-type squash when it is about 4"/10.2 cm in diameter. Pick summer squash every 2 or 3 days; wait much more than that, and you'll have a few baseball bats waiting for you among the garden rows. (Large summer squash become woody, and less tasty – another reason to harvest early.) Frequent harvest also keeps plants producing. To increase storage life, leave a 1"–2"/2.5–5 cm-long stem on each fruit when you cut it from the plants.

Q **Last summer, I picked what seemed like a bushel of zucchini and summer squash every other day. What can I do this year to spread out the summer-squash crop?**

A For one thing, start with fewer plants: Two plants per family member will produce a big crop. To spread out the harvest, start half your crop from transplants and then direct-sow seed for the rest of the crop on the same day you move transplants to the garden. (Gardeners from Zone 7 south have time to plant several crops.)

Q How can I tell when winter squash is ready?

A Wait until the fruit is fully colored, whether that means orange, blue-gray, white, or another hue. You can also look at the stem, which begins to shrivel and turns hard when the fruit is ripe. Yet another clue is the rind: It should be hard enough that you can't dent or puncture it with a fingernail. If in doubt, leave winter squash and pumpkins to ripen for another week or so, since the fruit isn't harmed by leaving it in the garden. Do bring in winter squash if a hard frost is predicted: Although the fruits won't be completely ruined by a freeze, they won't store well, and you'll need to use them right away. Cut winter squash from the vines, and leave at least a 2"/5 cm-long stem attached to each fruit.

Q I want to store my winter squash. Is there special treatment that will make them last longer?

A If you want to store pumpkins or winter squash for more than 3 or 4 weeks, cure them before putting them away. If the weather is still quite warm and humid, just cut them from the vines and leave them in the garden for 10 days. Otherwise, set them in a warm (85°F/29.4°C), humid spot for 10 days. A spot next to the furnace in the basement works fine, or an enclosed sun porch may heat up enough late in the season to provide a warm spot for them. Don't wash fruit you plan to store, but to control mold that may mar the surface, wipe them with a solution of one part bleach to ten parts water. Store cured fruit in a cool (50°F/10°C), well-ventilated spot.

Problem Patrol

I don't see any fruit forming. What do I do now?

A Pumpkins and squash begin producing male flowers a week or so before they produce the first female flowers. Be patient, and look for female flowers, which have small, preformed fruit located just beneath the flower petals. If you have female flowers but no fruit that has begun to grow, check for pollinators, since pollination requires that bees or other insects transfer pollen from male flowers to female ones. You can hand-pollinate flowers by picking a male flower, carefully removing the petals, and transferring pollen to the female flower.

Q **My plants wilt every afternoon, even though they're well watered. What's the problem?**

A The larvae of squash vine borers tunnel through the stems, eventually causing plants to wilt, at first in the afternoon during the heat of the day, but eventually, permanently. Look for a small hole and sawdustlike excrement at the base of the stem. If you don't see a hole, cut into one of the wilted vines. If it's full of milky, gummy sap, then the problem is bacterial wilt, and there is no cure. Pull up the plants and dispose of them in the garbage, not onto the compost pile. Cucumber beetles transmit bacterial wilt, so concentrate on controlling them.

SEE ALSO: *For squash-vine borer control, and for more information on bacterial wilt, pages 158–159.*

Q **The flowers and little squashes in my garden are covered with ugly gray bugs. What should I do?**

A Squash bugs have found your vines, and it can be hard to get rid of them. Try spraying them with insecticidal soap.

SEE ALSO: *For more control measures and to learn how to prevent squash bugs from invading next year's crop, pages 148–149.*

My pumpkins look lopsided. How do you grow nicely shaped ones?

Gently turn pumpkins occasionally to encourage them to grow symmetrically.

My squash is rotted on the bottom! What should I have done to prevent this?

A Once fruit begins to set, slide a board under each fruit to keep it up off the ground and dry on the bottom.

Sweet Potatoes (*Ipomoea batatas*)

MORNING GLORY FAMILY, CONVOLVULACEAE

TIPS FOR SUCCESS

- Give plants full sun in cooler climates but a spot in light afternoon shade in hot climates.
- Wait until the soil has warmed to at least 55°F/12.8°C before planting sweet potatoes; 65°F/18.3°C or warmer is ideal.
- Cut back the tops at harvest time, and begin digging 1'/.3 m away from the crowns to avoid damaging the tubers.

Q How do I start sweet potatoes? Do I plant seeds indoors?

A Although you'll start your sweet potato crop indoors, you won't be sowing seeds. Sweet potatoes are started from slips, which are rooted shoots, not seed. You can buy slips of various cultivars from mail-order suppliers or buy them from a local nursery.

Q Can I start my own sweet potato slips?

A If you have a sweet potato that overwintered from your garden or a neighbor's garden, it's easy to start your own slips. (Don't try starting them from grocery-store sweet potatoes.) Plan on starting 3 months before the last spring frost date. Use toothpicks to support sweet potato in a jar that's half full of water, so that only the bottom third is submerged. Set the jar in a warm (75°F/23.9°C), sunny spot, and you'll see sprouts forming in a couple of weeks. When the sprouts are 6"/15.2 cm long, gently pull them off, and stick them in damp sand to root. Harden off the slips as you would any transplant before moving them to the garden.

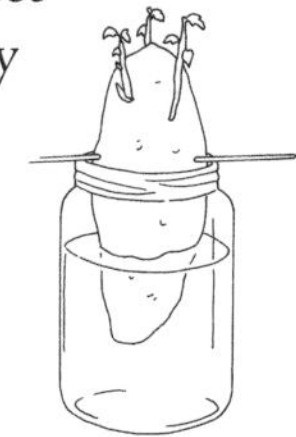

Starting sweet potato slips

SEE ALSO: *For advice on how to harden off, page 54.*

Q I'm a southerner, and I remember sweet potatoes from my father's garden. I'm currently living outside Lincoln, Nebraska (Zone 5). Can I grow them?

A Sweet potatoes need a long, hot growing season to produce well, and they can be tough to grow north of USDA Zone 6. Most need over 100 days of hot weather to produce well. If you want to try them, prewarm the soil with black- or clear-plastic mulch, and start with short-season cultivars like 'Georgia Jet' or 'Beauregard'. Leave plastic in place when you plant, and make slits through it to insert the plants.

I live in Springfield, Missouri (Zone 6). When do I move my sweet potato slips to the garden?

A Sweet potatoes are warm-weather plants, so don't be in a hurry to plant them outside. Two weeks before the last frost date, loosen the soil to 10"–12"/25.4–30.5 cm, and work in some finished compost. Then cover the site with black or clear plastic to prewarm it. Transplant slips to the garden 2 weeks after the last frost date, once the soil temperature is at least 55°F/12.8°C; 65°F/18.3°C is even better.

Q I seem to remember that my grandfather grew his sweet potatoes in mounds or hills. Is my memory accurate?

A Yes. Hilling or mounding up the soil along the row provides perfect conditions for growing sweet potatoes, since the soil warms up more quickly and also is well drained. The hills don't need to be enormous – 1'/.3 m wide and about 8"/20.3 cm tall is fine. Space the rows of hilled soil about 3'/.9 m apart. Plant the sets from 1'-1½'/.3-.45 m apart.

Care and Harvesting Tips

What care do sweet potatoes need during the summer?

A Once temperatures are settled consistently in the 70s/21.1-26.1°C, sweet potatoes grow happily with little care. Keep them weeded, but don't worry much about watering or feeding, since they are fairly drought tolerant and need water only in very dry weather.

Q **How do I tell when they're ready to harvest?**

A You can begin digging sweet potatoes as soon as they are large enough to use. For best flavor, though, wait until daytime temperatures dip into the 50s/10–15°C (for sweet potatoes, this qualifies as "freezing" weather). Carefully dig tubers with a fork. Use any that are damaged by digging immediately, since they will not store well. Harvest immediately if you see any leaf blackening, and don't wait until frost kills the vines, since cool soil (in the 40s/4.4–9.4°C overnight) damages the quality of the tubers.

Q **When I dug up my sweet potatoes, I found roots everywhere along the vines, but not many tubers. What happened?**

A The sweet potatoes you harvest are actually a type of fleshy root, and they form only on the main roots of the plants. But if given a chance, sweet potato plants also sprout small feeder roots from the leaf nodes all along the vines. For the best crop, it's important to discourage the production of these small feeder roots, since they won't produce any potatoes. To do this, periodically lift up the vines and carefully cultivate the soil under them throughout the season.

Q Can I just pack sweet potatoes away next to my regular potatoes for storage?

A Sweet potatoes need warmer storage conditions than potatoes: Store them in a cool (55°F/12.8°C), dry place. Before storing them, cure sweet potatoes by spreading them out in a warm (80°F/26.7°C), sunny spot for a day, then hold them in a warm, humid spot out of direct sunlight for an additional 2 weeks.

Tomatoes (*Lycopersicon esculentum*)

NIGHTSHADE FAMILY, SOLANACEAE

TIPS FOR SUCCESS

- Provide warmth for early planted tomatoes by prewarming the soil with black plastic as well as wrapping cages in clear plastic or using cloches.
- Plant cultivars that resist or tolerate disease.
- Decide on a caging or trellising system in advance, and install it on the day you plant.

I have space for only four tomato plants. How do I figure out which ones are best to grow?

For starters, there are three major types of tomato fruit, and even if you are growing only a few plants,

you'll probably want to grow at least one of each. It's a good idea to ask friends and neighbors as well as your local Cooperative Extension Service for suggestions on favorite cultivars that grow well in your climate. Early season types are best in areas with short, cool growing seasons, while gardeners in southern zones need plants that can tolerate hot summer weather. Also ask what diseases and disorders are most common in your area, and look for cultivars that are resistant or tolerant.

- **SLICING TOMATOES.** Also considered to be all-purpose tomatoes, these include beefsteak types, with huge fruit that ranges from 1–2 pounds/.5–.9 kg apiece, as well as hundreds of cultivars with small- to medium-size fruit. Slicing tomatoes come in traditional red, the color that typically signals the most intense flavor, but there also are yellow slicers, as well as pink, orange, purple-red, yellow-and-white, white, and green-striped ones.
- **PASTE OR PROCESSING TOMATOES.** These have thicker walls and fewer seeds than slicers, making them more suitable for making sauce and for canning and freezing. They're also great for slicing up and adding to a salad, though.

Slicing tomato

Beefsteak tomato

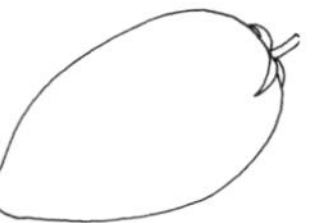

Paste tomato

Cherry tomato

- **CHERRY TOMATOES.** Great for salads and snacking, cherry tomatoes typically bear round, 1"–2"/2.5–5 cm-wide fruit (currant tomatoes bear tiny ½"/1.3 cm-wide fruit), but there are also small-fruited tomatoes that bear pear-shaped fruit ('Red Pear' and 'Yellow Pear'), as well as the popular grape tomatoes, which bear sweet, oval-shaped fruit.

Q How long does it take to grow tomatoes?

A Tomato cultivars are designated as early, midseason, and late. Early season cultivars usually are ready to harvest from about 65 days on, midseason types from 66 to 79 days, and late-season types from 80 days onward. Days to maturity are from transplanting, so add 6 to 8 weeks (42 to 56 days) to the schedule if you are starting your own plants. Keep in mind that tomatoes produce and ripen more slowly in cool and cloudy weather — daytime temperatures from the upper 70s to the low 80s/25–28.3°C) are ideal for fruit production. As a result, plants take longer to produce fruit in areas with cool or cloudy weather. An unusually cool spring also slows production, since plants won't really begin to grow until the soil and weather warm up.

A Sensible Sampling Strategy

WHILE VARIETY IS ONE OF THE DELIGHTS of a backyard garden, you could easily plant 50 or 60 tomato plants and still not try all the cultivars available. Instead, try to select at least three different cultivars to grow each year, and make sure one of those is a variety that you've never grown before. Since you can always buy typical round, red-orange tomatoes at farmers' markets or even the grocery store, you may want to concentrate on unusual colors, shapes, and sizes so you can grow some that are a bit more unusual than the average fare. For snack-size fruit, consider the cherry tomato 'Gold Nugget', which bears golden yellow, 1"/2.5 cm fruit on determinate plants; old-fashioned 'Yellow Pear', an indeterminate cultivar with sweet, 1"/2.5 cm-wide, pear-shaped fruits; or one of the currant tomatoes, 'Red Currant' or 'White Currant', with clusters of ½"/1.3 cm fruit on indeterminate plants. Unusual full-size tomatoes (all indeterminate) to consider include 'Cherokee Purple', with fruits that are red with a purple cast; 'Pineapple', with large yellow-and-red-striped fruit; or 'Costoluto Genovese', which produces large, ribbed fruits that have an outstanding taste.

Q **I want tomatoes for fresh eating, but my family also likes to put up some sauce and whole tomatoes. How many plants do I need?**

A While two plants per person should supply enough ripe tomatoes for fresh eating in most households, plant at least six extra plants – processing or paste types – if you plan on putting up whole tomatoes or sauce.

Q **I'm reading through catalogs, and they all specify whether a cultivar is determinate or indeterminate. What does that mean?**

A These terms refer to growth habits, and you'll find them used in plant descriptions and on plant labels. Both types require the same basic growing conditions, but they require different trellising or support systems.

Indeterminate tomatoes are large, sprawling plants that have long, vinelike stems ranging from 6'/1.8 m to as much as 20'/6 m in length. Most gardeners grow them in large cages or stake them. Indeterminates generally produce a larger harvest than determinate types do and continue producing flowers and fruit – and growing taller – all season long until they are killed by frost.

Determinate tomatoes have short main stems, form fairly compact bushes, and take up less space in the garden. They tend to bear their flowers and fruit all at the same time. Determinate tomatoes can be caged, staked, or allowed to sprawl. Most decline after they fruit, although modern cultivars (sometimes called vigorous determinates) may continue to bear all season long or produce a second crop after the first one, especially if they are cut back once the first crop is picked.

You may want to grow some of both kinds. Determinate types are a good choice for producing a large crop all at once, which is beneficial if you plan to can or freeze and want one big harvest. They're also best if space is at a premium. Indeterminate tomatoes are a good choice for spreading out your tomato harvest over the season. Plants that are staked or grown in cages do need regular training to keep them growing in the right direction, and in this matter determinates are a bit easier to care for. Early and short-season cultivars are determinate types, so you may want to plant a couple of these for early harvest, along with a main crop of indeterminates. Finally, the decision to grow indeterminate or determinate plants affects the support system your plants need, as well as the best spacing for optimum production. For the best fruit production – and to prevent plants from sprawling all over the garden – indeterminate types need to be staked or contained in large, tall cages. Determinates can be allowed to sprawl but are typically grown in cages or staked to use space most efficiently.

Q **Will tomatoes grow in containers? I don't have space for an in-ground garden.**

A For many gardeners, containers are a great option. They make it possible to grow a crop on balconies, decks, patios, or even along the driveway. You can grow slicing, paste, or cherry tomatoes in containers, but for best results with full-size cultivars, use at least a 10-gallon/37.9 L container for each plant.

For smaller containers, look for dwarf or miniature cultivars. Don't make the mistake of assuming that small fruit means small plants: cherry tomatoes are small, but they're usually produced on very large, full-size plants. For patio-size plants, look for cultivars where space-saving or overall size are mentioned in the plant description. Truly tiny cultivars include 'Patio F/Hybrid', 'Red Robin' 'Micro-Tom', 'Florida Petite', 'Florida Basket', 'Tiny Tim', and 'Yellow Canary'. You'll get a larger harvest from slightly bigger plants, though, such as 'Elfin', 'Tumbler Hybrid', 'Sprite', 'Sugary', and 'Sweet Baby Girl'. These larger selections can be grown in the ground or in at least 5-gallon/18.9 L containers.

Container-grown tomatoes require more attention than in-ground plants. Plan on watering daily or even twice daily in hot weather. The soil should be moist but not wet and should never be allowed to dry out. All but the tiniest cultivars require staking or caging. Use cages, stakes planted firmly in the containers, or another trellising method. One option is to group three containers, each with a stake in the soil next to the tomato plant, then lash together the tops of the stakes to create a sturdy teepee.

Perfect Planting

What kind of soil will give me a bumper crop of tomatoes?

A Tomatoes aren't picky. All they need is average, well-drained soil. Work a couple of shovelfuls of compost into each hole at planting time. Loosen the soil to at least 1'/.3 m to encourage roots to grow down into it deeply.

I live near Austin, Texas, and my tomatoes fry in the summer! Do they really need full sun?

A If you live in the South or Southwest – Zones 8 to 10 – where summers are long and hot, tomatoes manage with as little as 5 hours of sun. Many gardeners in those areas prefer a site that receives sun in the morning and late afternoon, but is shaded a bit during the hottest part of the day. The midday shade helps protect plants from excessive heat. Since the growing season is long in Zones 8 to 10, keep in mind that you can also grow two crops of tomatoes, one in spring to early summer and a second from midsummer into the fall. Double-cropping allows you to avoid trying to keep plants alive during sweltering summer heat.

Q **I don't have a spot that offers even 6 hours of sun. Are there any tomatoes I can grow?**

A Most cherry tomatoes will bear at least a partial crop with as little as 4 hours of sun per day. It won't be as large a crop as they would produce in full sun, but you'll still get some to enjoy. Early-bearing tomatoes also can produce at least a partial crop when grown with less-than-ideal sun exposure. Try 'Early Girl', 'Stupice', or one of the other early-season cultivars. Keep in mind that tomatoes growing in partial shade take longer to produce ripe fruit than plants in full sun. For this reason, gardeners in areas with short, cool summers will be less successful growing tomatoes in partial shade than gardeners in hot, southern zones.

Q **I want to grow my tomatoes from seed this year. When do I need to get started? Are they hard to grow?**

Tomatoes are easy to grow, and you'll need to have seeds on hand for sowing 6 to 8 weeks before the last spring frost date. Don't start earlier than that, since young, compact seedlings will outpace tall, lanky ones in the garden every time. Sow two seeds per pot and germinate them at about 75°F/23.9°C. Once they're up, keep them at 65°F/18.3°C; 55°F/12.8°C at night. Cut off the smaller seedling once they both have at least one true leaf. Move seedlings to larger pots as necessary to eliminate potbound roots. When you repot, set seedlings deeper than they were growing before, so the first true leaf is just above the soil surface. This encourages plants to form new roots along the buried stem.

When are seedlings ready for transplanting?

Move tomato transplants to the garden about 2 weeks after the last spring frost date, once soil temperatures have reached 60°F/15.6°C. Be sure to harden off transplants beginning about a week before it's time to transplant.

I want to get an early start this year. Can I plant my tomato seedlings out extra early?

Early planting only works if you protect your transplants from cold temperatures. For the earliest start – up to about 3 weeks before the last spring frost date – do the following:

- **WARM SOIL.** Prewarm the soil by covering it with black plastic beginning about 2 weeks before planting outside. Also, plant into a raised bed, since raised soil warms up more quickly than in-ground beds.
- **TEST FOR TEMPERATURE.** Don't move transplants until the soil is 60°F/15.6°C under the plastic.
- **PROTECT YOUR BABIES.** Use Wall-O-Waters or hot caps, or wrap tomato cages with plastic to protect the plants from cold wind. Wall-O-Water is a double-walled plastic teepee-shaped protector that holds an insulating layer of water around transplants. To use it, set it up around transplants and fill the sides with water. Wall-O-Waters insulate transplants to about 20°F/–6.7°C.
- **WATER WARM.** When you need to water your seedlings, use warm water to reduce shock.
- **DON'T BABY TOO LONG.** Once warmer spring weather arrives, remove extra protection to avoid overheating plants.

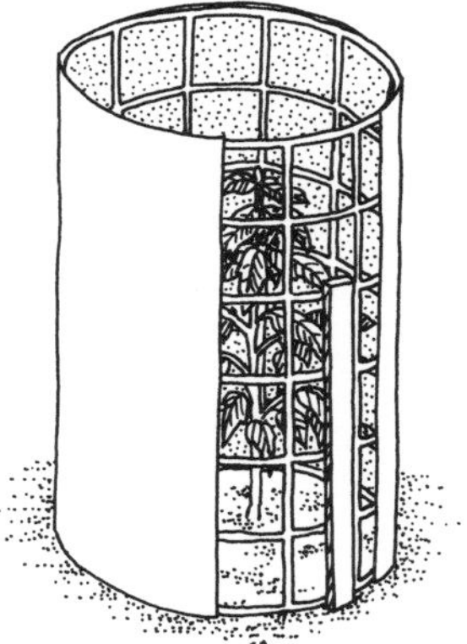

Plastic-wrapped tomato cage

Q How much space does each tomato plant need?

A Proper spacing is determined by how you are training and managing your tomatoes. Plant determinate tomatoes 3'–4'/.9–1.2 m apart if they are going to be allowed to sprawl, without caging or staking. Tomatoes — both indeterminates and determinates — grown in sturdy, 2'/.6 m-diameter cages can be spaced 4'/1.2 m apart. Space staked tomatoes 2'/.6 m apart. If you tend to let your tomatoes go over the summer, meaning you don't train them or prune away excess growth regularly, wider spacing is best. That's because a healthy tomato planting will be quite junglelike by the end of the season, and it can be hard to find the fruit at harvest time. If you are conscientious in pruning and training throughout the season, somewhat closer spacing will work just fine.

SEE ALSO: *To learn the difference between determinate and indeterminate tomatoes, pages 387–388.*

Care Tips

Q Do tomatoes need fertilizing?

A If you have fairly good soil and incorporated a couple of shovelfuls of organic matter into the soil at planting time, your plants are probably fine without supplemental feeding. If your soil isn't in topnotch form, water weekly with a dilute solution of fish emulsion until flowers appear.

Q **Why do gardeners use stakes or cages? Can't you let tomato plants sprawl on the ground?**

A Staking or caging tomatoes helps save space in the garden and generally makes the plants easier to manage. It also gets the fruit up off the ground so it is exposed to more sunlight and is easier to harvest. In addition, staking or caging increases air circulation and thus reduces problems with diseases. In hot, dry, windy climates, however, tomatoes are better off left to sprawl over the ground, since dry winds can damage both foliage and fruit.

Q **If I decide to stake my tomatoes, what size stakes do I need?**

It depends on whether you're growing determinate or indetermate varieties:

- **FOR INDETERMINATE TOMATOES,** use 8'/2.4 m-long stakes that are ¾"/1.9 cm square. Set the posts at least 1'/.3 m in the ground. Another option is 10'/3 m sections of ½"/1.3 cm rebar, which can be hammered

2'/.6 m into the ground to make a really sturdy support. Plant a transplant at the base of each stake, and tie it with soft strips of cloth as it grows. Another option is to plant between the stakes, then weave strings along the row between the posts, tying up the plants in the process.

- **FOR DETERMINATE TOMATOES,** use 5'–6'/1.5–1.8 m-long stakes. Set stakes before you move transplants to the garden, and sink the base 8"/20.3 cm deep. Tie plants loosely to the stake with strips of T-shirts, panty hose, or soft string. You'll probably want to prune out some of the suckers to keep plants manageable, but leave some in the middle and top of the plant to shade the fruit and prevent sunscald. Pinch back the top of the plant once it reaches the top of the stake to encourage branching and more fruit.

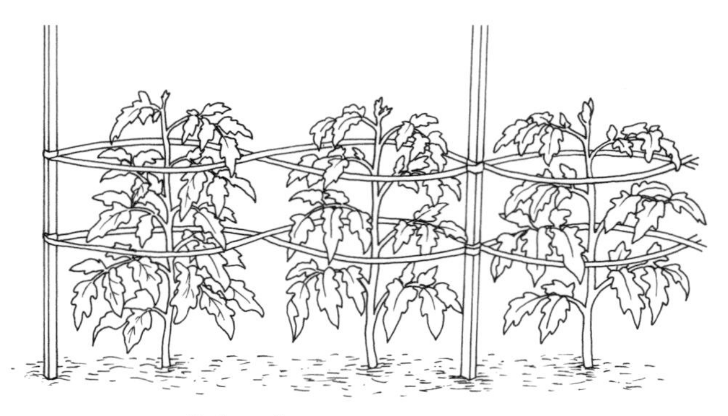

Stake and weave tomato support

Q I want to stake my plants, but does that mean I have to have only one main stem?

A You can install two stakes next to each plant and let the first main sucker that appears grow out. Train the main stem to one stake and the first sucker to the second stake. After that, train the plant as you would a single-stemmed staked plant.

Q What is a sucker, and how do I prune them out?

A Suckers are side shoots that form on the plant's main stem in the leaf axils (the point where the leaf meets the main stem). To remove it, grab the sucker between your thumb and forefinger and wiggle it back and forth. The sucker will break off near where it arose from the main stem. If you need to use scissors, use them, but try to remove suckers before they get this big. If you are considering pruning, here are some guidelines to follow:

- **INDETERMINATE TOMATOES.** If you're using cages, you can leave side shoots on the plant, since they'll produce flowers and fruit. Pinch side shoots back once they grow beyond the bounds of the cage. Also

Pinching tomato side shoot

remove enough side shoots to open up the center of the plant to allow light and air in.

- **DETERMINATE TOMATOES.** Don't prune determinates, unless they form a really dense mass of foliage inside the cage. Keep in mind that the plants need plenty of leaves to support fruit growth and also to shade the tomatoes as they form and prevent sunscald.

Q Can I make my own tomato cages?

A Make mesh tomato cages from concrete reinforcing mesh that has 6"/15.2 cm-square openings. Home improvement stores carry rolls of this heavy-duty mesh; mesh that's 5'/1.5 m or more wide is best for making tomato cages.

1. Buy 8'/2.4 m of mesh for each cage. You'll also need heavy-duty bolt cutters to cut it. (Alternatively, have the mesh cut into 8'/2.4 m-long sections at the store.)

2. To cut the mesh, spread it out on a driveway or other relatively flat surface. Measure out an 8'/2.4 m section, then weight down both ends of it with cement blocks or other heavy objects.

Otherwise, it will spring back quickly when cut and can be quite dangerous.

3. Use bolt cutters to clip off wires that stick out on the end of the section of mesh, so the piece ends with a smooth, vertical wire.

4. To cut the 8'/2.4 m-long section (16 squares), cut across the width of the mesh along the outside of one row of the 6"×6"/15.2×15.2 cm squares. You want both ends of the 8-foot section to end in a smooth, vertical wire that doesn't have any sections of wire that stick out.

5. Bring the two cut ends of the mesh together to make a cylinder, then fasten the ends together with wire or plastic wire ties. You'll have a sturdy cage that's about 2½'/.75 m across and 5'/1.5 m tall.

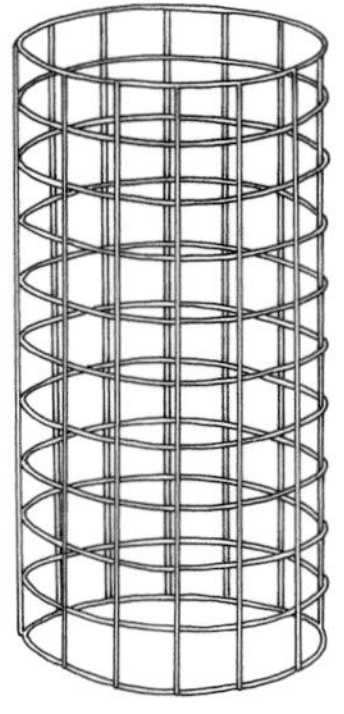

Mesh cylinder tomato cage

6. To install cages in the garden, set them in place, then secure them with stakes on either side, because full-size plants laden with fruit will tip them over.

I've seen cages made using PVC pipes. How can I make those myself?

Using ¾"/1.9 cm PVC pipe and ordinary pipe fittings, you can fashion large cages that will last for years. You'll also need a hacksaw or a PVC pipe cutter and some sandpaper.

1. Cut PVC pipe to the lengths shown in the illustration below. Especially if you're using a hacksaw, you'll need to sand the ends of the cuts so they are smooth and fit easily into the pipe fittings.

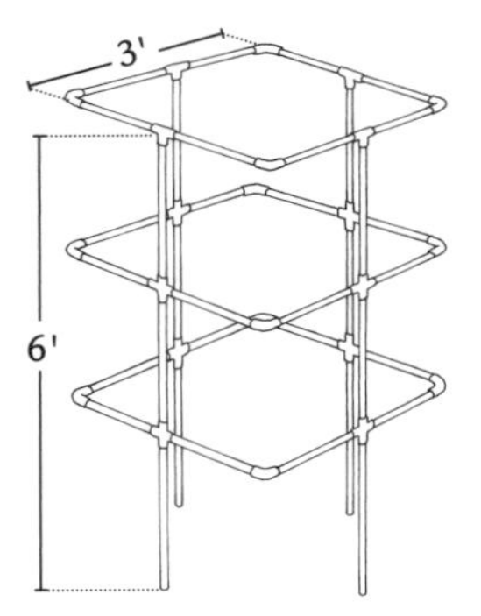

PVC pipe tomato cage

2. Check the fit of the pieces of pipe by assembling them (using the pipe fittings but no glue) to make sure lengths are correct and the cage fits together properly.
3. Take the cage apart, then reassemble it using plumber's cement to permanently connect all the pieces.

Q **I want to store my tomato cages in the garage over the winter. Do I have to take them apart?**

A If you use wire ties to connect the ends of the concrete reinforcing mesh when you make the cages, you can cut the ties off at the end of the season and nest all the sheets together for the winter. For easy handling during storage, connect all the sheets with wire ties or use heavy-duty string to tie them together into a single cylinder. Another option is to start with varying lengths of mesh (7'8"/2.3 m, 8'/2.4 m, 8'6"/2.6 m, and 9'/2.7 m, assuming a 6"×6"/15.2×15.2 cm mesh). The resulting cages should fit one inside the other.

Q **How often do I have to train my tomatoes?**

A While caged tomatoes do just fine with occasional attention to redirect a wayward stem so it stays supported and inside the cage, tomatoes that are staked or grown by one of the other systems need regular maintenance to keep them in bounds. Check plants every few days to remove extra suckers, redirect stems, and tie branches in place. If you attend to them regularly, this shouldn't be too much of a chore, but if they get out of hand and you're trying to wrangle branches that are several feet long, tying them back in place can be a real headache.

Gathering the Harvest

How do I tell when my tomatoes are perfectly ripe but still firm enough to slice?

Rich red-orange is the classic mark of a fully ripe tomato, but large-size heirloom types sometimes are ripe before the tops of the fruit have turned fully red-orange. The fruit also doesn't ripen properly if temperatures exceed 85°F/29.4°C. In that case, pick nearly ripe fruit and ripen it indoors at room temperature out of direct sunlight. Don't store fruit in the refrigerator, since cool temperatures destroy the flavor and texture.

We're going to get an early cold snap tonight. Anything I can do to save my tomatoes?

If frost threatens, but you expect the weather to warm up after a cold snap, cover your plants with blankets or tarps at nighttime to keep them warm. Uncover them when temperatures are warmer during the daytime. Since the season is nearly over, consider pruning away a good bit of the foliage to expose the fruit to sunlight, and thereby speed ripening. Once daytime temperatures are routinely below 60°F/15.6°C, pick all the fruit that has turned from dark to lighter green. Mature fruit – those that have turned color – will ripen indoors.

Q I live in North Dakota, and our first frost always comes too soon! Is there any way I can lengthen the tomato-growing season?

A Try growing a few plants in large containers, and set the containers on dollies or in a children's wagon. That way you can wheel the plants into a garage or shed when cool weather threatens and back outside again on warm days.

Problem Patrol

My plants have loads of leaves but no flowers. What did I do wrong?

A Check the label on your fertilizer bag. In good soil, tomatoes don't need much in the way of supplemental feeding, and they especially don't need high-nitrogen fertilizer (like the kind sold for lawn grass). Too much nitrogen encourages the formation of all foliage and no fruit.

Q **My tomatoes looked fine last week, but it rained over the weekend, and now the fruit is cracked. What happened?**

A Tomatoes need soil that remains evenly moist for the fruit to develop properly. If soil moisture varies too much – if the soil gets too dry and then it rains, for example – the fruit can crack. Pick off the cracked fruit and keep the soil evenly moist but not wet, even during dry weather.

Q **I moved to Washington State 2 years ago, and my tomatoes don't seem to bear as heavily as they did where we lived before. What is the problem?**

A Tomato plants don't produce as many fruits in areas where they do not receive ample summer heat as they do in areas with warm summers. Start with a minimum of four plants per person if you live in an area with cool summers such as the Pacific Northwest or New England.

My tomatoes are rotting on the bottom, but the tops look great. What's going on?

Blossom-end rot is the culprit, and although it looks like a disease, it's actually a physiological condition. When the weather is cool, the plants can't transport nutrients as efficiently as they can when the weather is warm. Blossom-end rot is caused by a calcium deficiency – the calcium is present in the soil; it's just not being transported to the fruits where it is needed. Blossom-end rot usually affects the first fruits of the year, especially when the weather has been cool and wet. Once temperatures warm up and nutrients begin moving around, the plants begin to produce normal fruit, provided they're growing in well-prepared soil. Pick off the rotting fruit, and discard it.

Q **My tomatoes look perfect on the outside, but they're rotten and fuzzy on the inside!**

A Sometimes blossom-end rot affects just the inside of the fruit. Wait for the weather to warm up, and the plants should begin producing normal fruit.

Q **My tomato plants looked fine until just before the first batch of fruit was nearly ripe, then they turned yellow and wilted. Should I have fed them more?**

A Provided you worked a good dose of compost into the soil at planting time, your plants probably didn't die because of insufficient fertilization. Instead, they probably succumbed to one of the major tomato diseases such as fusarium or verticillium wilt. While plants can become infected with these diseases early in the season, symptoms often don't show up until fruits begin to ripen, and the plant is under stress. Next year, look for cultivars that resist diseases like these.

Early and late blight are fungal diseases that are problems in some parts of the country: early blight during warm, humid weather and late blight when days are warm and humid and nights are cool. These diseases seem to be able to infect many standard blight-resistant tomato cultivars, causing spots on lower leaves first. Early blight causes spots with concentric rings (you may need a magnifying glass to see the rings), and late blight causes water-soaked spots that turn purplish or black on the leaves.

Breeders are working to introduce new cultivars that resist these blights, so watch for them in garden catalogs. Inspect plants every other day when the weather is warm and humid for signs of these diseases. If you suspect early blight, pick off infected leaves and discard them in the trash, mulch plants to prevent fungal spores from splashing up onto plants, and spray plants with compost tea or *Bacillus subtilis.* If late blight is the problem, pull up infected plants immediately, place them in a plastic bag, and discard them in the trash. To avoid spreading the spores, wash your hands and change your clothes before returning to the garden.

Q **The flowers on my tomato plants are dropping off without forming fruit. What should I do?**

A Tomatoes don't set fruit when temperatures are below 55°F/12.8°C or above 100°F/37.8°C. Row covers provide a bit of protection from weather that is too cold. Use them in spring until the weather warms up. Too much nitrogen also affects fruit set.

Q **I live in South Georgia, and my tomatoes produced a pretty good crop in spring and early summer, but then they succumbed to hot summer weather. Is that the end for tomatoes for me this year?**

A If you live in Zones 8 to 10, there's still plenty of time to start a second fall crop of tomatoes. Start seeds yourself in midsummer, look for transplants at a local nursery, or root suckers from healthy plants still in your garden as you would cuttings. (For fastest rooting, look along the stem of the sucker for telltale bumps that indicate roots that need only the encouragement of being in contact with moist vermiculite to form.) Plant tomatoes out in late summer, and enjoy a long season until the first frost!

Glossary

Anaerobic bacteria Bacteria that live or are active only in the absence of oxygen.

Biennial A plant that takes 2 years to complete its life cycle. Several vegetables, including leeks and cabbage, are biennials, although they're grown as annuals. These germinate, produce leaves, and generally are harvested the first year, but if left in the ground flower, set seed, and die the second year.

Bolt, bolting To form flowers and seeds prematurely, usually because of exposure to excess heat. This term is most often used to refer to biennial crops, such as cabbage, that flower too soon. Lettuce and spinach also commonly bolt in response to warm temperatures.

Bract Leaf- or scalelike structures borne at the base of individual flowers, flower clusters, or where a new shoot emerges on a stem. Bracts are actually modified leaves. The scales that make up an artichoke are bracts, and each bract has a morsel of edible flesh at the base. They surround the hairy "choke," which is actually the artichoke flower.

Cell pack A lightweight plastic container typically comprised of four, six, or eight small blocks; used to grow transplants of vegetables, herbs, annuals, and other small plants.

Cloche A cover, much like a tiny greenhouse, designed to protect a plant or group of plants from cold weather. Historically, cloches were glass bell jars. Modern-day gardeners can buy paper or plastic cloches.

Compost tea A dilute liquid fertilizer made from compost.

Cover crop A crop, usually a grass or a legume, grown specifically to cover the soil surface and prevent erosion by wind or rain. Cover crops also keep raindrops from beating down on soil and compacting it; in addition, they help control weeds. Use them to fill unplanted beds or fill in around crops, or sow them between rows. Although the terms *green manure* and *cover crop* are often used interchangeably, strictly speaking, a cover crop differs from a green-manure crop in that it is not tilled or dug into the soil.

Cotyledon Seed leaf *See* True leaf.

Crop rotation Altering the location where a particular crop is grown from season to season. This technique helps keep soil fertile, makes efficient use of soil nutrients, and combats crop-specific soilborne diseases. Basic principles include avoid planting a crop in the same spot it grew the year before; avoid planting crops with similar pest and disease problems in the same spot (such as crops that belong to the same plant family); and avoid planting crops with similar nutritional needs in the same spot year after year. One simple system involves grouping crops in four categories and rotating them from year to year: Fruit crops (tomatoes, peppers, eggplants, broccoli, squash, corn), followed by leaf crops (lettuce, spinach, cabbage, kale), followed by root crops (carrots, onions, potatoes), followed by legumes (peas and beans). Keeping records of what grew where is essential.

Crown The portion of a perennial where the stems and the roots meet. Asparagus is a vegetable that grows from a crown.

Cultivar A cultivated variety. A particular, distinct form of a plant that originated and is maintained in cultivation by either sexual or asexual propagation. The terms *cultivar* and *variety* are commonly used interchangeably. See also Variety.

Cuttings A portion of a stem, leaf, root, bud, or modified stem (such as a rhizome) that is separated from a parent plant, induced to form adventitious roots, and eventually grown into a new plant. Taking and rooting cuttings is a form of vegetative, or asexual, propagation that duplicates the parent plant exactly.

Dibble A small hand tool designed to poke holes in soil for seeds, seedlings, or other small plants.

Disease-resistant/tolerant A term used to describe a plant that can continue growing and bearing a crop, showing minimal or no symptoms, despite being infected by a disease organism.

Drip line The line on the soil (either real or imaginary) where rain drips to the ground from the outermost leaves of a plant.

Double digging A soil-preparation technique that deeply loosens the soil, incorporates organic matter, improves soil drainage, and also encourages plants to grow deep, wide-spreading roots.

Flat A shallow tray that holds pots. Flats can be open at the bottom to allow water to drain away, or they can hold water. The standard size is roughly 12"×20" (30.5×50.8 cm) long.

Green manure A crop that is grown and then dug or tilled into the soil to increase soil organic matter and improve soil fertility. Green manures can be sown in fall and tilled under in spring or planted any time during the growing season. Use them to fill empty planting beds or as living mulches under row crops.

Hardening off A technique used to gradually expose seedlings, cuttings, or other plants to the conditions they will encounter outdoors in the garden.

Hot cap A small, disposable cloche (cover for an individual plant) made of waxed paper.

Inoculant A treatment for seeds that ensures the presence of certain beneficial bacteria that allow peas, beans, and other legumes to transform atmospheric nitrogen, which plants can't use, into ammonia nitrogen, a form they can readily absorb. Inoculation increases yields and increases the amount of nitrogen left in the soil from legume-plant residue. Inoculants are crop specific, but seed companies also sell inoculant mixes that contain strains appropriate for all major crops. If you have inoculated your soil in previous years, sufficient bacteria are probably already present.

Intensive gardening Gardening systems that use a variety of techniques designed to maximize harvests by making the best use of available space. Most intensive systems grow crops in raised beds and use close spacing between individual plants. They also use succession planting and crop rotation and pay special attention to building soil and maintaining soil fertility. A well-planned, well-cared-for intensive garden can produce from four to ten times the harvest of a conventional vegetable garden planted in rows. The French intensive and biodynamic gardening systems are best known.

Legume Any member of the pea family (Fabaceae, formerly Leguminosae).

Organic gardening A method of gardening that uses natural systems and cycles to care for plants without the use of synthetic chemical pesticides, herbicides, fungicides, or fertilizers. "Feed the soil and let the soil feed the plants" is an organic-gardening adage pointing to the fact that soil-building techniques are at the heart of organic gardens. Organic gardeners use compost, animal manures, green manures, and crop rotation along with techniques such as double digging and mulching to build and maintain rich soil to support their crops. They use natural rock powders and materials such as fish emulsion to provide nutrients. Organic gardeners also foster a rich population of beneficial insects and other organisms to reduce the need for artificial pest control. They use naturally occurring substances to control insects and diseases only as a last resort.

Paper pot Also called newspaper pots, these are homemade pots made from strips of black-and-white newsprint. Two-piece molds are available to make these. Simply roll a strip of newspaper of the length and width specified around the mold and crush the bottom of the "pot" into the bottom of the mold. Pop the pot free. Fill the pots with premoistened medium and fit them snugly into a flat. To make larger pots (for large seedlings like squashes and pumpkins), simply wrap larger, thicker, strips of newspaper around cans or other containers to form your pots. Move seedlings to the garden, pot and all. There's no need to tear off the top of the pots (see Peat pot), and they won't wick water out of the soil.

Parasitic nematodes Also called beneficial nematodes, these are threadlike microscopic soil animals that attack other soil-dwelling organisms, including a variety of crop pests.

Parasitic wasps These beneficial insects lay eggs on the body of a host insect, such as a caterpillar, and the wasp larvae feed on the insect from within, eventually killing it.

Peat pot A container made of compressed peat moss and designed for growing seedlings. Roots easily penetrate moist peat pots, which are used to start difficult-to-transplant seeds. Seedlings can be planted right into the garden, pot and all, to minimize transplant stress. When transplanting, tear off the top of the pot to prevent the entire pot from drying out and the roots from penetrating the pot.

Pelleted or pelletized seed Seed that has been coated with inert materials to make it uniform in size and easier to handle when sowing. Crops with very small seeds, such as carrots and lettuce, often are sold as pelleted seed, which makes the seed easier to sow thinly and reduces the need to thin. Depending on the material used, pelleted seed may contain pesticides or other materials not acceptable in an organic garden, but organic pelleted seed is also available.

Perennial A plant that persists for more than 2 years. Technically, shrubs, trees, and woody vines are perennials, but gardeners and horticulturists generally use this term specifically to refer to non-woody, or herbaceous, species.

Perlite Small white pellets of volcanic rock that have been popped like popcorn. Perlite is added to potting mixes to improve aeration.

pH A measure of the acidity or alkalinity of soil, indicated on a scale that runs from 0 to 14. Soil pH determines which nutrients can dissolve in soil water and are thus available to plants. It also influences the activity of soil organisms. A reading of 7 indicates neutral pH. Numbers below that indicate acid soil, numbers above 7 signify alkaline soil. A range near neutral (roughly 6.5 to 7.0) is considered ideal for the majority of garden plants because most nutrients are in forms plants can use. Above or below this range, certain nutrients bond with others to form compounds that are not available to plants. To determine the pH of your soil, take a soil sample and either test it using a home test kit or send it out to a lab.

Potbound The condition of a container-grown plant that has filled all the available space with roots. Potbound plants dry out much more quickly than ones that are not, and this condition eventually stunts growth. Tipping a potbound plant out of its container reveals a dense mat of roots circling the root ball; roots sticking out the bottom of the pot are also a sign of a plant that has been in the same pot too long. When planting potbound specimens, score (cut) the sides of the root ball with a knife and tease out roots to encourage them to spread into the surrounding soil.

Pregerminating Sprouting seeds before they are planted to give crops a head start on the growing season or to provide extra control over the germinating process.

Propagate, propagation To cause new plants to be produced from existing ones. Gardeners use many different techniques for propagation, including taking cuttings, dividing plants, layering, grafting, and seed sowing.

Rhizome A specialized horizontal stem that runs underground or on the surface of the soil. Since it is a stem, a rhizome contains nodes and internodes. It produces both roots and shoots at the nodes.

Season extension Lengthening the number of days a vegetable garden is productive, in both spring and fall. Season extension involves activities such as prewarming soil, starting seeds indoors, using cloches or row covers to protect transplants, protecting full-size plants or rows of plants in fall with temporary covers such as plastic stretched over hoops, and growing crops in cold frames and greenhouses outside the usual growing season.

Sidedress A method of applying fertilizer, primarily used with row crops. To sidedress a crop, pull back any mulch that covers the soil, then spread the fertilizer along the row or around an individual plant, keeping it away from stems and leaves. Use a rake or cultivating fork to work the fertilizer into the top 2"/5 cm of soil.

Soil structure The manner in which individual soil particles clump together, or aggregate. The sizes and shapes of soil aggregates determine pore space and thus how water and air move through the soil. Ideal garden soil, that which is rich in organic matter, has plenty of aggregates that form a loose, granular, or crumblike structure. Soil structure isn't a static characteristic: It can be improved or destroyed. Walking on soil, driving or parking cars on it, digging or disturbing it when it is too wet or too dry, or leaving it exposed (unmulched) to heavy rain all break down aggregates and compact the soil structure, making it hard for air, water, and roots to penetrate it. To improve the structure of any soil, promote the formation of aggregates by adding plenty of leaf mold, compost, or other organic matter.

Soil texture The relative proportions of sand, silt, and clay particles in soil, which determine how coarse or fine it is. Texture plays a large role in determining how well soil holds water and nutrients. Soils are classified according to the percentage of each particle they contain.

Thinning As a planting technique, thinning is the act of reducing the number of seedlings planted in a given area to allow enough room for the remaining plants to thrive. Thinning is beneficial because overcrowded seedlings can become stunted, grow more slowly, and are vulnerable to pests and diseases because of reduced air circulation. To thin a planting, pull up or cut off extra seedlings so the remaining plants are at the recommended spacing. Although destroying perfectly healthy seedlings seems like the antithesis of gardening, thinning is necessary to give the remaining plants the room they need to grow.

Topdressing An application method for fertilizer, used to enrich an entire bed of plants. To top-dress, spread the fertilizer evenly over the entire bed prior to planting and use a rake or other tool to lightly work the fertilizer into the top few inches of soil.

Train, training The process of shaping a young plant to a desired form or directing its growth so that it will climb a trellis or grow within a cage or along a garden stake.

True leaf The first leaf or leaves a seedling produces after the seed leaves (cotyledons). True leaves resemble, or somewhat resemble, the leaves of the mature plant.

Variety The definition of this term depends on who is using it. A scientist who studies plant relationships would say that a variety is a group of naturally occurring plants that are different from the species but not distinct enough to be recognized as a separate species. Plant breeders, farmers, and gardeners, however, use the terms "cultivar" and "variety" interchangeably to refer to a distinct form of a plant that originated and is maintained in cultivation by either sexual or asexual propagation.

Vermiculite A micalike mineral that is expanded at high temperatures to form lightweight, pelletlike granules that retain water but also provide good aeration when added to various potting mixes.

How Much Should I Plant?

Sowing entire packets of seed for each crop you want to grow will leave you swimming in produce. To avoid drowning in a river of lettuce, tomatoes, and zucchini, use this chart to determine how many plants or how many feet of row of each crop to plant to feed your household. Quantities listed are for fresh eating; plant more if you plan to can or freeze your produce. If you're planting in succession, quantities listed are the amount to plant at each planting. Be sure to adjust your estimates according to how enthusiastic family members are about a particular vegetable, and plan on growing a couple of different cultivars to make up the total for each crop. Have some fun and experiment a bit!

CROP	NUMBER OF PLANTS PER PERSON	COMMENTS
Artichokes	2	For a first crop, try a small planting to see how well artichokes grow in your climate.
Asparagus	6-7	For a dioecious cultivar, plant 12 to 14 plants per person.
Beans, bush	10-12	Succession plant every 2-3 weeks.
Beans, pole	7-8	
Beets	12-15	Succession plant every 2-3 weeks in spring, early summer, and late summer/fall.

CROP	NUMBER OF PLANTS PER PERSON	COMMENTS
Broccoli	5–6	Plant in spring and again in fall.
Brussels sprouts	3	
Cabbage	5–6	Plant in spring and again in fall.
Carrots	25–30	Succession plant every 2–3 weeks in spring, early summer, and late summer/fall.
Cauliflower	3–5	
Celery	5–6	
Collards	3–4	
Corn	15	Succession plant every 3–4 weeks until about 75 days before first fall frost.
Cucumbers, bush	2–3	Succession plant every 4 weeks until about 2 months before first fall frost.
Cucumbers, vining	1	Succession plant every 4 weeks until about 2 months before first fall frost.
Cucumbers, pickling	15–20	

CROP	NUMBER OF PLANTS PER PERSON	COMMENTS
Eggplants	2–3	
Garlic	6–7	
Kale	5–6	
Kohlrabi	6–7	Plant in spring and again in fall.
Leeks	10	
Lettuce	5–10	Succession plant every 3 weeks in spring and fall (try heat-tolerant varieties in summer).
Melons	2–3	Plant a second crop 3–5 weeks after the first planting if your growing season allows.
Okra	2–3	
Onions, bulbing	30–35	
Onions, scallions	12–15	
Parsnips	10	
Peas	15–20	Succession plant every 10 days in spring, early summer, and late summer/fall.
Peppers, hot	1–2	
Peppers, sweet	4–5	

CROP	NUMBER OF PLANTS PER PERSON	COMMENTS
Potatoes	10	Succession plant or make a single planting using a mix of early, midseason, and late cultivars.
Pumpkins	1–2	
Radishes	6–12	Succession plant spring radishes every 10 days in spring, late summer, and fall.
Rutabagas	8–9	
Spinach	10–15	Succession plant every 2 weeks from spring until early summer and again in fall.
Squash, summer	1–2	Succession plant every 2–3 weeks until about 2 months before first fall frost.
Squash, winter	1	
Sweet potatoes	6–7	
Tomatoes	3–5	
Turnips	12–15	Succession plant every 2–3 weeks in spring and fall.
Watermelons	2–3	

Gardening Online

Here are a few of the best and most stable online resources for gardening information:

USDA COOPERATIVE EXTENSION SERVICES. This government agency offers a wealth of local information on home gardening through county-based offices staffed by Extension agents and volunteer Master Gardeners. Use the following link to locate the websites of Extension offices throughout the United States: *www.csrees.usda.gov/Extension/*

THE ORGANIC AGRICULTURAL CENTRE OF CANADA. This government agency participates in field studies across the country and offers programs and information for farmers and vegetable gardeners alike on a wide range of topics. *www.organicagcentre.ca/Extension/horticulture.asp*

GARDEN FORUMS. There are many forums on the Internet where you can post questions or read postings by backyard gardeners. These offer users a community of gardeners that extends around the world. Here are three of the best:

> **The Garden Web.** Read the postings on the forums along with the very useful FAQs (frequently asked questions). There are forums on several hundred different topics from composting, seed saving, and vegetable gardening to tomatoes, hot peppers, and market gardener. There also are forums for gardeners in many different specific regions from Florida to Canada. You need to join Garden Web to post your own questions. *http://forums.gardenweb.com/forums*

Dave's Garden. Another extensive website, Dave's Garden has forums on many different topics, plus a bug-identification database. Both free and paid subscriptions are available and allow access to many of the forums.
http://davesgarden.com

Gardening with the Helpful Gardener. This website features forums on vegetable gardening as well as many other gardening topics. Users who register have access to more services than those who don't, but you can read posts and post questions even if you are not registered.
www.helpfulgardener.com

Books

The following books are some of the best sources of information for growing and managing a vegetable garden and dealing with insect pests and other problems.

Bartholomew, Mel. *All-New Square Foot Gardening.* Franklin, TN: Cool Springs Press, 2006.

Bartley, Jennifer R. *Designing the New Kitchen Garden: An American Potager Handbook.* Portland, OR: Timber Press, 2006.

Bradley, Fern Marshall. *Rodale's Vegetable Garden Problem Solver.* Emmaus, PA: Rodale Press, 2007.

Coleman, Eliot. *Four-Season Harvest: Organic Vegetables from Your Home Garden All Year Around.* White River Junction, VT: Chelsea Green Publishing, 1999.

Cranshaw, Whitney. *Garden Insects of North America.* Princeton, NJ: Princeton University Press, 2004.

Cutler, Karan Davis. *Burpee: The Complete Vegetable & Herb Gardener.* Indianapolis, IN: Wiley Publishing, 2007.

Denckla, Tanya L. K. *The Gardener's A-Z Guide to Growing Organic Food.* North Adams, MA: Storey Publishing, 1994.

Ellis, Barbara W., and Fern Marshall Bradley, eds. *The Organic Gardener's Handbook of Natural Insect and Disease Control.* Emmaus, PA: Rodale Press, 1992.

Greenwood, Pippa, Andrew Halstead, A. R. Chase, and Daniel Gilrein. *American Horticultural Society Pests and Diseases.* New York: Dorling Kindersley Publishing, Inc., 2000.

McGee, Rose Marie Nichols, and Maggie Stuckey. *McGee & Stuckey's Bountiful Container: Create Container Gardens of Vegetables, Herbs, Fruits and Edible Flowers.* New York: Workman Publishing, 2002.

Nick, Jean M. A., and Fern Marshall Bradley, eds. *Growing Fruits & Vegetables Organically.* Emmaus, PA: Rodale Press, 1994.

Smith, Edward C. *Incredible Vegetables from Self-Watering Containers.* North Adams, MA: Storey Publishing, 2006.

Smith, Edward C. *The Vegetable Gardener's Bible.* North Adams, MA: Storey Publishing, 2000.

Index

Page numbers in *italics* indicate drawings; page numbers in **bold** indicate charts.

D

T

Other Storey Titles You Will Enjoy

The Big Book of Preserving the Harvest, by Carol W. Costenbader.
A revised edition of a classic primer on freezing, canning, drying, and pickling fruits and vegetables. 352 pages. Paper. ISBN 978-1-58017-458-9.

Carrots Love Tomatoes, by Louise Riotte.
A classic companion planting guide that shows how to use plants' natural partnerships to produce bigger and better harvests.
224 pages. Paper. ISBN 978-1-58017-027-7.

The Complete Compost Gardening Guide,
by Barbara Pleasant & Deborah L. Martin.
Everything a gardener needs to know to produce the best compost, nourishment for abundant, flavorful vegetables.
320 pages. Paper. ISBN 978-1-58017-702-3.

The Gardener's A–Z Guide to Growing Organic Food, by Tanya L. K. Denckla.
An invaluable resource about growing, harvesting, and storing for 765 varieties of vegetables, fruits, herbs, and nuts.
496 pages. Paper. ISBN 978-1-58017-370-4.

Incredible Vegetables from Self-Watering Containers, by Edward C. Smith.
A foolproof method to produce a bountiful harvest without the trouble of a traditional earth garden. 256 pages. Paper. ISBN 978-1-58017-556-2.
Hardcover. ISBN 978-1-58017-557-9.

The Vegetable Gardener's Bible, by Edward C. Smith.
A reinvention of vegetable gardening that shows how to have your most successful garden ever. 320 pages. Paper. ISBN 978-1-58017-212-7.

Serving Up the Harvest, by Andrea Chesman.
A collection of 175 recipes to bring out the best in garden-fresh vegetables, with 14 master recipes that can accommodate whatever happens to be in your produce basket.
516 pages. Paper. ISBN 978-1-58017-663-7.